SHAPING WELFARE CONSENSUS

U.S. CATHOLIC BISHOPS' CONTRIBUTION

PHILIP S. LAND, S.J.

FOREWORD BY
ARCHBISHOP REMBERT WEAKLAND, O.S.B.

EDITED BY
C. WILLIAM MICHAELS, ESQ.

CENTER OF CONCERN
WASHINGTON, D.C.

THE CENTER OF CONCERN would like to express sincere gratitude to Missionhurst -C.I.C.M., Rome, Adelaide and Daniel Schlafly of St. Louis, Babs and Lou Fischer of Philadelphia, and the Cambridge Center for Social Studies of the Jesuit Conference, Washington, D.C., whose generous support assisted in the publication of this book.

To Pedro Arrupe, S.J.

As Superior General of the Society of Jesus, he encouraged me, as so many others, to embrace without misgivings Vatican II's vision of a Church deeply committed to the world, working for peace and justice as significant dimensions of the Reign of God among us.

ACKNOWLEDGEMENTS

For their generous financial support of my work I am especially indebted Adelaide and Daniel Schlafly of St. Louis, Babs and Lou Fischer of Philadelphia, the Cambridge Center for Social Studies of the Jesuit Conference, Washington D.C., and Missionhurst C.I.C.M., Rome.

My associates at the Center of Concern have been most helpful and supportive. I must single David Simmons, Administrative Director, and Lucien Chauvin, who shepherded the book through publication; Andrea Pi-Sunyer who spent many, many hours patiently and expertly transferring and editing rough drafts; and Judy Mladineo who, besides resolving computer problems, produced the index.

At the half-way mark of my work, a reading of the text by Sharon Daly, Director of the Office of Domestic Social Development at the United States Catholic Conference, and several hours discussion with her, both encouraged pursuit of the project and shed light on the intricacies of welfare problems.

I am enormously indebted to the long-time Executive Director of the Center of Concern, Peter Henriot, who plunged his energies into overall shaping of this book. Peter at once showed me encouraging strengths of my manuscript but just as insightfully helped me see its weaknesses. If this book ends in a reasonably coherent account of the welfare debate, my colleague deserves much of the credit.

FOREWORD

Often at hearings on the Economic Pastoral Letter of the U.S. Bishops'
Economic Justice for All, I would listen to the people present say phrases
like the following: "Welfare is certainly the heart of the matter; anything
you can do to help would be appreciated." Or: "Whatever you can do to
help us get a grasp on this whole welfare question would be appreciated." Welfare was recognized as a sign that the system was not function-
ing well and that help was needed.

But there were also others with a totally different view. They felt
comfortable if the Bishops remained on the level of moral theory or biblical vision; they became very uneasy, however, when the Bishops talked
about more specific questions like that of welfare and said quite openly
that the Bishops were entering a territory that was outside of their competency.

The discussion of the degree of specificity that should characterize the
pastoral letter of the Bishops, one could say, plagued the process of writing the pastorals. The constant and nagging question that was repeated
was: to what degree of specificity should the Bishops come to in
responding to any economic issue? Moral principles were considered as
being within their competency, but even here some felt that there was
not a real guide in the scriptures and tradition that could be brought to
bear on economic issues. The moral questions in that area, some felt,
would be an analysis of the action of individuals, not the critique of the
inherent structures in the system. The American Bishops felt that there
was much that could be said about economic systems from both the biblical perspective as well as from the moral tradition of the natural law.

The next level of discourse was that of middle axioms, descriptions of
how moral principles could be worked out in society without at the same
time giving actual specific wordings of laws to be passed. The fine line

of division here was not always easy to maintain, but in many areas—the international, for example—that procedure was held to. Some commentors were, even in this middle axiom area, a bit nervous about the Bishops' intrusion.

To avoid confusion with regard to the weight of the teaching authority of the Bishops in this type of discourse, the major pastoral letters of the Bishops point out that the Bishops place their full teaching authority behind the statements they make when reiterating perennial teaching of the Church; they also state that this authority is reduced as they descend to particulars because of the contingency of details and the inability to control the data in question. This does not imply that they see morality only as an abstract discourse and that actions and decisions do not have moral content. There has always been a tradition of judging actions according to their moral content in an objective way and without attributing to the individual in question guilt or non-guilt. Objective and subjective morality have always been kept distinct in Catholic teaching.

One could well understand, however, why there may have been some hesitancy about the Bishops speaking out on concrete solutions if it was felt that they were teaching that one and only one solution could be the moral choice to solve concrete cases. In such cases of specificity it is often easier to say when a solution does not meet criteria than to suggest a solution that does so to perfection.

In the four areas treated more specifically in the Economic Pastoral Letter, that is, where the Bishops give concrete cases of positive solutions that meet the moral criteria they had laid out, they did so because they felt that the a Church had had more experience in those areas and could well contribute to the national or international debate. The four areas were: employment, poverty (welfare is treated in this section), food and agriculture, and the U.S. economy and the developing nations.

The Church has been dealing with the poor for centuries and has accumulated a vast amount of experience about human nature and its relationships to the work ethic. In more recent times in our own nation the Church has developed a vast network of social services that involve millions of dollars per year. The Church, too, has been involved in this country for over a century in a school system that has educated vast numbers of the poor and given them a chance to move ahead in society. It would only be right that the Church, thus, share with other citizens of this nation the results of that experience and not be deprived of that opportunity. One could say that the bishops felt more at ease in talking about this area of poverty, its causes, and its remedies that they would have in many other areas (high finance and banking, for example).

It would have been, it seems to me, a misfortune if the Bishops had been persuaded not to offer their advice in these areas because of some theory that Bishops must only speak in theoretical terms. They would be depriving their fellow citizens of the knowledge learned through years of experience, hands-on experience, that is invaluable.

Father Philip Land is well-acquainted with Catholic social teaching and its application. No better mind could be found in our society to analyze the Church's teaching in this area and the concrete suggestions given by the Bishops. I am sure that the members of the Church in the United States and other citizens of goodwill will appreciate his keen endeavor.

Rembert G. Weakland, O.S.B.
Archbishop of Milwaukee

Archbishop Weakland was Chairman of the National Conference of Catholic Bishops' *ad hoc* Committee that drafted the U.S. Catholic bishops' pastoral letter, *Economic Justice for All: Catholic Social Teaching and the U.S. Economy.*

TABLE OF CONTENTS

INTRODUCTION

I trust that you did not buy this book under the impression that you were getting something quite other than the thesis presented within these covers. You may have different—somewhat or altogether different—ideas about welfare and welfare consensus than what this book supports. My reason for this candid warning is that shortly after my studies had revealed the existence of an expert consensus on welfare, one which I wholly embraced, I fell upon another consensus which was decidedly not to my liking.

It was recognition of that first convergence of opinion, standing in close agreement with Catholic social principles, that almost persuaded me to incorporate the word "consensus" into the title of my study of welfare and the U.S. Catholic Bishops' Pastoral Letter, *Economic Justice for All: Catholic Social Teaching and the U.S. Economy.* But subsequent encounter with a welfare consensus warmly embraced by an opposing camp gave me pause, at first, about enshrining the word "consensus" in the title to this book. But only at first, as I shall explain.

The existence of the two opposing camps on welfare was in a way signaled within the span of two months (February and March, 1987) by lengthy articles in *Time* magazine. In the first article *Time* reported the existence of a public consensus which supported the Reagan Administration's belief that welfare had been an unmitigated disaster. The second reported that the public widely held that the Administration had been plain wrong-headed in its war on welfare.

Just prior to these two conflicting articles in *Time*, two major studies appeared. One was in the camp of *Time's* negative consensus, the other on the side of *Time's* positive consensus. The first, *Up From Dependency,* appeared at the end of 1986. It was a report of experts convened at President Reagan's request to produce for him a program of welfare reform. In early 1987, the second appeared, *Work and Welfare: New*

Directions in National Policy. This was produced by the Washington, D.C.-based Center for National Policy.

This latter study—together with *Fighting Poverty,* a book to which much attention will be given in the pages that follow—firmed my conviction that I wanted to write a study showing that both Catholic social thought in general and the U.S. Catholic Bishops' Economic Pastoral in particular were to be found within that positive welfare consensus. It also convinced me to stick to my title of "Building A Welfare Consensus" despite possible confusion of my consensus with that of the opposing camp. Celebration of the positive consensus warranted, I believed, running the risk of some initial confusion.

One further nomination for welfare consensus was announced just as I was doing my final editing. This was the headline of a mid-June, 1988 editorial in the *New York Times* heralding the vote on Senator Daniel Patrick Moynihan's legislative proposals for welfare reform. The Senate had massively said "yes" to Moynihan and the House had before it legislative proposals akin to those of Moynihan. The Moynihan legislation has considerable affinity with *Up From Dependency*, even embracing the Reagan Administration's insistence that work requirements be more stringent. (All the documents referred to in this introduction will be amply reviewed in the chapters to follow.)

At least twenty-four national organizations and churches have condemned the Moynihan bill in its present form. This includes the United States Catholic Conference, Catholic Charities USA, and NETWORK, the Catholic social justice lobby. I personally share the misgivings of all these groups that the Senate's bill will not do much for the poor nor will it move the country into a true transformation of welfare.

This leads me to make a second preliminary observation. This current study is not confined to welfare in the narrow sense of assistance to welfare mothers, e.g., Aid For Families With Dependent Children (AFDC), food stamps, medical assistance. It rather expands the concept to embrace all the poor who may be in need of assistance of whatever kind—for example, the working poor.

Another preliminary note. Does the consensus I embrace provide space for alternative thinking? Is it in any way transformative? I think here in particular of those welfare proponents who look to a day when welfare might be more community based. That means, for example, more reliance on co-ops, community-child-care for children of working women, local housing initiatives, etc. Does the consensus provide room for exploration and experimentation with such pioneering new efforts? Even within the system which will probably be with us in some degree for the foreseeable future, do the contemplated changes constitute something transformative, albeit in a minor key? Or are the proposals only a shoring up of a failed system, a tinkering with a creaking and inoperable machine?

These very important questions are at least tentatively explored in my postscript. I also raise there the question of "first-best" versus "second-best" approaches. The former brings jobs to people and people to jobs; the latter relies on more generous governmental transfers of income. While opting for the "first-best," I do recognize the inevitable role for a long time to come of the "second-best." That being so, I call for much more generous programs than the last few years have seen.

A final note is on "How-You-Might-Read-This-Book." There are five major parts to this study. One: (Chapter I) This responds to the general challenge that the U.S. Catholic Bishops have no business writing about economics, that they have neither the right to do so nor the competence. Two: (Chapter II) This surveys the more philosophical aspects of the welfare debate between conservatives and liberals. Three: (Chapters III, IV, and V) This analyzes the charges that welfare causes poverty, family break-up, and the black underclass. All are shown to be myths. Four: (Chapters VI and VII) Here I first survey at length the literature that suggests to me the growing welfare consensus among professional researchers, welfare workers, and administrators. Then I analyze three strands of proposed national legislation, which are fitted into the opposing consensus camps. Five: (Chapters VIII, IX, and X) This presents an overview of Catholic social thought and then the teaching found in the Economic Pastoral. I argue that the Bishops' position is solidly within the new consensus and contributes significantly to the debate.

As a suggestion, the reader might skim Chapter I, setting aside the analysis for later reading. Similarly, the philosophical discussions of Chapter II might be omitted until later. Chapter VII's treatment of welfare legislation at the national level could also be postponed. The heart of this study, I believe, is the examination of the charges against welfare, the exploration of the new consensus, and the exploration of the Bishops' role in building that consensus.

The U.S. Catholic Bishops began their consultation process on the Economic Pastoral in early 1984. Their succeeding drafts, roundly criticized by many within the Church and in the wider public, boldly challenged many U.S. welfare myths. This challenge was made in the face of the strong support of the myths by the Reagan Administration. I wondered frequently at the Bishops' courage in holding on to their positions. They were right to do so. That they were right is what I hope emerges from this book, along with an appreciation of the major contribution they thereby made to a human and Christian addressing of a serious crisis facing the people of the United States today.

1

WELFARE:

THE BISHOPS AND

THEIR CRITICS

A primary concern for those interested in the development of Catholic social teaching and the contribution this teaching can make to the public discussion of urgent social issues is the credibility and authority with which this social teaching is received, both by Catholics and by the general public. A document from a Church body or organization, or even from the Vatican, may pose critically important comments and recommendations about crucial human problems. But if the document itself is considered of little value, its contribution to addressing those problems, and its effect upon them, will certainly be slight. Such a dilemma has faced an essential document of social teaching from the United States Catholic Bishops.

The 1986 Pastoral Letter by the Bishops, *Economic Justice for All: Catholic Social Teaching and the U.S. Economy,* was one of the most comprehensive statements ever issued by any national group of Catholic Bishops on the economic issues. It examined exhaustively several problems, challenges, and social concerns underlying the generally agreed-upon public goal of building a better economic life for all citizens.

Yet even before the Economic Pastoral was officially published—in fact, when the process for the document was first announced in 1980—it was criticized from many quarters. Some of these criticisms the Bishops addressed as the document went through its drafting process. Other criticisms, however, bespeak a broader social debate on how the economic challenges of American society are viewed, on the role of the state in shaping the approaches to those problems, and on the minimal standards for a good and healthy economic life—not only for U.S. citizens but for all world citizens. Nowhere was this situation more plain than on the topic of welfare, which is both a notion and a group of programs that have been at the core of social and political debate for decades in the United States.

This broader social debate was clearly reflected in several of the unfounded criticisms leveled at the Pastoral Letter's treatment of welfare and recommendations for welfare reform. The Pastoral is clearly on target with respect to welfare, and in this is faithful to the scope and direction of Catholic social thought on human needs, human rights, and human responsibilities. To say that, however, hardly tells the whole story about the Bishops, their critics, and welfare in the United States.

Adequate examination of these criticisms is an interesting study in the contrasts and conflicting directions that surround welfare and the nature of the U.S. economic debate. So to do justice to the Bishops and their Pastoral and to its critics involves considering a number of things, including: the social assumptions underlying those criticisms, the current state of the debate on welfare, the approaches to the notion of poverty in this society, the prospects for U.S. attitudes about the poor, and the outlook for welfare policy—with a view toward how this policy would be affected if the Bishops' comments and recommendations were taken into account.

I. CRITICISMS OF THE PASTORAL BY SOME MAJOR OPPONENTS

Criticism of the Economic Pastoral was leveled directly at the document by some critics, indirectly by others through charges and studies that supposedly refuted the Bishops' positions. Perhaps the most prominent criticism was by way of the "American Catholic Lay Letter," issued by a panel of conservative Catholics prior to the issuance of the Pastoral.

Throughout this body of criticism, there appear five fundamental complaints: (1) the Bishops have no right to address economic matters, (2) the Bishops have no competence in economic analysis, (3) the welfare proposals are overly detailed, (4) the fundamental welfare thrust of the Pastoral is misguided, and (5) in their support of a "welfare state," the Bishops dismiss the virtues of the U.S. economic system by focussing on distribution rather than production and by favoring such supposedly dangerous notions as "economic rights" and "economic democracy."

These five charges were made to one or other of the early drafts of the Pastoral, and many of them persisted after the final version. That some criticisms were at least partially valid was acknowledged by the Bishops' drafting committee in the process. Since most of those making the charges have not in the main declared their satisfaction with the amendments or with the final document, it can safely be assumed that they remain dissatisfied with the Pastoral itself in its tone, approach, and direction. Before concentrating on the welfare debate, it may be worthwhile to take up some of these more general charges in order to demonstrate that the Pastoral does have intrinsic value as a major document of U.S. Catholic social teaching.[1]

Some critics were totally dissatisfied with the document and remain so. For example, conservative columnist and writer Charles

Krauthammer finds the tone of the Pastoral lacking in humility and moving beyond prophecy to open advocacy of the poor. Its content, he claims, is "routine acceptance of liberal assumptions."[2] Krauthammer contends that "the poverty of their [the Bishops'] analysis is due to a profound naivete."[3]

Then too, the Bishops are also guilty of the "absurd banishment of the paradox that there is no non-inflationary economic policy," according to Krauthammer and those who take his position. Further, on welfare comes the direct assault: "Where have they been for twenty-five years? We have had a generation of experience with liberal social programs and the Bishops appear just to have discovered them."

And there were still more criticisms, in pages, forums, panels, articles, statements, documents, studies, reports, editorials, and the like. It would not be possible or even productive to list them all at this juncture.[4] Even the Jesuit magazine *America*, speaking of the document's first draft, charged that its practical suggestions are out of touch with mainstream liberal economists.[5]

However, the Pastoral did not lack its supporters either. Equally strong as the critical voices were the voices of many prominent economists who came to the defense of the Bishops.

Two eminent supporters were Nobel-prize winners James Tobin of Yale and Lawrence Klein of the University of Pennsylvania. Both economists testified in Congress on the Pastoral. Klein said the Bishops had engaged in a "careful, scholarly assessment." More, "they have done a great service by raising many questions."[6] Klein remarked that the Bishops' concerns "go right down to the fundamental units of our society." He said the Bishops have pointed out that our social priorities "seem misplaced and it is this lack of quality of life in our economic life that comes through."

Finally, turning to the Bishops' much maligned proposals on employing the jobless, Klein said, "I would advocate the provision of increased support for direct job creation. I would also support their proposal for job training and apprenticeship programs in the private sector." The Bishops, he concluded, "have put the present economic debate on a new plane."[7] Months later Klein returned to the topic in an academic forum, giving the same endorsement.

Tobin stated in the same Congressional testimony that he found the Bishops' values to be "of universal appeal." He recognized that many economists criticized the Pastoral as lacking an appreciation of our economic system and of the realistic requirements for its operation. Nonetheless, Tobin treated the Bishops' proposals with respect, even some enthusiasm, while pointing out some of the economic reasoning still required to make some proposals operable. For example, addressing the need of incentives if the Pastoral's proposals are to be carried out, he called for "ones that work for, rather than against, their objectives."[8]

As for the Bishops' unemployment objectives, "they are not unreasonable." Like Klein, Tobin applauded the Bishops' call for "direct job creation by government." And, as if in answer to conservative Catholic critics of the Pastoral, Tobin argued, "while throwing money at the problems didn't solve them, not throwing money at them doesn't solve them, either."[9]

Leonard Silk of the *New York Times* affirmed that "many economists will conclude that the Bishops have brought together competent economic analysis." They will also applaud the Bishops for "hitting so hard and challenging the nation to rethink its policies."[10]

Thus the debate was joined, as it had been before the Pastoral Letter was even being considered by the Bishops themselves. The Pastoral has served—through the criticisms regarding its welfare positions, for example—as a focal point for some of the sharpest debates on some of the most critical areas of national social policy.

However scholarly and well-meaning these criticisms have been, the Pastoral does withstand their scrutiny. It is important in an examination of these criticisms to keep in mind that the Pastoral is certainly not the only Catholic social teaching on economics or economic principles.

In fact, the Pastoral could hardly have been issued had it not been for the body of modern Catholic social thought developed in this century in applying biblical, theological, and philosophical concepts of justice and rightness to contemporary human life. It must also be noted that criticism of the Pastoral is not only directed at the political issues such as welfare that are dealt with in the document, but also reflects the social and moral positions and assumptions from which the comments and criticisms emanate, be they negative or positive.

A review of the more specific criticisms on the welfare debate is therefore a review not only of the political scope of the welfare issue but also the different attitudes that have grown up around the issue in the past several years among politicians, social economists, commentators, and other observers. This review is a demanding and rewarding task, one which indicates how far the country has to go in its perception and ability to address fully the problems associated with welfare. More importantly, this review of the Bishops and welfare indicates the contribution the Pastoral Letter itself has made and can continue to make to the discussion.

1. The Bishops Have No Right to Speak

Dissidents against the Pastoral declare in unison that the Bishops have no authority to speak on economic issues. The Pastoral, they charge, should confine itself to moral pronouncements and leave the details of economic matters to the laity.

What right, indeed, do the Bishops have to speak on such concrete public issues as economic policy? A right no more or less strong than the right of the Church itself to speak.

In modern Church social teaching, that right can be traced directly to major Papal encyclicals. John XXIII, in his *Christianity and Social Progress* (1961), referring to Pius XI's encyclical, *The Reconstruction of the Social Order* (1931), says the earlier encyclical confirmed "the right and duty of the Catholic Church to makes its irreplaceable contribution to the correct solution of the pressing and grave problems that beset the entire human family."[11] That encyclical, in turn, is replete with concrete proposals for a better economic order.

A series of other papal documents, not to mention the historic documents of the Second Vatican Council, preceded another central event in modern Church social teaching, the Synod of Bishops of 1971. That Synod proclaimed the obligation of the Church to denounce injustices.[12] For the Synod, the Gospel has an undeniable and crucial social dimension which must be addressed not only by Church authorities but also by all Catholics if the Gospel is truly to be lived and to be followed in its basic meaning for our lives and for the world.

At the same time, that Synod, as well as Church authorities more generally, acknowledged that the hierarchy has no competence on technical questions of economic policy. These matters, the Synod noted, were properly to be left to the laity whose special task is, in the words of Vatican II's *Constitution on the Church* (1965), "to illumine and organize temporal affairs."[13]

But this division of competencies cannot be used to deny ecclesial authorities the right and the obligation to suggest and to evaluate the options presented in the "temporal order" on social issues. There may also be a confusion about the Bishops', or more properly the Church's, "right to speak" on "political" questions because there is a tendency, in the United States especially, to separate the "political" from the "moral" components of social issues. The Bishops do not accept that approach. For there is no action that does not have moral consequences in the end chosen, the means used, the circumstances of the choosing, and in the effect of that action upon others.

However, it is precisely this moral aspect of all political action that makes it difficult to say concretely what it means to argue that Church and clergy should confine themselves to the moral message of the Gospel on social concerns while leaving the details of the application of moral teaching to the laity. As moral teachers, the Bishops must pursue the moral where it is actually imbedded in current affairs. The Bishops are charged with raising questions and with shedding Gospel light on concrete human choices. Although each in different manner, cleric and lay are both engaged in public life and must reflect that public life in their consideration of moral concerns.

Suffice it to say that within this debate there exists a clear and plain moral purpose and legitimate role for the Bishops, the U.S. Bishops certainly among them as part of the wider Church, to speak and to evaluate the moral aspects of "political" concerns. And there is certainly much to say when it comes to the U.S. economic system, so critical is this economic system to U.S. lives and so important in the way it affects the lives of others.

But if the Church has authority to speak on current questions, does this authority extend to national bodies of Bishops or does it remain with the Vatican? It was once thought that the Pope's duty was to solve all questions and the Bishops simply were to transmit these papal statements and conclusions to their own local dioceses or national conferences. In this view, the Bishops served chiefly as pipelines for centrally-issued Church proclamations. National episcopal conferences were not yet recognized. Individual Bishops spoke only by direct papal delegation.

Vatican II, however, transformed this thinking with the "Decree on the Bishops' Pastoral Office in the Church," which encouraged the establishment of national and regional conferences of Bishops.[14] Over the years the authority of these conferences has grown in relation to succeeding Popes—even while much of the Roman Curia remained deeply suspicious of local authority. Paul VI, however, supported the national conferences. In his 1971 *Call to Action*, another major papal document in modern Church social teaching, Paul VI gave this support a singular affirmation: "It is up to the Christian communities, in communion with the bishops, to analyze...the situation proper to their own countries."[15]

It appeared that a 1983 statement of Cardinal Joseph Ratzinger of the Sacred Congregation of the Faith disputed this authority of the Bishops' Conferences. [16] However, theologian Avery Dulles, S.J., answered this charge by noting that Canon Law itself says that Bishops "either individually or gathered together" are "authentic teachers."[17] Dulles added that Ratzinger, in a 1965 article, had himself insisted that collegiality—a structural term that seeks an organizational model of more shared responsibility and authority rather than authority being arranged in a pyramidal manner—should not be restricted to relations of all the Bishops under the Pope. True "collegiality" is also exercised by episcopal conferences. Dulles further noted that Rome repeatedly has approved statements emanating from episcopal conferences.

Even if this right of episcopal conferences to speak in the public forum clearly is affirmed within the Church, is this right denied by U.S. constitutional practice? Does the oft-cited phrase "separation of Church and State" mean that the First Amendment of the Constitution prevents a church body from speaking on issues of concern to the state? This question has been recently addressed by Archbishop John Quinn of San Francisco. The First Amendment's clause of separation of church and state is often popularly interpreted as denying the church a voice in the public arena. Quinn points out that the Amendment, however, only refuses political favor to any one church and requires that the state not provide any advantages or impose any disadvantages on any one church. But so far as the wider society is concerned, of which the government is only one segment, the Constitution does not deny the churches an active voice in the shaping of the public good.

This position Quinn finds reinforced in noting that constitutional practice favors the activity in the public sphere of voluntary associations. To the churches the Constitution and the government attribute the character of a voluntary association. The Supreme Court also has never stated that the separation of church and state as established in the First Amendment prevents churches or religious societies from making statements regarding moral perspectives about contemporary social issues.

2. The Bishops Are Not Competent to Speak.

Whether the Bishops have the authority or the opportunity or the responsibility to speak, the right of the Bishops to speak on political matters is also conditioned to a large degree on their competence. For though it may not be for the Bishops to enter into purely technical matters, the moral questions they address are in fact imbedded in the technical.

Thus the turn to economics, a subject which has never failed to live up to its image of being exceedingly complex. Questions endlessly abound when reviewing the values of an economic system. In arranging economic affairs as a nation and as a people, what economic theory is to be espoused? Free enterprise with its unconstrained free market? Keynsian approaches to limited government intervention in the market? Neo-Keynsian approaches to government regulation of the market in special instances? Marxist perspectives on the primacy of the worker as the pivotal element of the economic system? Variants or combinations of these? And how do we obtain and interpret the facts on unemployment, poverty, economic growth? How do we identify the causes of concerns within the economic situation? How do we structure the solutions to these concerns? How do we go about assessing the implications, hidden costs, and later effects of the solutions? And how do we go about imposing those solutions?

Three main points should be made at the outset. First, the Bishops have no right to speak on topics where they lack competence. But one surely can detect relevant human moral values at stake in social issues even if one does not comprehend the complete technical complexity of those issues. For example, unemployment carries immense human hurt. This leads to raising legitimate questions about increasing the human cost of unemployment as a solution to inflation. So the Bishops can take a strong stand on unemployment even if there remain ramifications that cannot fully be expressed.

Second, one who lacks competence can develop competence. For example, in preparing their earlier Pastoral on war and peace, *The Challenge of Peace: God's Promise and our Response* (1983)—which dealt in a truly comprehensive way with the moral questions surrounding nuclear weapons and the arms race—the Bishops studied diligently and consulted widely to make themselves competent on many, if not all, issues surrounding the moral implications of the development and continuation of the nuclear arms race. It was said by some that by the conclusion of this study and the issuance of the Pastoral Letter in 1983, many Bishops knew at least as much about nuclear weapons and nuclear war as many members of Congress.

The drafting committee for the Economic Pastoral followed the same procedure with a wide consultation process stretching across many months, utilizing many expert advisors and consultants. The committee took its task quite seriously. The Economic Pastoral is not a document drafted in a month or even in six months. It was a process that literally took years.

This question of competence leads to the third point. One can have a solid measure of competence and still deliver only a probable opinion. This is the nature of the prudential order in which political decisions are made. And the prudential—the order of concrete final decisions—is a field in which the Bishops are qualified to enter.

For this reason, in the Peace Pastoral, the Bishops carefully distinguished between general moral principles which the Catholic Church always upholds and which are always binding, and concrete actions in which judgments can and will differ. The Bishops recognized that people of equal good will might reasonably differ as to application of principles in a given situation. They recognized this freedom to differ even as they stated clearly their own moral conclusions.

So it is with the Economic Pastoral: "Our judgments and recommendations on specific economic issues, therefore, do not carry the same moral authority as our statements of universal moral principles and formal church teaching; the former are related to circumstances which can change or can be interpreted differently by people of good will. We expect and welcome debate on our specific policy recommendations. Nevertheless, we want our statements on these matters to be given serious consideration by Catholics as they determine whether their own moral judgments are consistent with the Gospel and with Catholic social teaching."[18]

Commentating on the Peace Pastoral, Father J. Bryan Hehir, then-director of the USCC Department of Social Development and World Peace, argued that the Bishops had the responsibility to be "thoroughly public in their participation in the wider life of society."[19] That surely may be said equally strongly of the Economic Pastoral. There may be, and indeed are, other views to be weighed against what the Bishops state. But if the Bishops have reflected and reasoned well on the values of the economic issues they address, they will have done the members of the Catholic Church and the general public a needed service.

Archbishop Quinn stated that "religious organizations must earn their way into the public debate by the quality of their positions."[20] That cannot be interpreted to mean that the Church may not enter the public arena unless it has the last word. Correctly, therefore, Hehir observed that in the Peace Pastoral the Bishops did not solve the moral problem of nuclear policy.[21] What they did do was "create explicit space in the public argument of a democratic society so that many voices now face the opportunity and necessity to address the moral question of nuclear policy."[22] That is what the Bishops have done, once again, in the field of economics and concerning the U.S. economic experience.

A final point of methodology is worth noting in passing. The Bishops contrast principles not against applications, but against policies. The former formulation is the familiar "natural law" approach, in which applications were presumed integrally and totally discoverable in the principles adequately understood. In the second formulation—that of the Pastoral—the search for appropriate policies, certainly conducted in the light of the principles, begins with fact-finding and social analysis.

James E. Hug, S.J. provides this thoughtful summation of the Pastoral's methodological process: "The open, participative process strengthened the document considerably by drawing upon the vast resources of the whole Catholic community. This is not simply a pastoral letter of the bishops. It is a pastoral letter of the church that was coordinated, formulated, and published by the bishops. For that very reason, a number of blanket criticisms of the letter arising from the complaint that the bishops are not economists and don't know what they are talking about miss the point. They are largely irrelevant. In this letter as in the Peace Pastoral, the participation and expertise of the whole community—including some of the best economists available—directly shaped Catholic teaching.

This participating process was consciously chosen to operationalize the Second Vatican Council's theological insight that the church is the People of God. It is not to be identified with the hierarchy of pope, bishops, and clergy."[23]

3. The Proposals Are Too Specific

Some commentators, without going so far as to challenge the economic analysis in the Pastoral, argue that its welfare recommendations are too specific. Those making these charges have in mind particularly the welfare sections of unemployment, poverty, and welfare reform.

But a reading of the precise proposals in the Pastoral does not reveal an excess of detail. On poverty, there are six such proposals. Heading the list is a healthy economy, followed by a call to fostering self-help among the poor and improving the quality of education. In addition, the Bishops urge "public spending" in partnership with local private groups to provide seed money as well as training and technical assistance for self-help projects.

More funding is proposed for child care for working parents, in part through tax relief for parents who pay for child care. Enterprises are also asked to provide day-care centers. The Pastoral states that women and minorities should receive full and equal employment and that tax burdens on the poor should be reduced.[24]

These proposals are not too detailed, nor, as a matter of fact, do they call excessively upon the state for their implementation.

On welfare reform, the Pastoral offers three principles, condemns certain myths about welfare recipients, and ends with six guidelines (to be taken up in more detail here in the later discussion on the Bishops and welfare). But such is not the stuff of excessive specificity. The Bishops' critics are here seeking to condemn the Economic Pastoral for its very presence on the scene of public welfare debate. It is only to be wondered what the critics would have said had there been no specific proposals at all.

Further, the relevant sections of John XXIII's *Peace on Earth* (1963) and John Paul II's *On Human Work* (1981)—both treating subjects that have been addressed by the Bishops—reveal that the Bishops are only somewhat more detailed than these encyclicals. That they are more detailed is not matter for surprise when it is remembered that the Popes are speaking on a much more universal level, and have inevitably to be more general than do the Bishops in addressing a particular national situation. Also, Paul VI's *Call to Action* (1971) explicitly invited local churches to analyze their own situation and develop their own solutions to the moral problems they identify.[25]

So those who would excise from the Bishops' Pastoral Letter all specifics on economic matters would logically have to remove from papal statements proposals such as the priority of labor, the need for trade unions, the primacy of a living family wage, the effect on the traditional wage contract of profit-sharing or stock-sharing in management, and the fundamental role of the option for the poor in structuring moral assessments of contemporary problems.

4. Welfare Proposals Are Misguided

Archbishop Rembert Weakland, chair of the NCCB *ad hoc* committee that prepared the Economic Pastoral, said after the first draft that two criticisms dominated: (1) the recommendations often represented discredited programs of the Great Society in the late 1960s, and (2) the recommendations were too similar to programs that have already caused difficulties in European nations. [26] Others speaking against the Pastoral have raised this now-familiar cry of "warmed-over socialism"[27] or "New Deal Redivivus."[28]

A strong voice of opposition to the Pastoral was noted Catholic sociologist, novelist, and commentator, Father Andrew Greeley. He condemned an earlier draft of the document for its supposed betrayal of the basic Catholic principle of "subsidiarity," which states that smaller, local entities should be helped by the state to be and to do for themselves.[29]

Greeley charged that the perspective of the drafters, as evidenced by an absence of a sense of the tradition of subsidiarity, was that this concept had nothing to contribute to the solution of contemporary social problems. He added that the drafters appeared to believe that the only way to solve the problems of the poor is to throw money at them. Money has its role, the prominent sociologist continued, but the document fails to empower the poor through participation in decision-making. This failure derives from the mentality of "the men who are behind the present draft."

The Pastoral, however, drawing upon a rich heritage of Catholic social teaching concerning human empowerment, thoroughly explores the need for empowerment of the poor. The concept of the "option for the poor" does not mean the "opportunity for the rich to feel better by giving money to the poor." Instead, it calls for systemic social and political change. In this, the poorest and most needy of society are not only served with regard to their immediate needs but are also given the skills and abilities, opportunities and directions, encouragement and dignity, to bring themselves fully to the mainstream of enjoyable, productive, healthy participation in a fully human society.

The proposals of the Pastoral, then, on welfare as well as on other economic issues, are neither too specific nor beyond the authority and proper role of the Bishops themselves. They are not only within the basic moral concepts of modern Catholic social teaching, but are a complete expression of the Bishops' authority to speak on such crucial moral questions as the structures, purposes, and programs of our economic system.

5. Bishops Support Economic Democracy and Economic Rights

The condemnation by conservative Catholics of the Bishops' support of the concepts of economic democracy and economic rights is such a fundamental challenge that it will be more thoroughly discussed in a later chapter of this study. Here it is sufficient to describe the challenges themselves.

Conservative Catholic commentator, author and columnist Michael Novak has been a leading critic of the Economic Pastoral. He co-chaired the Commission on the "Lay Letter" which in advance of the final document set forth some basic conservative Catholic viewpoints on the U.S. economy. His response to the document contains much that is typical of the attack upon the Pastoral with respect to "economic democracy" and "economic rights."

One such assault came in a televised debate with former Congressman Robert Drinan. Novak, while not calling the Pastoral a socialist document, asked Drinan why the Bishops, in the preliminary draft then under discussion, used the term "economic democracy." He roundly criticized the use of this term, calling it a favorite "slogan" of well-known American radicals Tom Hayden and Jane Fonda, and suggesting that it meant that the Bishops had totally capitulated to the viewpoints of the far left.[30]

For Novak and others, "economic democracy" necessarily connotes the despicable socialism of Marxism or of neo-Marxism. True, there are many socialists who support the notion of economic democracy. But economic democracy can mean many things, and mainly suggests a more participatory economy less dominated by corporate decisions, large investors, government regulation, and market determinations, and more open to change and to the involvement of those who are part of the economy.

True, many social democrats embrace economic democracy. One example is the Swedish Socialist party. But support for this concept is not remotely confined to socialists, much less to philosophical Marxists. Later, the case will be made that the Bishops, under pressure of the conservative attacks upon this term and the distortion made of the term, abandoned the label of "economic democracy" but decidedly did not abandon the content or the general thrust of the approach. Indeed, the latter could not be done, for this general thrust is fully contained in Catholic social thought.

Similarly, Novak leads the charge against the use of the term "economic rights."[31] This is chiefly due to his perception of the serious implications for government responsibility to meet and support the wide individual demands that supposedly could be made if such rights were to be recognized. Economic rights include the "right" to food, shelter, clothing, employment, livable wage, housing, education, and health care, in addition to private property, and individual initiative. This will also be addressed in a later chapter. But it should be noted briefly that these "rights" are fully within the concept of Catholic social teaching in its treatment of two central issues, the "dignity of the human person" and the "option for the poor."

6. The Bishops Denigrate the U.S. Economic System

Novak is reported to have said "the Lay Letter circled in on what to do for the poor more effectively than the Bishops, and, above all, we don't blame the American people."[32]

Whatever truth there may have been to the charge that the Pastoral in an earlier version failed to do justice to what is good and right in the U.S. cultural and economic systems, this criticism cannot be made of the final document. Indeed, it may here be true that Novak himself can take credit for the more positive tone on that topic in the final document.

As to specific comments in the Pastoral, for example, concerning business, the Pastoral notes that securing economic justice "depends heavily on the leadership of men and women in business." The Pastoral agrees with John Paul II that "the degree of economic well-being which society today enjoys would be unthinkable without the dynamic figure of the business person."[33] In this connection, some charge that the Pastoral is only concerned with redistribution of wealth and not with its production. But scattered throughout the document are demonstrations of an understanding of the productive process and the virtues supportive of that. Some of these pro-business comments are: private property contributes to economic health (115, 128);[34] innovation is important to economic growth (119); justice is measured in part by the ability of the system to deliver a sound and equal economy (137); developing markets are helped by foreign investment (323, 324); and economic freedom, personal initiative and free markets are essential to a healthy economy (295-297).

Despite this support of economic freedom and personal initiative, the Bishops are careful to note certain limitations: "we have increasingly come to recognize the inescapably social and political nature of the economy. The market is always imbedded in a specific social and political context"(313). The Bishops go on to list several political features of the economy, such as the tax system, defense policy, monetary policy, protection of the environment, and regulation of international trade.

Also, there is praise for the past. The Pastoral notes that the nation's founders "took daring steps to create the structures of participation, mutual accountability and widely distributed power" (297). This to ensure freedom and political rights. If this is all to the good, what is now needed is to expand economic participation, broaden a sharing of economic power (295). In a similar vein, the Bishops extol the great venture of the Founding Fathers to establish justice and promote the general welfare "of which those who live in this land are beneficiaries" (295). All that the Bishops challenge Catholics to do here is to make this ideal situation a reality for all U.S. citizens. The Bishops rightly point out that "a fair share in the general welfare is denied to many" (295).

Finally, there is praise for the power of the U.S. economy. The United States is "among the most economically powerful nations on earth." It has given "unprecedented standard of living for most" people. Also, the United States has created "productive work for millions"; it has likewise "encouraged citizens to bold ventures." And its citizenry "through hard work, self-sacrifice and cooperation" have brought "to flourish families, towns, cities, and a powerful nation" (6).

But this praise is also tempered with realism suggesting "sober humility." The U.S. experiment has involved "serious conflict and injustice." A series of these conflicts are then related. The Bishops note some of the contradictions that still haunt U.S. political and social history: treatment of the Indians, violent revolution, slavery, denial of the vote to women, denial of civil rights to blacks, the shame of child labor, the despair of the Great Depression (7).

On the question of economic democracy and the Bishops' supposed lack of support of the U.S. system, prominent Massachusetts Institute of Technology economist Lester Thurow, a vocal supporter of the Pastoral, has written language far less benign than the Bishops' concerning whether the degree to which free enterprise and the market are an organizing force for justice. He notes in *Zero-Sum Society* that he opposes the belief that the market can create fairness or that the conservative solution of cutting the standard of living of wage-earners is the proper means to international competitiveness.[35] Thurow also opposes limiting the role of government in urging fairness upon the economic landscape and seriously questions whether inequity is necessary to combat inflation.

So while the Bishops do not hesitate to point out the difficulties which have beset the U.S. economic system and the inequities which have driven it, their Pastoral is generous in its acclaim of the U.S. economy and of the opportunities it has afforded for upward mobility, for creating and sustaining a post-War middle class, and for its ability to meet the needs of consumers.

Yet the Pastoral would certainly be remiss in its purpose were it content with a glowing description of the U.S. economy. The Bishops seek to raise moral and social challenges, not be cheerleaders for the marketplace. The Pastoral, therefore, is particularly concerned with what the U.S. economy has *not* been able to do, and how to address those problems.

II. CRITICISMS WITHIN RANKS SUPPORTIVE OF THE PASTORAL

In addition to the critics who have largely or totally rejected the Bishops' work, there are others who, while strongly supportive of the Pastoral, have taken seriously the invitation of the drafting committee to help improve it. One such group is the Center of Concern, which made several recommendations for each draft of the Pastoral.[36]

The Center of Concern team felt that the theological method of the first draft appeared to be a speculative "biblicism". Its theological reflection, its appeal to the scriptures, were insufficiently grounded in the experiential. Moreover, the concept of Christian "discipleship" appeared excessively male. In general, more attention was urged on the role of women in the world of work, and on their needs and contributions. The first draft also ignored the negative impact of militarization of the economy. More attention should be directed, it was further suggested, to the disastrous consequences of our economy on the environment and on the.availability of natural resources.

The Center of Concern also raised the question of the document's excessive anthropocentrism. This theology of the human as crown of creation and overlord of nature seemed a limited vision of God's total creation. True, Vatican II's *Church in the Modern World* sets the tone for this focus on the human. "All things on earth should be related to [the human person] as their center and jewel."[37] It would have been too much to expect the Bishops to question this theology with its strong roots in the *Genesis* account of the creation mandate given to humankind. Certainly, one of the worst manifestations of that domination of nature by the human, ecological destruction, is condemned in the Pastoral. Still, one may wonder whether a long-term conservation program for humanity in the world of which it is inextricably a part does not call for a new language of regeneration of the whole biosphere—with the human in community *with*—and not set apart from or above—the rest of creation.

There were two other concerns expressed by the Center: first, the original drafts did not give the family the centrality in the economy that Catholic social thought accords it; second, the Pastoral in its attention to the poor seemed in danger of ignoring the middle class in the United States.

As to the family, fundamental to this concern is that U.S. liberals, fixated on an individualistic view of social interaction and personal rights, rather typically ignore the family. Their notion of welfare runs, not in terms of government support of families, but of state attention to needs of individuals.

There is, to be sure, an immoral familialism which turns the family in on itself, fostering a deplorable family individualism. There is also the fact that centering on the family can lead to neglect of those many people—and very many women—who by choice or necessity (much more the latter) do not live in nuclear families. Catholic social thought, with its strong emphasis on the family, has ignored these "singles." Both these issues need to be addressed further in a more comprehensive Catholic social teaching on the family. Both these acknowledgements made, the challenge still was legitimate that the earliest drafts of the Pastoral stood in danger of sounding too much like a liberal individualist approach rather than a proper recognition of the role of the family in society.

Turning to the industrial process, one meets a different attack on the family. Industrial economies have been structured in such a way as to make the family and its values peripheral, a private affair, public only as an object of media influence. As a result, the family is not accorded adequate treatment in political-economic debates. By not challenging that situation explicitly, and by not treating the family as central, the earliest draft of the Pastoral reinforced a private-public dualism.

Concern about the impact of the industrial process on the family—long hours outside the home for both spouses, forced geographic mobility, duration of unemployment—is also a concern about the attack on the family mounted by mass media, especially television. Television has become an extremely powerful social force and much of its programming has eroded healthy family images and healthy family interaction.

The final text of the Pastoral made note of these important concerns.[38] Competition has too many negative consequences for the family (345, 92 and 94); the economy "must support the family" (346); the breakdown of the family owes much to false television advertising (345). Social service, the document adds, "must be scrutinized in light of whether it ensures both individual dignity and family integrity"(93).

As for the middle class, the problem many saw was that the Bishops took seriously the plight of the poor but did not recognize the negative impact of the economy on the middle class. Most American Catholics are not poor, though subject to financial insecurity. They are, as the expression has it, one layoff, or one protracted illness away from financial crisis. Still, they pay taxes, contribute to the economy and often manage to put their children through college.

The first draft gave the impression that the Bishops thought of this middle class as somehow to be identified with the rich. The hierarchy was in danger of alienating a vast body from their project of having all Catholics answer the Pastoral's invitation to address U.S. economic inequities.

The Bishops rectified this impression in the second draft of the Pastoral. Eight paragraphs are directed to recognition of the middle class. This was done without diminishing the option for the poor that is such a crucial concept to the entire document (87-89), or at the expense of challenging the middle class to review, where necessary, an excessively affluent lifestyle. For example, the Pastoral states, "Many middle-class Americans feel themselves in the grip of economic demands and cultural processes" (23). More specifically, the Pastoral insists that the option for the poor is "not an adversarial slogan that pits one group or class against another"(88). Indeed, the Bishops are careful to link that option to the good of the whole society: the option is "to enable *all* to share in and contribute to the common good"(88; emphasis in original). That is, just as others, e.g., middle classes, share in the common good, so likewise should the poor. This relationship of classes sharing—with priority attention to the poor—gets an alternative statement: "The obligation to provide justice *for all* means that the poor have the most urgent claim..."(86; emphasis added).

In summary, this opening chapter has reviewed two classes of criticism of the Economic Pastoral in either its initial or final drafts. Why was this done? In the case of the first class of critics, more-or-less hostile, there was the need to confront their rejections of the Bishops' right and competence to speak. This was to keep the Pastoral from simply being laughed out of court. The charges against the Bishops have been shown to be completely unfounded. With regard to the second class of criticism—from those supportive of the document as it developed—the purpose was to celebrate the process adopted by the Bishops from the outset. That process was to welcome dialogue from whatever quarter and to be prepared to incorporate worthy emendations.

Thus the brief review of the core of the criticism of the Economic Pastoral substantiates the legitimacy that properly can be attributed to the Bishops' document. It also underscores the attention that should be paid to its concrete proposals, including and especially those on welfare.

ENDNOTES FOR CHAPTER I

[1] As I am editing these chapters, Pope John Paul II has just issued (February 19, 1988) his encyclical *The Social Concern of the Church* (Sollicitudo Rei Socialis), commemorating the 20th anniversary of Paul VI's remarkable encyclical *The Progress of Peoples*. That document was generally dismissed by the economic right. One heard, "It's only warmed-over socialism." Such was the same charge against the Bishops' Economic Pastoral. The guns have not yet begun to roll against the new encyclical. But when they do, the criticism of the U.S. Bishops will by comparison seem mild. For the Bishops come nowhere near the sweeping condemnation of liberal capitalism that characterizes the current papal teaching. There is nothing in the Bishops' Pastoral of the encyclical's severe condemnation of capitalism's (as well as the Eastern Bloc's) "sinful structures" of imperialist exploitation. Both sides are equally put to task.

[2] *New Republic*, December 24, 1985.

[3] Ibid.

[4] Writing in support of that first draft, November 1984, Peter Steinfels, then editor of *Commonweal* and now religious editor of the *New York Times*, gives a sampling of critics of that first draft. He tells us that William F. Buckley dismissed the draft as "an accumulation of lumpen cliches" and a "puree of...vapidity." Steinfels says further that George F. Will outdid Buckley in disdain. "The bishops," Will began, "discovered that God subscribes to the liberal agenda." And further:"...in the mental world to which the Bishops in their flight from complexity have immigrated, there are no intellectual difficulties, no insoluble problems— there are only shortages of good will." The pundit goes on: "Their letter is marinated in conventional wisdom." Steinfels, *Dissent*, Spring 1985, 177 ff.

William Simon, former Secretary of the Treasury under President Nixon, and Michael Novak, writer at the American Enterprise Institute, wrote in anticipation of the first draft the conservative "Lay Letter":

Toward the Future: Catholic Social Thought and the U.S. Economy (New York: Lay Commission on Catholic Social Teaching, 1984).

[5] Thomas J. Reese, *America,* February 2, 1985, writing on the first draft.

[6] Testimony before Congress, March 19, 1985. All quotations in this paragraph except the last are from this testimony.

[7] Ibid.

[8] Tobin testifying before Congress, March 19, 1985.

[9] Ibid.

[10] Leonard Silk, *New York Times.*

[11] Christianity and Social Progress, 16. For full texts of key papal documents of 1961-1975, see Joseph Gremillion, *The Gospel of Peace and Justice* (Maryknoll, N.Y.: Orbis Books 1975). Reconstruction was written to celebrate the sixtieth anniversary of Leo XIII's pioneering social encyclical, *Rerum Novarum,* 1891.

[12] *Justice in the World*, produced by the 1971 Synod of Bishops, proved one of the most influential documents of official church teaching on social questions. The synod had been strongly influenced by the 1968 teaching on justice by the Bishops of all Latin America, meeting in Medellin, Colombia. The Synod's methodology is that of "reading the signs of the times" to discover where God is moving in our world.

[13] Dogmatic Constitution on the Church, in Walter Abbott, S.J., ed., The Documents of Vatican II (New York: America Press, 1966), 31. The question is taken up more extensively by that same Council in its major document, *The Church in the Modern World,* 43.

[14] Recommendation of national and regional conferences of Bishops is to be found authoritatively in Vatican II's *Constitution on The Church,* in Abbott, op. cit., ch. 3, "Concerning the cooperation of bishops for the common good of many churches", especially sections 36-38. The latter section introduces the regional conference, recommending their cooperation where they have common cultures or concerns. An early example of such is the Conference of the Bishops of Latin America, begun in 1899.

The official body of U.S. Bishops, sanctioned by Vatican II, is the National Conference of Catholic Bishops (NCCB). Most people hear much more about the USCC, that is, the United States Catholic

Conference. The latter is the executive arm of the former. Through it the body of bishops relates to priests, religious and laity. The USCC has three departments: education, communications, and social development/world peace. These serve the church and the world through their respective episcopal committees and staff.

15 May 1971, *Call to Action.* This Apostolic Letter commemorates the eightieth anniversary of *Rerum Novarum.*

16 Cited by Avery Dulles, S.J., *America,* June 11, 1983. Cardinal Ratzinger is president of the Vatican's Sacred Congregation of the Faith, known before the Vatican II as The Holy Office.

17 Ibid.

18 *Economic Justice for All,* 135. The equivalent is present also in *The Challenge of Peace,* 9 and 10. The Peace Pastoral, like the subsequent Economic Pastoral, was the fruit of many months of input from a variety of sources and of intense dialogue. Voices from many positions on the political spectrum were invited to help the Bishops explore the intricacies of a number of positions. The Bishops carried forward the debate into their own annual sessions for three years.

Like the later Economic Pastoral, so did the Peace Pastoral explore biblical sources, as well as the "signs of the times," in an effort to find God's word operative in our times. Both relevant traditions within the Catholic Church of the Just War theory and of Pacifism (together with non-violence and civil disobedience) were explored.

Despite their grave misgivings about nuclear missiles, the Bishops opted finally for a "strictly conditioned moral acceptance of nuclear deterrence" (e.g., 186). Given the misgivings of many within the ranks of the Bishops and the world outside the episcopal ranks over whether their conditions for moral acceptance could or would be accepted, the Conference, after publication of its work in 1983, set up an episcopal commission to review their "strictly conditioned moral acceptance."

19 J. Bryan Hehir, Commencement address at Catholic University of America, *Origins* (vol.14, no.3) May 31, 1984.

20 Address to the Yale Club "Several Meanings of Religion and Politics," *Origins* (vol.14, no.14) September 20, 1984.

21 Hehir, loc.cit.

22 Ibid.

[23] "Church Influence in the Economics of Health Care: Implications of Economic Justice for All: Pastoral Letter on Catholic Social Teaching and the U.S. Economy," in James E. Hug, S.J., ed., *Promoting Catholic Health Care Ministry* (St. Louis: Catholic Health Association, forthcoming).

[24] *Economic Justice For All*, 196-206.

[25] *Call To Action*, 4.

[26] *America*, September 21, 1985. This Jesuit weekly had devoted the entire issue of January 5-12, 1985, to the Economic Pastoral. Joseph Califano, who had helped President Johnson draft that Administration's welfare proposals, in his article of that issue said disparagingly that the Pastoral "sounds like one of the legislative messages I helped draft."

[27] This charge, of course, has frequently been made against recent papal social encyclicals.

[28] Michael Novak, of the American Enterprise Institute, on several occasions challenged the views advanced in the Economic Pastoral toward U.S. free enterprise, much of its social philosophy and its welfare proposals. In particular, he judged to be misconceived the support of welfare as a human right. (This will be explored further in Chapter VIII on "Catholic Social Thought and Welfare.")

[29] *America*, November 9, 1985. Greeley is an associate of the National Opinion Research Center of Chicago and a professor at the University of Arizona.

[30] Televised debate with former Congressman Robert Drinan, November 20, 1985, before the Roosevelt Center for American Policy Studies, Washington D.C.

[31] "Economic Rights: The Servile State," *Catholicism in Crisis*, October 1985.

[32] "Patriotism" is often used by conservative writers to squelch criticism of U.S. programs and actions.

[33] *Economic Justice for All*, 110; see also 117.

[34] In this and the three paragraphs that follow all references in parentheses are to the Economic Pastoral.

[35] *Zero-Sum Society* (New York, Basic Books, 1985). All references in parentheses are to Zero-Sum Society. Thurow, one of the bright lights among younger and more progressive economists, is author of several books in economics, a columnist, and widely sought after for consultation.

[36] See Memoranda from Center of Concern, Washington D.C., 1984-86.

[37] Pastoral Constitution on the Church in the Modern World, Gremillion, 12.

[38] All subsequent references in parentheses are to the Economic Pastoral.

2

FOUNDATIONS

OF THE

WELFARE DEBATE

When the New Deal began a new era of government involvement in the economics of public life, there was a dearth of welfare experience in the United States. Even in the 1960s, there was only rudimentary analysis of the impact of Great Society programs. Most of what was known or thought to be known about welfare, its role, its extent, and its impact was based on the same suppositions from which a particular perspective was offered. Although in some degree underlying suppositions still affect the direction taken by a particular commentary, at least by the 1980s there are plenty of statistics for everybody.

This second round of debate about welfare in this country began with the entry of the Reagan Administration into politics and the New Right's doctrine of the "truly needy" and their beliefs that less government involvement in the economy will be most beneficial and welfare really has not worked anyway. This debate is still underway. But beyond the suppositions critics and supporters alike can now turn to a vast body of social research on welfare, dealing in a variety of ways with the various forms of welfare and with those who receive it.

These studies, abetted by ideologies, have brought about the consensus averted to in the introduction to this book. Was there no consensus at all during the New Deal (1930s) and Great Society (1960s) eras? There was, but not at the philosophical level. Ideological antagonism ruled the day, as much or more than in our times. What consensus there was had the character of a left-leaning, liberal-dominated agreement on the part of the U.S. public generally, a populist consensus. Conservatives never could countenance anything of that consensus, for they already regarded any welfare as misguided.

This situation, still in existence in a basic way today, emphasizes the bipolar nature of the U.S. discussion of welfare. An examination of this discussion in its basic philosophical/ideological foundations provides a background for a review of the Bishops' recommendations on welfare.

I. TWO FUNDAMENTAL POSITIONS

Essentially, what is evident in the strikingly divergent approaches to economic policy and welfare has been—and remains—the difference in the assumptions to be made about national political direction. These assumptions concern basic values such as: the importance of authority, the role of the state, the responsibility of the individual for his or her own fate, the extent of governmental responsibility and capacity to affect the complex factors accounting for poverty, and individual responsibility to the poor. The Bishops' Pastoral provides an opportunity for these viewpoints to be gathered into a discussion of poverty, U.S. economic policy, and the role of welfare.

Also evident in this examination of the alternative philosophical approaches to welfare are social and political foundations emanating from Enlightenment and Utilitarian development in Europe. Historically, these philosophies have contributed fundamentally to political and social attitudes in the United States. This country was born of Enlightenment ideals about the social contract the rights of the people versus the state, and the independence of nations. While it is not possible to give extensive treatment of each of these philosophical approaches, a brief description of the most pertinent ones will serve to provide background for the debate on U.S. welfare policy.

Very helpful in fixing the essentials of the long-standing bipolarity of welfare philosophy is the 1985 book *Habits of the Heart* by Robert Bellah and associates.[1] The authors compare two basic poles in economic thought: what they term on the right, "Neo-Capitalism," and on the left, "Welfare Capitalism." This nomenclature is eminently serviceable, even though others have alternative titles for these perspectives. It must also be remembered that these perspectives are in turn a reflection of a world view and an orientation that are based on many other social forces and influences. So one often speaks of far more than economics when addressing economic issues, particularly when facts or statistics are subject to varying interpretations.

Bellah's socio-economic foundations for these ideologies is drawn from the radically changed circumstances following the 1929 collapse of the private corporate economy in the United States. The emerging debate then, as now, pitted a revived Capitalism or Neo-Capitalism against the vision of some form of welfare gradually evolving out of the various New Deal policies. The roots of both perspectives are much earlier.

The central issue for these contesting economic viewpoints, as it still is before the U.S. public today, was how best to secure material well-being for citizens, while also securing as much individual choice as possible in decision about one's goals. Both camps carried forward the U.S.

enthusiasm for industrial and technical progress. The Neo-Capitalist vision derived more immediately from the creed of corporate business of the Nineteenth century, as business began to free itself from the confining strictures of local political communities.

Business, proclaiming itself to be the true guarantor of the better life, decidedly rejected public action in the economy. According to Bellah, the rhetoric of a 1980s Ronald Reagan now epitomizes the mood of the Neo-Capitalist. For Reagan the true mission of life is to build "a new consensus of all those across this land who share a community of values imbedded in these words: family, work, neighborhood, peace and freedom."

But for Reagan, as Bellah also points out, these words are an evocation of private rather than of public virtues. Work is economic activity pursued by self-reliant individuals in the interest of themselves and their families. Indeed, says Reagan,"We, the people, are special interest groups." These are made up "of men and women who raise our food, patrol our streets, man our mines and factories, keep our homes and heal us when we are sick.[2]

The flaw in this, argues Bellah, is defining the U.S. people by occupation. Reagan names us by who we are economically, not politically. We are a collection of interest groups, chiefly preoccupied with "a healthy, growing economy that provides equal opportunity for all Americans." However, this is not the full picture.

For example, the Reagan economic view often applauds neighborhood action. But, says Bellah, neighborhood activity is always a purely voluntary association of neighbors who know one another and freely express concern for one another. Reagan's association remains a purely private affair, in no way a public form of association. If this form of human interaction retains some relation to the Nineteenth Century town, it is only on the narrow view of the town as foundation for a private life. Finally, the dynamic of the free market in this view remains the sole effective means of integrating the national society.

And what of government's role in this Neo-Capitalist perspective? It is primarily to promote the peace and security needed to establish a framework wherein self-reliant individuals can undertake their pursuit of largely economic aims in freedom. For the Reagan approach, Bellah affirms, a government attempting to provide more than such essentials is overgrown. There may be a need for a minimal "safety net" for individuals who fail in their quest for self-sufficiency—presumably through no fault of their own. But such a safety net would be geared only to the protection of the "truly needy." Consistent with this, Reagan believes that concern for those disadvantaged people who are not—in his perception—truly needy should be pursued as a matter of private virtue and not as a public responsibility.

Welfare Liberalism has two approaches to providing individuals with the means for pursuing their private ends. First, some degree of administration by the national government is needed to keep in balance market operations in the interest of economic growth and social harmony. Welfare Liberalism, no less than Neo-Capitalism, accepts the capitalist market and its private institutions as the core mechanism of growth of material abundance. Welfare Liberalism's second approach distinguishes it from Neo-Capitalism. This is to expand government's role beyond simply that of administrative machinery corrective of the market. The state should also function as provider of an entire range of services perceived as needed. This, of course, is the history of the Roosevelt effort in the early 1930s.

The economic success of the post-World War II period made it possible for great growth of such government programs. Those programs were also encouraged by a near total liberal consensus of the U.S. public in support of welfare. But this consensus was never shared by Neo-Capitalism except for a small and more progressive wing that went along with the Liberals—up to a point. The more right-wing of the Neo-Capitalists simply bided their time, waiting for their chance to reverse the welfare momentum when the economy would turn down and disadvantaged people would grow cold on the "shell-out" for welfare.

That moment came toward the end of the 1970s. A variety of factors led the country into extremely unsettling and nearly disastrous periods of inflation and recession, triggered in particular by the high cost of crucial imports such as foreign oil. Economic discontent led to a rethinking of governmental spending policies on social programs, even while a new political conservatism re-established the priority of spending on national defense and national security, thus reinforcing the cuts on programs for the poor.

For Welfare Liberalism, in Bellah's view, the public good or national harmony is seen as a fair sharing in the fruits of economic growth. Governments exist to promote the economic growth that guarantees individuals a fair chance and an equal opportunity to benefit from that growth. Such equality connotes an equal chance to engage in economic competition, free from exploitation.

In Bellah's reading, the debate between Neo-Capitalism and Welfare Liberalism is not over fostering individual self-reliance, but over the means to achieve it. For the Welfare Liberal, this goal could only be accomplished under two conditions: the economy must be managed by bureaucratic agencies, guided by experts and social scientists; and the disadvantaged must be given governmental assistance to enable them to compete on an equal basis for the fruits of economic opportunity.

For those who fail in the competition, Welfare Liberalism offers much the same ethical solace as Neo-Capitalism: compassion. However, this compassion differs from the Neo-Capitalist's in that there is reliance on the state to do something to respond to the misery of unfortunate individuals. Still this compassion and some accompanying sense of justice were inadequate to fend off the attack from the Right at a moment when the Liberals were vulnerable. That moment arrived when the economic growth the Liberals rely on was turned off. Then, the Welfare Liberals could only withdraw as the Right lashed out at their "do-goodism" which supposedly was "ruining the country" and "impoverishing the middle class." It is fine to express compassion, sneered the Right, with other people's money.

The economic downturn of the late 1970s triggered just such crisis for Welfare Liberalism and educed just the reaction described in the preceding paragraph. Neo-Capitalism, up on top, pushed with breezy confidence its program. Bellah rightly perceived the Liberal vulnerability to rest, at this moment of challenge, in their lack of a philosophy of public good: an articulated good for the totality of the citizenry and not just for an accumulation of individual goods. To be sure, a number of Liberals have themselves been the first to point out this gap in Liberal social philosophy. A few will be mentioned shortly. Still, Bellah is correct in his conclusion that Liberals, along with Neo-Conservative individuals, had lost the sense of an earlier U.S. view of the public good—what Catholic social teaching calls, as will be described later, the "common good." The Liberals had lost the "republican" virtues that promoted the public good, virtues deep within the U.S. political consciousness.

II. COMMON PHILOSOPHICAL ROOTS
OF RIGHT AND LEFT

There is nearly as much that holds Right and Left together as separates them. This commonality has its source in the philosophies of the Enlightenment and of Utilitarianism. Since Catholic social teaching (and therefore the U.S. Bishops' welfare proposals) is grounded in a totally different tradition, these philosophies themselves and their influence on the approach of Left and Right to welfare need to be described.

This exploration, in turn, requires an inquiry into the curious twist by which the word consistently used in Europe to designate the Right—"liberalism"—has in its voyage across the Atlantic become in the United States the word to designate the Left. Oddly, in their sense of the word "liberal," U.S. progressives have moved back to the very earliest source of the term—the human effort to throw off the shackles of institutions that chained human freedom. Such was the European movement of "liberalism." Those who attacked prevailing institutions, whether of a secular or religious nature, were designated "Liberals." These recognized the need for emancipation from inhibiting cultures that, along with princes and bishops, obstinately refused to see any good in the new developments of science, technology, and philosophy.

How then did this "liberalism," supported at one time by all sides in what would now be the U.S. political spectrum, become the appellation of one wing of emancipators, rejected by the other? It came through a joining of economics and physics. Economic philosophers rejected in business affairs rules made by governments. They viewed these as crippling new energies and modern visions and prospects. Enamored of the methods of Newtonian physics in its description of natural phenomena, the liberal economists of Europe declared that human associations should be arranged and governed according to the free flow of human energies. One of these economic philosophers, Adam Smith, proposed a Newtonian application to the world of producing and trading in unfettered, free markets.

Thus, the liberal view was to allow capitalism to develop according to its own "natural" laws of accumulation of goods and providing of services solely through free human enterprise. The best results would be achieved by leaving the market alone (*laissez-faire*—from which comes the term "Laissez-Faire Capitalism"). The more religiously-inclined among the liberal European economic philosophers viewed these "forces of economic nature" as being in effect the working out of an order willed by God. It was a physiocratic world, wound up, as it were, by the Supreme Being to operate as a finely-tuned, purposeful mechanism.

The product of early economic liberalism, laissez-faire capitalism, became branded by the rest of the original emancipators as "Liberal Capitalism." To describe themselves, on the other hand, this second school of Liberalism possessed no single name. Some called themselves "Progressives." Some denominated themselves "Social Thinkers," others "Social Democrats," still others, "Socialists."

Catholic social thinkers massively opposed the Liberal Capitalism of the time, as they still do today. The social encyclicals of the popes joined in this opposition and in various ways called for a social framing of the market and for state involvement in it.

On the other side of the Atlantic, in the United States, "progressives" along European lines had, in view of the original core truth of Liberalism as emancipation from the shackles of unjust systems, no difficulty in being known as "Liberals." What European Progressives knew as "Liberals" and "Liberal Capitalism," U.S. progressives came to call "Conservatives" and "Conservative Capitalism." With that twist of nomenclature straightened out, one can proceed to explore the common root metaphors on which rest both "conservative" and "liberal" visions.

Liberalism and Laissez-faire Capitalism or classic Conservatism in the United States have common roots in both the Enlightenment of the Seventeenth and Eighteenth Centuries and in that era's Utilitarianism.[3]

Enlightenment philosophy demanded freeing of the individual from all restraints: economic control exercised by the earlier Mercantile state, political monarchy, thought control imposed by traditional cultures, and, finally, religion, which was perceived as linked to and in league with those same inhibiting forces. In place of all such restraint, the Enlightenment proposed the "domination" of human reason over nature, over traditional culture, over the power of the throne, and over the dehumanizing controls many forms of religion sought to impose. Alongside reason, the Enlightenment enthroned science and progress.

The Utilitarians, including such famous figures as Jeremy Bentham and John Locke, added other elements which in turn strongly influenced modern social thought, including early U.S. political development.[4] They also had some impact on Catholic social teaching, including that of Leo XIII. (Locke over time modified his Utilitarianism.)

Basically, Utilitarianism taught that the useful or the pleasurable is the good and goal of life. Each individual—as individual—seeks to maximize pleasure (utility) over pain (disutility). The highest accomplishment for a nation is to achieve the greatest good for the greatest number (of individuals—again as individuals.) However large the aggregate of goods might become, it never constitutes the common good of the collectivity or community of persons. The good must be viewed and defined always at the individual level. For Bentham and Locke, government is best when it best meets the interests and desires of individuals.

Out of this common focus on the individual, espoused by the Enlightenment and Utilitarianism, as well as European "progressivism," U.S. liberalism began to forget its humanitarian stance within Individualism. Liberals were very much moved by compassion for the victims of an individualistic society, those hurt by the mechanism of a laissez-faire economy. Liberals also recognized that capitalism, while professing free markets, had in fact moved strongly into monopoly power that could be cruel and disastrous to the weak.

U.S. liberals also recognized that trade unions had to take the road of power to meet this challenge by industry. They perceived that this head-on clash of powers—capital and labor—would force the modern state to develop a countervailing power. All this the liberal economist John Kenneth Galbraith would raise to a theory of society under the aegis of "countervailing power".[5] Compassion (in part) moved one branch of Individualism into the progressiveness that Americans (contrary to Europeans) designate Liberalism. But Conservatives for their part dismissed the state as guardian of the individual's goods, in confidence that the market would best address individual needs. Conservatives, also true inheritors of the Enlightenment and Utilitarianism, sought to maximize the good of individuals—as did the "Liberals"—always as individuals. The only difference was that where the progressive liberal forces relied very considerably on government to achieve the good of individuals, the conservative groups believed that with only a little alteration here and there the free market was fully adequate to the task.

Against this Conservative assurance, Liberals saw with clearer perception over time that a central social problem was that of meeting the need of *disadvantaged* individuals. Toward this goal there was need of managing the economy. There was need also of allowing for some countervailing government power to aid the weak and marginal in the power battle of the titans of capital and labor. The Utilitarian concept of countervailing power, gradually imbedded in U.S. Liberalism, in no way resembles the "common good" found in Catholic social thought. Liberal notions of countervailing power, to repeat, are as individualistic and utilitarian as are those of the Right. Liberals, further, give more acceptance than does Catholic social thought to the market and private institutions as means to material abundance. Society for the Liberals is a collective of individuals and individual interest groups, pushed into social harmony by two forces. First is competition among their collective interests, a competition which prevents any one group from dominating. Second is state action on the economy as the state exercises its response to the countervailing powers spoken of above.

For U.S. Liberals, no more than for Conservatives, there is an intrinsic ordering of the protagonists of society and their social functions. There is no organic integration of social components. There is only mechanistic balancing, as weight shifts from one individual or interest-group component to another, given various times and various issues. This approach harkens back to the Enlightenment's enthronement of Newtonian physics as the model of how a society operates. Society is made up of isolated clusters or blocks of free flowing, atomistic parts creating a continual and dynamic interaction of individual or group interests, each seeking to realize its own goal.

By contrast, modern Catholic social thought, particularly the social documents and Papal encyclicals of the past three decades, has considered the social order more in terms of an organic whole. Each of the parts has its rights and responsibilities for the growth and improvement of the social order as a whole. From that social good each individual has a right to draw, and this not only in the political and civil order but also in the social and economic order.

Catholic social thought also limits the extent of governmental authority over individuals. Thus, Catholic social teaching shares key concepts with Liberals and with Conservatives, while possessing perspectives not found in either. The Church's social teaching stands apart from each of the poles of the commonly recognized political spectrum.

With this understanding of the common philosophical core of Right and Left, a more precise exploration can now be made of the varieties of

Neo-Capitalism and Welfare Liberalism, the two poles with which this discussion began. In effect, the question here is how some of these approaches produce a spectrum of positions on welfare.

III. THE RIGHT'S PERSPECTIVES ON WELFARE

1. Market Welfare

The first and most radical Right position argues that the market can and must be allowed to procure welfare. If allowed to function freely, the market provides maximum welfare for all. This appears to be the position of Milton and Rose Friedman in their *Free To Choose* "Most of the present welfare programs should never have been enacted."[6] Some "free marketers" are prepared to admit that a redistributive function may be called for where the market fails to provide some satisfactory degree of equality. Nevertheless, they would still maintain that the market has the virtue at least of achieving a maximization of the Gross National Product (GNP) from which society can then shape distribution as it sees fit-- hopefully in line with neo-conservative values.

2. Supply-side Economics

This position mounts a somewhat different attack on welfare. The U.S. economy will not be firmly set on the tracks of enduring recovery unless more savings are promoted that can flow into more productive investment. On this will depend the United States' competitiveness in the world. Supply-siders thus shift decisively away from any Keynesian emphasis on increased consumption to get the nation out of recession.

Keynesianism! Before going on with Supply-siders a word must be said about Keynesianism, since it figures so strongly in the Right's—and Supply-siders'—attack on welfare. Keynesianism underwent such an onslaught in the 1970s that some declared its death-knell. But it is currently staging a strong comeback, as the attacks on it sound every day less convincing. In the process, a more naive Keynesianism on the part of some has yielded to a Keynesianism which, while retaining its solid traditional core, has learned to embrace what truth is discoverable in opposing ideas.

An excellent account of this history can be found in Alan Blinder's *Hard Heads, Soft Hearts*.[7] Keynesianism of today may be seen as embracing several economic and political notions:

a) There is faith in governmental fiscal power to stabilize public demand for goods and services. Thus, government may exercise some measure of control over either unemployment or inflation as desired. These cyclically alternating developments, each posing danger if allowed to go unchecked, must be adjusted alternately. The government, in choosing to reduce inflation, must accept some degree of unemployment; yet to seek full employment, there must be some degree of inflation.

Blinder notes that many of today's Keynesians are open to the possibility, at least in the long run, of affecting positively at one and the same time both unemployment and inflation. In any event, Keynesians are committed to reducing unemployment as a primary goal.

b) The money supply plays an important role in taxing and spending policies. Towards affecting aggregate demand, Keynesians accept from Monetarists the notion of the crucial role of the money supply, alongside fiscal policies of taxing and spending. But unlike Monetarists, Keynesians believe that fiscal policy is at least as important as monetary policy (that is, governmental spending priorities as important as increasing or decreasing the money supply). They are also skeptical about the benefits of stability and predictability in the growth of the money supply as controller of inflation—the crux of Monetarism. Keynesians believe that an infusion of new money into the demand stream at any given moment, as circumstances require, can get an economy moving. They are prepared to accept this even at the risk of inflation, hoping the latter can be controlled.

c) Public expectations are a major factor in economic health. The Keynesians have introduced into their system the role of expectations, a lesson learned from other economic adversaries, this time the "Rational Expectationalists." These had scorned earlier Keynesians for assuming that future economic behavior would follow in the path of past behavior of demand for and spending on goods and services. But, for example, past inflationary experiences are not necessarily good predictors of how and when future inflationary episodes will occur. Now, with their critics, new Keynesians accept a role for changes in public expectations, although some still question the practical value of this theoretical insight.

d) Alterations in supply can change public expectations. Keynesians have introduced into their equation alongside their demand focus the recognition of a role—a passive one—for supply. They had missed the importance of this aspect in the 1972-74 period of failure of the supply of food and oil. But, they add, influencing supply is far more difficult than influencing demand.

e) The classic "Invisible Hand" notion of Adam Smith and others is rejected. Smith and his followers contended that if each person pursues their own individual self-interest, the result will be an economy that serves the needs and interests of all. Individual pursuits collectively "guide" the economy like an "invisible hand." Keynesians still reject the idea that the private economy is a huge auction hall guided exclusively by individual bids of supply and demand. They reject equally the notion that such an economy can regulate itself or will develop either smoothly or reliably.

    f) Taxing can reduce debts and deficits. When, whether, how, and to what extent public debt and deficits are to be reduced is a core debate in economics today. While Keynesians remain expansionists—government economic policy must expand, not contract—they also believe that the debt and deficit must be reduced. For that reduction they rely mainly on tax increases.

But now to return to the discussion of the Supply-siders, after this brief explanation of today's Keynesianism. Where will one find the extra savings required to stabilize the economy through increased investment? This is the fundamental thrust of the Supply-siders' economics. Their "obvious" answer: divert to private savings/investment the tax money presently expended on unemployment compensation, aid to dependent children, and other welfare programs. That shift of "released funds" to investment will bring increased productivity, and more jobs and wages. And from this economic expansion, individuals and families will be better able to care for themselves—thus reducing the welfare burden on government. If there remain any truly needy—but only the truly needy—these would have government help.

3. Laffler's Supply-side

As an extension of Supply-side, conservative economist Arthur Laffler, in a view wholly embraced by the Reagan Administration, explains that a large reduction in personal income taxes would provide such strong incentive to work and to invest that the economy would realize tremendous growth. The lost tax receipts would be more than recouped through the enlarged tax base that would result from the productivity engendered by the initial tax relief.[8] In 1981, the Kemp-Roth legislation put this theory into practice through a personal tax reduction.

Five years later, far from that tax loss being recouped, federal debt had grown to astronomical figures. Nor had personal savings been increased.[9] Private investment as a percentage of GNP actually declined.[10] Consequent to these declines there was a turndown of growth in the GNP in 1982-84, from the period of 1977-80.[11] Blinder says of this episode: "Thus, something between a gimmick and a slogan became the official economic policy of the greatest economic power in the world. P.T. Barnum would have been proud."[12]

Parenthetically, had the Laffler thesis been borne out, other conservatives would have been enraged. For they judge that recouped taxes would simply mean a return to the government spending that is anathema to them!

4. "Reverse Welfare."

To round out the Right's positions on welfare, another perspective needs to be added—though the Right would probably reject the inference and the title. There are those industrialists who fear, or profess to fear, that their business will collapse unless the government bails them out.[13] But their own call upon government for aid clearly competes with the call from the poor. For the good of the country, in their belief, if a choice must be made, tax money must be shifted from welfare to industrial bail-outs because entire businesses or banks have higher priority measured by the effect of their prospective failure than has assisting non-productive welfare recipients.

This completes a brief review of the more prominent perspectives of the Right concerning welfare. The basic perspectives of the Left remain to be described.

IV. VARIATIONS ON WELFARE FROM THE LEFT

1. Humanitarian Left

This name, unlike other titles that follow, lacks scientific foundation. It is a simple recognition that millions of people, not all of whom would count themselves "leftists," are moved by compassion for the poor and needy. Most people in this group would not think of themselves as "do-gooders," although that is the label attached to them by their detractors. Rather, this group sees the need to go beyond economics in addressing the problems of poverty. Their view is that compassion powerfully moves them, and that is as it should be. If they are Christians, they think spontaneously of Jesus' response to the needs of the hungry: "I have compassion on my people" (MT 15:32).

2. Welfare Liberalism

This differs from the Humanitarian Left in that its welfare approach goes beyond the affective compassion of the former to root itself in a more developed social philosophy. Since this was dealt with at length above in the reflection on Bellah and analysis of the traditions of Enlightenment and Utilitarianism, only a brief summary needs to be made here.

Welfare Liberalism shares the individualism of Neo-Capitalism. It too believes in private, free initiative and a free market. It also believes that these are forces in achieving the good—the good of the individual. That good depends in turn on economic abundance. Welfare Liberalism differs from Conservative Capitalism only in calling for a fair chance for all to share in that abundance.

Finally, whereas in Neo-Capitalism this abundance can be jeopardized and the individual threatened by the state, in the view of Welfare Liberalism the individual's search for a share in economic abundance

and the existence of that abundance can both be decidedly enhanced by
governmental action.

3. Welfare State Expansionism

Many Liberals go further and seek to expand the Welfare state. They do
so mainly because they regard such expansion as necessary if there is to
be the economic growth on which they rely for financing of the welfare
programs they believe in. Consider, they say, the eight to nine million
unemployed in 1987. Welfare State Expansionists contend that far more
economic growth than presently projected will be necessary if all these
are to be re-employed, and at wages equivalent to those they were paid
in their lost jobs.

Because the present moment appears to be one of expanding employment, it is imperative to dwell for a moment on the reservations this
evokes. The picture is still disturbing.[14] In 1985, nearly 25 million
employed worked only part-time. Many of these desired and needed
full-time employment to gain enough income to survive and support a
family. In addition, at the end of 1985, 40 percent of the employed
worked in service industries, which include retail trade and health
care—occupations whose earnings are only 44 percent of wages in manufacturing. Finally, add to all these potential or "hidden" job-seekers
those whom conservative welfare reformists want to remove from
welfare ranks and add to the employment pool.

4. Re-industrialization

Re-industrialization, of course, is endorsed not just by the Left; very
many on the Right equally endorse it. But there is a big difference
between the views of these two groups. The underlying thrust of both is
the belief that reversing the recent decline in American productivity (the
need is disputed by some) and restoring America's supposed lost capacity to compete successfully in world markets can no longer be left to the
economy itself to resolve. Government must take the lead. Liberal
Welfarists support government intervention to revive American productivity and competitiveness in the conviction that this is the only way to
reduce unemployment and thereby shift as many as possible welfare
recipients into the independence associated with having paying jobs.
Those on the Right who approve of re-industrialization and government's role in it typically argue, as seen above, that the United States
does not have the financial resources both to re-industrialize and to support welfare programs.

5. Workplace Democracy

Another category hints at transformation. It is a "yes" to the Welfare
State, but a look at the same time to a transformation that moves beyond

this. Supporters of this approach characterize it as workplace democracy. They further designate their position as "radical left," which may suggest to some a Marxist Socialism. But their position, far from being Marxist-leaning, is not even in the line of the European socialist emphasis on the role of the state. What in the European experience it would applaud would be efforts to realize economic democracy.

Exemplifying this view are writings such as *A New Social Contract*, by Martin Carnoy, Derek Shearer and Russell Rumberger.[15] The authors support welfare—it seems provisionally.[16] They are against President Reagan's "new Federalism" offensive against welfare. They observe that decentralization of such transfer payments as welfare benefits, food stamps and more than forty other items from the federal government to the states would mean fifty different policies, fifty different standards, fifty different levels of benefits. Hence, they urge that welfare be left in the hands of the federal government. Given that, they would then democratize the process through "economic democracy." (They rely on the same democratic controls to guide government in investment policy.)[17]

Reagan's federalism is, for these authors, primarily a smokescreen for cutting federal social welfare and shifting responsibility for funding and administration to state and local governments. The state and local governments, they maintain, have neither the financial nor administrative resources to maintain these programs even at current levels.[18]

Advocates of Workplace Democracy are also concerned that Reagan-style federalism reduces rather than increases democracy. This is so because Reagan's brand of local control means that "dynamic" and "efficient" private enterprise and the market will decide how communities provide welfare, education and health care. In effect, this "New Federalism" ends up giving less—certainly not more—power to workers and consumers at the local level. And corporations, powerful as they now are over Congress, will be enabled to exercise even more control over welfare because of their enormously increased power over state legislatures.

In the Reagan philosophy, Workplace Democracy advocates note, citizens are presumed to exercise the greatest influence over resource allocation and over distribution when they act as individual producers and consumers.[19] The fact is that such individual control has, among other evils, historically led to a sharp drop in the quality of services delivered to different income groups.[20] "No one has to take care of the collectivity because it is mysteriously taken care of by all of us doing the best we can individually."[21]

But equally, Workplace Democracy rejects Liberal support of "tripartite boards" consisting of corporate-government-labor participation in search for new economic growth and new economic policies—arguing that corporate management will dominate such boards. Neo-Liberals advancing this approach "place all their confidence in the very same big-

business community that contributed and is contributing so actively to
the present crisis."[22]

Against Reagan's New Federalism and against the Neo-liberal tripartite solution comes the call for a "true economic democracy." This would
begin with local control and democratic planning from the bottom up.
Consumers, workers, home-owners and small businesses, acting through
their elected officials and planning councils, would control local and
state development.[23]

This calls too for democratization of large corporations through worker representation on corporate boards. Thus workers would be given
democratic rights. But such reform would still need the federal government to develop national guidelines for policies in such areas as income
assistance, affirmative action, non-discriminatory wage policy, and
health care.

However, all this is not sufficient to revitalize U.S. society. For such
revitalization, local and regional government units require enough clout
and popular backing in order to become effective planners and investors
in the public interest.[24] There must also be room for the state government, democratically, to share as entrepreneur and planner.[25] Here
again, any exclusive reliance on private entrepreneurs to set society's priorities is rejected.

Finally, with all this, there must be a mix of market operation and economic planning to guide the course of the economy. Rather than permit
largely unaccountable private corporations to do the planning for society,
democratic institutions at all levels should through democratic proce-
dures lay out priorities and guidelines. Market relations can be carried on
within a set of publicly agreed rules.[26]

Barbara Ehrenreich sums up the Radical Left position with special
reference to their belief in the provisional character of welfare: "I do not
propose an extended Welfare State as an ultimate social goal but as a
pragmatic step that circumstances have forced on us."[27]

6. The Good Society

A view similar in general scope to that of economic democracy or workplace democracy is offered by another thoughtful social scientist, Theda
Skocpol.[28] She rejects the "practical liberalism" of the New Deal which
understood the Welfare State as "merely a convenient instrument for pursuit of individual benefits."[29] This approach, Skocpol argues, missed the
proper sense of welfare as a public interest and as the common well-
being of all. She suggests, in contrast to Liberal Welfare, a post-Liberal
or radical Liberalism or, perhaps more accurately, a social democracy.
All of this is in line with what has been described earlier. But Skocpol
adds more.

The new social democracy will seek societal health and communality, while recognizing the need for coalition-building that will embrace middle-class and middle-income people. Her "good society" will need, on the part of the state, coordination of various interventions, plus democratically-undertaken economic planning. According to her, social democracy will operate within the framework of a reformed Capitalism and will provide a social democratic legitimation for a welfare function of the state.

7. A New Welfare

Possibly yet more radical is a group exemplified by Steven Wineman. In his *The Ethics of Human Services: A Radical Alternative to the Welfare State*,[30] Wineman recognizes, as do those like Ehrenreich and Skocpol, that welfare may have to continue under present circumstances. Indeed, he calls for restitution of the welfare cuts made under the Reagan Administration. He goes further to call for selective expansion of programs that can concretely improve the material and social condition of the recipients.[31]

Wineman, nevertheless, makes several charges against the Welfare State. First, it is no better than corporate capitalism at tackling structural unemployment, stratification of power, predominance of giant corporations and the like. Second, the Welfare State pits the underclass of welfare poor against the middle class and upper working class, by proposing work programs for welfare poor. These programs threaten the jobs on which the upper working class rely to maintain their standard of living, and encourage resentment of the middle class that bears much of the tax burden for welfare recipients.[32]

Wineman is most critical of the Welfare State as dehumanizing in its capitalist assumptions. If you need help it is because, as the system is administered, you have been proven to be an economic and productive failure. A strong social stigma attaches to public assistance, no matter how benevolently provided. Worse, it renders beneficiaries dependent. In a word, the Welfare State remains a system that internally degrades and disempowers its recipients.[33]

Against all Liberalism rooted in individualism and against all "leftist centralism," Wineman proposes a "society of federated small socio-economic and political units in which local control and participatory processes empower people and create vibrant community life."[34] This radically decentralized, participatory society will provide alternative human services.

Wineman takes pains to differentiate his position from that of Reagan's New Federalism which he views as serving corporate interests and directing corporate influence to the state level (where this influence is more strongly felt). Wineman's world will be one of urban and local neighborhoods as primary social units in which people can assume individual and collective control over production and consumption even while they define for themselves their needs of housing, health, social services.

Wineman reviews existing social welfare programs to show how local communities—supported at the political levels of state and nation—could meet their welfare needs. While writing out of the Liberal tradition, Wineman proposes an alternative which sweeps beyond nearly all other liberal positions in the welfare debate. (Exceptions there surely are—notably Skocpol and Ehrenreich.)

Digging to deeper philosophical depths, Wineman insists that social needs must be met holistically and as inextricably integrated in human lives. Mutuality must be allowed to live alongside individual autonomy. The tools people will work with must be comprehensible and usable. Here he refers to E.F. Schumacher's *Small Is Beautiful*. They must also be culturally beneficial, as emphasized by Ivan Illich in his *Tools Of Conviviality* and other writings.[35]

V. THREE ADDITIONAL CONSIDERATIONS

In a summary way, review has been made of the more notable positions of both liberal and conservative camps on the overall approaches to the welfare debate. It will soon be seen that these positions further crystallize when it comes to translating and categorizing the statistics and studies done over recent years on welfare.

At this point, three additional considerations will be helpful in clarifying the philosophical aspects of the welfare debate.

First Note: Noted economist Lester Thurow has entered into this debate on a presumed need to choose between competitiveness of the economy and welfare—in its wider sense. In his *The Zero-Sum Society: Building a World-Class American Economy,*[36] he takes issue with the conservative presumption that wages will have to yield to the need for the United States to be competitive. In particular, he attacks the widely-held belief exemplified in economist Arthur Okun's thesis that productivity cannot exist together with equity and that for the sake of productivity, therefore, wages must be sacrificed.[37]

Thurow also rejects the positions adopted by the Brookings Institute's Robert Lawrence. Lawrence had argued that there is no problem of becoming more competitive. What is needed to make U.S. exports cheaper is a lowering of the wages and standards of living of U.S. workers—as much as may be required. And the required decrease may possibly be 35 percent.[38]

For Thurow, such a proposal in the supposed name of U.S. competitiveness is plain economic injustice. He proposes taking a lesson from the Japanese, without imitating them. This is to set up tripartite boards in industries. On these boards, Government, as one member, would partici-pate by giving leads and financial support. Capital and Labor would together be prepared to propose and implement whatever temporary sac-rifices may be needed to regain competitiveness.[39]

Thurow's proposals may gain more and more attention, as U.S. politi-cal and economic leaders and observers attempt to grapple with an ever-fluctuating picture of U.S. competitiveness, trade prospects, and eco-nomic difficulties. How welfare will fit into this larger picture is one of the pivotal economic debates for the remainder of the century.

Second Note: A thread running through many of the liberal positions outlined above is the question of whether the Welfare State in reality exists to support capitalism. This debate continues to flare in liberal cir-cles. One approach to this question is presented by Joe Holland and Peter Henriot, S.J., in *Social Analysis: Linking Faith and Justice*.[40] The authors portray three stages of industrial development: Laissez-Faire Industrial Capitalism, Social Welfare Industrial Capitalism, and National Security Industrial Capitalism.[41]

The second stage, Social Welfare Capitalism, builds technologically and as an industrial system on the move away from laissez-faire compe-tition. It moves from trading "among the many" to monopoly or virtual monopoly. This is a sort of competition, but among the few—indeed, the very few. As capital became national in scope of operation, workers began to organize into national labor unions. These unions began to pressure their industries for concessions on wages and conditions of work. The monopoly national corporations were able to meet the work-ers' demands because their monopoly position freed them from fear of being undercut by maverick competitors.

The result was, perhaps uncharacteristically, a strong labor-manage-ment alliance in an industrial state economy. Technology favored this capital-labor balance as it stimulated production of more goods over which to bargain. The auto industry exemplifies this trend. Henry Ford produced a car that even his workers could afford, a product the price of which declined over time in real terms.

For Holland and Henriot, three consequences of this situation fol-lowed.[42] Economically, the industrial working class found itself better off, as demand for labor accompanied the drive for increased productivi-ty. Where exploitation had dominated the first stage, labor-shared pros-perity became the new basic trend. Politically, the national consolidation of capitalism required a state system that could support the national scope of industry. That in turn entailed emergence of a national regula-tory state involved in activities like interstate commerce, national bank-ing, and nationwide stock market controls. This new regulatory state was also pressured by workers's movements and other social welfare lobbies to enact the progressive social welfare legislation present today with its social security, minimum wage, unemployment compensation, collective bargaining, and so on.

And culturally, freedom ceased to connote a solely negative form of personal license to do whatever one would do. Instead, it came to signify positive opportunity for large sectors of the public. Culturally, this second stage of capitalism is a "social liberalism," in contrast to the preceding laissez-faire stage. Henriot and Holland would be in agreement with Bellah that this Liberalism, culturally, is freedom purely of individuals to do as they see fit, the state supporting them.

A number of Liberals would agree with this analysis, but would go further to say that the Welfare State, in this logic, exists only to shore up capitalism and to legitimate it against potentially explosive labor rejection. They would call for state action in the direction of disrupting the mechanism which thus permits capitalism to dominate labor and society more generally. Frances Fox Piven and Richard A. Cloward explain this position—which they eventually reject—in *The New Class War: Reagan's Attack on the Welfare State and Its Consequences.*[43]

Welfare programs emanate from capitalist society's need, on the one hand, to ensure profitability and capital accumulation, and on the other, to maintain sufficient social harmony to legitimate their class society and class state. Social welfare programs are seen to support profitability by lowering the cost to employers of maintaining a healthy and skilled workforce. Without such programs employers would have either to pay directly for health and worker education or to raise wages.[44]

In addition, welfare programs exercise their legitimating function by removing ground for discontent--particularly the discontent generated by the process of economic concentration, an economic concentration which is seen as creating a pool of unemployed labor. Other writers are preoccupied more by the support the Welfare State gives capitalism by its contribution to the necessary continuous increase of aggregate demand for industry's products.

Piven and Cloward reject this second explanation. Welfare, on the contrary, strengthens labor, not capital, by providing the means of subsistence beyond what the market offers. Welfare, by shifting wages and profit share in favor of labor, thus intervenes in the process by which capital dominates labor.

Unemployment compensation, add Piven and Cloward, protects those unemployed who hope to return to their old job and at their old wage and protects them from competition by the still worse-off unemployed.[45] Thus these factors of social intervention by government must continue rather than be eliminated for they serve essentially therapeutic roles in the socio-economic landscape.

Third Note: After reviewing the major Liberal positions on welfare, one would conclude that much of the Left (some exceptions were noted), if it has its heart in the right place, often has its head in the wrong place. This problem in particular occurred when economic development did not go forward according to their positions or did not favor their perspectives. In the last four Left positions there are Welfare Liberals of different shades who are at one in rejecting the typical liberal individualism. These advocates have strong affinities with the philosophy to be explored in the discussion to follow in this study on Catholic social teaching and welfare.

To the last four Left positions on the spectrum there should be added one more. This is Princeton University's Michael Walzer, who would reasonably be placed within the liberal tradition. In his contribution to Irving Howe's book *Behind the Welfare State*,[46] Walzer firmly recognizes the need for a welfare function of the state. He notes: "We once thought of the state exclusively as a place of communing. We now know that the state ought to do for us."[47] The state became more legitimized as more people felt content that it had met their wants.[48] The state had made citizens cease to be an invisible mass. Class or interest groups formed to interact with the state. People began to share more widely and participate more fully in political membership.

Walzer is aware of the attacks mounted against the Welfare State, but is particularly concerned with the Utilitarianism which roots so much of Liberalism.[49] Utilitarianism argued that the state exists to take care of individual wants. Once these wants are satisfied, interest groups can dissolve, cease political activity, and their members turn to the pursuit of purely individual interests. Individuals are permitted to have needs, but not plans of their own. It is not theirs to say where welfare is to go. Once needed welfare legislation is in place, action shifts away from the electorate—even from the legislator—to the welfare administrator, who knows what is best for us and how best to achieve it.[50] Our role is to be happy beneficiaries, quiet and unassertive. Those who do not comprehend the system become patronized by it.

In his reform of this Utilitarian view of the Welfare State, Walzer manifests some affinity with alternative models and with modern Catholic social teaching. He rejects the permanent political destiny for a segment of society of being simply provided for. He equally rejects the theory that social life consists purely in private pursuits. Even enhanced by the state, private pursuits cannot sustain a significant human culture. Even family life cannot exhaust the human mind and passion for active public life. Politics is more than welfare production. It is a vital world of work and striving, of initiative and discussion, of collective effort and social achievement.

Walzer thus affirms the communal nature of the human experience, as does Catholic social teaching. The individual is central to that experience, but is not the ultimate value. There are goods and goals to be sought and enjoyed together: education, culture, community health, community planning, foreign policy. These goods are to be shared and not merely distributed according to some formula.[51] Walzer also shows affinity for alternative approaches. For the state cannot by itself achieve all goods and all goals. These goods and goals also require a human scale, a smaller scale, accessible to social aspirations, responsive to individual decisions.[52]

These conclusions, however, are not a call for dismantling the Welfare State. Rather, they lead to limiting the role of welfare, removing, wherever necessary, usurped power. This allows intermediary groups to play their proper roles. Walzer's position should be kept in mind when Catholic social teaching is addressed later in this study.

After this review of the welfare debate in its various perspectives and philosophies, it is appropriate to turn now to its more sociological and statistical aspects. This brings up the major criticisms leveled against welfare and—implicitly or explicitly—against the Economic Pastoral's support of welfare.

ENDNOTES FOR CHAPTER II

[1] Robert N. Bellah, Richard Madsen, William M. Sullivan, Ann Swidler, and Steven M. Tipton, *Habits of the Heart: Individualism and Commitment in American Life* (Berkeley, CA: University of California Press, 1985). The paperback edition is used for the references in these notes: New York: Harper and Row, 1985.

[2] Ibid., 263

[3] See, e.g., *The New Catholic Encyclopedia* (New York: McGraw and Hill, 1966): "Enlightenment "(vol. 5); "Utilitarianism" (vol. 14).

[4] On the Utilitarian bases of much of Liberalism as understood in the United States, see Michael Walzer, *Politics in the Welfare State: Concerning the Role of American Radicals*, in Irving Howe, ed., Beyond the Welfare State (New York: Schoken Books, 1974).

[5] *The New Industrial State* (Boston: Houghton-Mifflin, 1967).

[6] *Free To Choose* (New York: Harcourt, Brace and Jovanvich, 1980), 119.

7 Alan Blinder, *Hard Heads, Soft Hearts: Tough-Minded Economics for a Just Society* (Reading, MA: Addison-Wesley, 1987).

8 The arguments of Arthur Laffler along with other supply-side economists are thoroughly explored in Lester C. Thurow, *Dangerous Currents: The State of Economics* (New York: Random House, 1983); see especially "the Laffler curve," 133-37.

9 Blinder, op. cit., 86-90 and 99; Thurow, op. cit., 133-137.

10 See Thurow and Blinder in sections noted in previous footnote.

11 Blinder op.cit. 88 ff; 96 ff.

12 Blinder op. cit. 90.

13 Blinder op.cit., 95; Thurow op. cit., 263 ff. A 1985 study, Aid for Dependent Corporations (Washington, D.C.: Public Citizens' Congress Watch), reports what it terms "The Fiscal 1986 Corporate Welfare Budget." This details Federal subsidies to industries (tax breaks, direct subsidies, credit subsidies, law subsidies). The irony will not escape anyone of the acronym AFDC being shifted from Aid to Families with Dependent Children—an aid much of the corporate world calls a giveaway—to Aid For Dependent Corporations.

14 All the facts cited in the rest of the paragraph are taken from Ward Morehouse, President of the Council on Public Affairs, and David Dembo, the Council's program coordinator, in a letter to the *New York Times*, February 14, 1986. The Council has extensively studied unemployment and underemployment. Much the same story is told more extensively by Barry Bluestone and Bennett Harrison in a study prepared for the Joint Economic Committee, U.S. Congress, December 1986.

The Wall Street Journal disputes their evidence. Relying on a January 1988 report of the Bureau of Labor Statistics, the Journal claims that 320,000 jobs were created in December 1987, and of these more than 40 percent were in the high income category with fewer than 10 percent in lower-paying categories. The bulk of the analysis on this appears to favor the Bluestone-Harrison side of the argument. Others note that of those 320,000 jobs, 80 percent were part-time. People seeking full-time employment had to rest content with part-time.

It should be observed that even at 60 hours a week pay at present minimum wages single persons would fall below the poverty level if they had to pay for housing. See also the December 1986 study reported by the Joint Economic Committee of the U.S. Congress, *The Growth of Poverty: 1979-85 and Demographic Factors*, especially the section on work, wages and poverty.

[15] New York, *Harper and Row*, 1983.

[16] Ibid., 49 ff; 200

[17] Ibid., 169

[18] Ibid., 195.

[19] Ibid., 197.

[20] Ibid.

[21] Ibid., 156.

[22] Ibid., 151.

[23] Ibid., 199.

[24] Ibid.

[25] Ibid., 209 ff.

[26] Ibid., 213.

[27] *The Nation*, February 26, 1983.

[28] *Legacies of the New Deal Liberalism*, in Douglas MacLean and Claudia Mills, eds., Liberalism Re-Considered.

[29] Ibid.

[30] Boston, South End Press, 1984.

[31] Ibid., 41.

[32] Ibid., 36.

[33] Ibid., 42.

[34] Ibid., 51.

[35] E.F. Schumacher, *Small is Beautiful: Economics as if People Mattered* (New York: Harper and Row, 1973); Ivan Illich, *Deschooling Society* (New York, Harper and Row, 1971); and Ivan Illich, *Tools For Conviviality* (New York, Harper and Row, 1973).

[36] New York: Simon and Schuster, 1985. Besides Thurow, there has been an outpouring of other writings on re-industrialization. A few titles: Ronald E. Muller, *Revitalizing America* (New York: Simon and Schuster, 1980); Barry Bluestone and Bennett Harrison, *The De-industrialization of America*, (New York: Basic Books, 1982); Gar Alperovitz and Jeff Faux, *Rebuilding America* (New York: Pantheon Books, 1984); Ira C. Magaziner and Robert Reich, *Minding America's Business* (New York: Vintage-Random, 1982); Robert Reich, *The Next American Frontier* (New York: Penguin, 1984).

[37] This is also substantively treated by Robert Kuttner, *The Economic Illusion: False Choices Between Prosperity and Social Justice* (Boston, Houghton Mifflin, 1984).

[38] Thurow, op. cit., 95-102

[39] Ibid., 158-60, 262-301

[40] Maryknoll, N.Y.: Orbis Books, and Washington, D.C.: Center of Concern, 1983.

[41] The three stages are discussed in Chapter 4, pp. 64-88.

[42] Ibid., 74.

[43] New York, Pantheon, 1982.

[44] Ibid., 30.

[45] Ibid., 31 ff.

[46] New York, Schocken Books, 1982.

[47] Ibid., 131.

[48] Ibid., 130.

[49] Ibid., 130-33, 143.

[50] Ibid., 133.

[51] Ibid., 145.

[52] Ibid., 146.

3

DOES WELFARE
CREATE POVERTY?

The spectrum of ideological positions on the Welfare State has been examined. Believers in these perspectives would reject the charge that their positions rely largely on deductive logic with minimal empirical basis. Yet a close reading of their works discloses little significant reporting of facts or extensive social analysis. The positions largely reflect other basic convictions about the poor and poverty. (Whether this is also true, as alleged, of the U.S. Catholic Bishops will be addressed later.) But gathering credible support for one's position is critical if one is seriously to influence economic dialogue and political decisions.

This review of the welfare debate now shifts from examining the overall philosophic or ideological approaches to welfare to analyzing a number of empirical studies and reports which have been conducted on welfare. This chapter does two things. First, it demonstrates the growth of poverty. Second, it rejects the conservative myth that welfare causes poverty. A vast array of current studies have sifted the statistics to reveal with striking clarity the contemporary picture of poverty in the United States.

I. A LOOK AT THE POVERTY PICTURE

An overview of poverty in the United States indicates three main groupings: (1)the elderly and incapacitated poor, (2) the working poor, and (3) the non-elderly and non-working poor. Much of the welfare debate focuses on the last group, but concern must be shown equally for the second. The first group, the elderly poor, has largely been freed from the crushing effects of chronic poverty by social security—a topic deserving full treatment in its own right.

A first pair of questions to be faced are: Is the increase in poverty in the United States owed mainly to welfare programs or to other independent causes? What avenues are to be taken by U.S. society to meet the problem of poverty?

President Reagan has taken the view that welfare is a contributor to, rather than a barrier against, poverty. Reagan's statements have included: "After hundreds of billions of dollars in poverty programs, the plight of the poor grows more painful." And: "In 1968, as Lyndon Johnson left office, 13 percent of Americans were poor...Over the next twelve years, our expenditures on social welfare quadrupled. And, in 1980, the percentage of poor Americans was 13 percent.[1]" For the Reagan Administration, it was the Great Society that brought a tragic halt to economic progress for the poor in the United States.

Charles Murray, the welfare critic on whom the Reagan Administration relies most, says in his controversial 1984 book *Losing Ground*: "As federal cash for the needy increased, more Americans became impoverished."[2] Murray goes further to say that welfare measures in 1967-74 pulled people deeper into poverty. Another prominent conservative voice, the Heritage Foundation, maintains that high post-1979 poverty rates "have nothing to do with economic policies" and "everything to do with" deep cultural and demographic trends.[3]

One initial study to note in reviewing the U.S. poverty picture is the comprehensive 1986 study of the Joint Economic Committee of Congress.[4] According to this study, after nearly two decades of success in the fight against poverty, poverty rates began to rise in 1979 and then increased dramatically in 1982 and 1983. Although now slightly down from peak figures, the poverty rates have not returned to anywhere near the pre-1979 levels. The Bishops' Economic Pastoral also notes that official poverty has increased remarkably in the decade of 1974-84.

Relying on figures from the U.S. Census Bureau, the U.S. Bishops' Economics Pastoral puts the poverty figure at 33 million.[5] That is one person in seven for the entire United States population, a one-third increase over 1973. In a footnote, the Bishops add that some observers would estimate those below the poverty line as closer to 50 million. This jump would stem, in part, from the fact that the poverty line as a percentage of median family income has sharply declined from 1959 to 1983.

The statistical aspect of the rise in poverty over recent years can be viewed in still another way, one which raises questions about what the poverty figure would be under alternative methods of computation. The official definition of poverty utilized by the Bishops and others because of its comparability from year to year was first established in the mid-1960s. This poverty definition is based upon the Department of Agriculture's estimate of the cost of a nutritionally adequate diet. This figure is multiplied by three, since the average household spends about one-third of its income on food. The resulting figure is indexed for inflation. This is a pre-tax figure, generally including any "cash transfers" from government such as Supplemental Security Income (SSI), although not "in-kind" transfers such as medical aid, food stamps, or housing assistance.

The Joint Economic Committee's January 1987 Democratic Staff Report stated that the poverty line, thus defined, for a family of four in 1979 was an annual gross income of $7,386. In 1985, the figure was $10,987.In 1979, 10 percent of the U.S. population fell below the poverty line; 14 percent fell below the correspondending figure in 1985.[6]

The picture grows still darker with time. A family of three headed by a person working full time at the current minimum wage ($3.35 per hour) would fall 20 percent below the 1985 poverty line. By contrast, in 1979 that family would have had enough to meet, if barely, the poverty level. Even a mother with a single child working full-time in 1985 at the current minimum wage would not receive enough income to reach the 1985 poverty level.[7]

II. CASH TRANSFERS AND THE POVERTY PICTURE

Some believe that a poverty figure which does not take into account in-kind transfers like food stamps and medical care grossly over-estimates poverty. But one Congressional study argued that if in-kind transfers were added, the figure for those falling below the poverty level in 1982 would not have been significantly lower.[8]

Others agree that the level of in-kind transfers was so low that the difference would have been slight. In 1985, some 20 million non-elderly families received food stamps, but average benefits were low—less than $40 per person per month. Therefore, if food stamps had been treated as income in that year, the number of non-elderly poor would have fallen from 30.6 million to only 29.1 million.[9] A report of the Center on Budget and Policy Priorities goes even further with respect to in-kind transfers and their treatment in arriving at a poverty figure. Based on census data through 1985, the report indicates that, even with non-cash benefits included, the poverty situation worsens. This is because it is precisely in these benefits that federal government cuts have been the most drastic and where state government payments have not kept pace with inflation.[10] The conclusion is based on detailed studies of the affected programs.

Isabel Sawhill of the Urban Institute, in a discussion of the pros and cons of adding in-kind payments like food stamps to a computation of a basic poverty figure, observes that any possible drop in poverty by employing a more inclusive figure must be counterbalanced by the increase in poverty due to the fact that until very recently a large part of the income of the poor was taxable.[11] Sawhill, in turn, offers this picture of poverty. She starts with the same government figure utilized by the Bishops in the Economic Pastoral—33 million people—and then notes that this is 14 percent of the U.S. population. She contrasts that figure with 1978's 18.6 million or 11.4 percent. The current level of American poverty is higher than any year of the 1970s, almost as high as when the War on Poverty was inaugurated in the 1960s.[12]

Has the Reagan Administration identified a real problem? Anti-poverty programs have poured millions of dollars in aid to the poor in the U.S. and yet the poverty picture remains as bleak as when the War on Poverty began. Is it possible that the War on Poverty failed to address the real causes of poverty? In fact the War on Poverty did bring about a fall in poverty from 22 percent to 13 percent — a figure that remained rather constant for a period of time.[13] But then the poverty rate in the early 1980s rose sharply due to many other factors, including the fact that the economy experienced back-to-back recessions and the Reagan budget cutbacks.[14]

Because the question of including cash transfers continues to be such a large part of the debate over poverty figures, a few more words should be said on this. Social economists David T. Ellwood and Lawrence H. Summers have contrasted poverty figures *without* any government cash transfers with poverty figures after cash transfers. They do not take into account in-kind benefits, (e.g., health care, food stamps) because these are not incorporated in the official poverty definition.[15] The poverty "without transfers" rate showed an increase—not large in numbers, but important in impact—over two decades: in 1965 it stood at 21.3 percent, and in 1983 at 24.2 percent. The "with transfers" poverty rates showed a very slight decline. In 1965, official poverty was 17.3 percent and in 1983, 15.2 percent.

Why doesn't cash assistance from the government reduce poverty? Cash transfers, e.g., social security, certainly do account for dramatic reductions in poverty, particularly that of the elderly. Government expenditures are heavily in favor of the elderly. But for the non-elderly, cash assistance has been and remains very small—mostly for the disabled rather than for female-headed families who are such an important component of the non-elderly poverty picture.[16]

For all non-elderly, cash assistance programs were $20 billion in 1982, up from $5 billion in 1960 (Reagan's "quadruple" figure). But this is still less than one percent of the Gross National Product (GNP) and only two percent of the entire federal budget.[17] Ellwood and Summers estimate such cash transfers to be too small to significantly affect measured poverty over time.

In fact, cash transfers actually moved only five percent of poor people out of poverty. For single parents, benefits came to $100 per month, a sum that cannot appreciably make a dent in a chronic state of personal poverty.

Moreover, between 1970 and 1980, annual real expenditures per non-elderly person rose just $93, nearly all of which went to the disabled.[18]

In addition, expenditures for Aid to Families with Dependent Children (AFDC), a centerpiece welfare program, showed no growth in the 1970s. Rather, AFDC expenditures fell sharply in real terms. Despite a rise in the number of people living in single parent families, fewer persons were to be found in AFDC programs. This was because a smaller number were qualifying after more rigid qualifying standards were instituted.

It is noteworthy that in the mid-1960s a family of four at the poverty line had an income close to one-half the average for all four-person families but in the mid-1980s a comparable family had only one-third of the average income of four-person families.[19] At stake here is relative, not absolute, poverty. The reason for relative poverty worsening more than official poverty is that the poor live in an economy of normally rising average standards of living, and poverty programs have not kept up. The poor are linked by status comparisons to rising income that they do not share.[20]

III. THE POOR UNDER WELFARE

At this point, it is important to look at some of the specific segments of the "poor" and how they have fared, according to both critics and supporters, under various welfare-type programs. The major population segments are (1) the elderly, (2) the "working poor," and (3) one of the most basic images of American poverty as well as a major subject of the welfare debate—female-headed households.

1. The Elderly
The attack upon welfare is mounted in significant measure on the claim that anti-poverty programs account for increased poverty, betraying the very people the programs are intended to rescue. An Ellwood and Summers study reviewed the situation of the elderly poor and the non-elderly, dividing the latter into other categories.[21] Concerning the elderly poor, their study noted a major change in status. For those over 65, there was dramatic and relatively continued progress up to 1974, some modest progress through to 1978, and a relatively level poverty rate after that time.[22]

But even with this somewhat stable situation, there is a remarkable decline for the over-65 poor population from 1959. Further, if Medicare is added to cash transfers, which accounts for most elderly being removed from the poverty rolls, the poverty index for this group drops from a present 7 percent to 3 percent. The elderly thus receive "entitlement" payments through Social Security and other programs that are unlikely to be altered. Even if altered, they will not affect the situation of the current elderly population in the U.S. The elderly's rather low and stabilized poverty rate, then, effectively brings them out of the current discussion about poverty and welfare.[23]

It is to be noted that in the 1960s and 1970s, all the poor were lumped together and given the benefit of the negative income tax, which divides the poor into categories of those not expected to work and those expected to work. In the former category are, of course, elderly and disabled, and, until recently, mothers of preschool children. Mothers of preschool children living in poverty today total 1.8 million, or 13 percent of the total American poor.[24]

2. The Working Poor

The second overall category is the working poor. They are working because they always have worked, and want to, and are expected to. These working poor number nearly seven million, about 47 percent of the total poor. There is also a group of welfare-dependent women who have no preschool-age children. This group is the prime object of many welfare reform proposals. Sawhill observes that a consensus now seems to have emerged that, wherever possible, work should be substituted for welfare among women as long as they have no preschool-agers. She adds that this group in 1984 represented 700,000, or 5.2 percent of all poor, but this group is growing.[25]

The Bishops' Pastoral, in its welfare section, gives considerable attention to the working poor as well as to recipients of welfare transfers. The attitude toward the welfare recipients of many conservative thinkers and politicians is that they are poor because they are too lazy to work. Yet overwhelmingly the people expected to work are in fact working or seeking work, except where they have dropped out of the workforce because they are discouraged by the unavailability of jobs.

Ben W. Heineman Jr., a director of the Center for National Policy which produced "Work and Welfare," refers to the working poor as having been the hardest hit by Federal cuts of the last six years as well as by high unemployment. They are trying to make it without much help from their government.[26] Reischauer describes still further this category of working poor. In 1985, they totalled 3.6 million poor families.[27] That amounts to 6 percent of all families but about 50 percent of poor families. In addition, there were another 2.5 million working poor who were unrelated individuals—not in family households.[28]

To this group can be added a somewhat recent category of growing concern: the working *near*-poor. These 1.6 million families and 0.8 million individuals had incomes below 125 percent of the poverty line, that is, just above it. Of these, 84 percent have school-age children, 37 percent were headed by women, 23 percent were black.[29] The number of working near-poor has declined only slightly since attaining a peak in 1983. Looking at the decade, the working near-poor show substantial growth. From 1975 to 1985, there was a one-third growth for families and a 40 percent growth for unrelated individuals.[30]

From 1979 to 1984 the fraction of working near-poor whose income would be unable to keep a family of four out of poverty increased from 19.7 to 26 percent.[31] Barry Bluestone and Bennett Harrison say that one-half of the net increase of jobs created from 1978 to 1984 were jobs paying less than $7,000 in 1984 dollars.

Important to this situation is the loss of real value in the minimum wage of $3.35 per hour. Since January of 1981, the basic wage lost 25 percent of its purchasing power due to inflation. Returning to the expectations of conservative and some liberal reformers that putting welfare mothers to work will end the need of welfare, the fact must be faced that a woman with only one child, working for a minimum wage full-time and year-round, could not lift herself and child out of poverty.[32]

In 1985, one-sixth of all jobs were part-time. Some people want part-time work. But for most poor who needed full-time jobs, it was an additional cause of frustration and poverty. In 1984, 29 percent of households in the category of poor working families held part-time jobs, as did 45 percent of poor working unrelated individuals.[33] Similar to part-time work is not finding work for a full year. In 1984, two-thirds of poor working families and 55 percent of poor unrelated individuals did not have full-time year-round jobs due to periods of unemployment.

3. Families Headed by Single Women
In the chapter to follow, on welfare and the family, the third category of poor will be further studied where the charge is examined that welfare destroys the family. Here these female-headed families are introduced only to round out the spectrum of all those in poverty. A few statistics offer a gravely disturbing picture. First of all, of all working women, how many are in poverty? In 1986, 60 percent of all mothers with the youngest child between three and five were employed outside the home. For many of these women in two-parent families, their presence in the workforce was imperative if the families were to stave off poverty.

Indeed, of all two-parent families, one-third more would have fallen below the poverty level were the wives not working. This reveals a shockingly inadequate earning capacity of males, as can be seen reflected in just one age bracket: of all 20-22 year-old working males, only 43 percent in 1985 earned enough to keep a family of three above the poverty level of $8,700.

Turning specifically to female-headed families, in 1986 37 percent of these families were below the poverty level. Still another way to perceive the extent of the poverty of female-headed families is to compare them with the universe of all families in poverty. On this basis, 46 percent of these families are female-headed (1982).

In concluding this look at three categories of the poor, it is helpful to note what other impacts there are on the lives of the poor. First, in various ways, taxes affect poverty. To mention only the most obvious way, there is the regressivity of taxes themselves.[34] An example is the rapid growth of payroll taxes at all levels which affect the poor disproportionately. In 1983, a family of four at the poverty line was paying more than 16 percent of its income in direct taxes, almost double the percentage paid in 1965. (A discussion of this factor of taxes will be taken up further in the chapter on welfare and the family.) Second, if government taking from the poor in taxes has hurt the poor, so have government cutbacks in poverty programs proved crippling. Some believe that such curtailment accounts for one half of recent impoverishment.[35]

IV. DOES WELFARE CAUSE POVERTY?

For Reagan and Murray, as already noted, the increase in poverty following the War on Poverty was directly owing to that war and its irresponsible anti-poverty programs. Their supporters add that demographic factors of changing family compositions—as originated in and owing to poverty programs—have also kept the poor from moving up.[36]

Against their assumption stands a very large majority of scholars who maintain that poverty mirrors the unfolding, general situation of the U.S. economy. Poverty marches with our economic ups and downs, and the poor are perhaps affected more sharply than other segments of the population. Poverty marches too with the willingness and unwillingness of the public or government to help the poor.

(A peripheral question is whether the poor can themselves be the cause of their own poverty. This surely can not be denied. But the poor's possible contribution to their poverty is nothing comparable to the well-to-do's contribution. Disparity of income between rich and poor in the U.S., far exceeding that of any other industrial country, has increased in 1988. Possessors of high wealth and income like to think they earned every penny of it and in so doing made all U.S citizens richer. More objective surveyors of the U.S. scene find quite exaggerated the price which capital demands for its cooperation.

An answer to the Reagan-Murray challenge is imbedded in the poverty profile already outlined—if it be taken in its historical perspective. That historical perspective is very well presented in several of the essays in *Fighting Poverty*.

Here, in brief, is the record. When the War on Poverty was declared in 1964, 19 percent of the U.S. population was poor. That level of poverty then quickly declined in the 1960s during the robust expansion of the economy which was attributable in part to the Vietnam War. Poverty continued edging down to a low of 11.1 percent in 1973. For the balance of the 1970s, the poverty rate fluctuated at around 11.5 percent.

Then, a major recession was brought about by a confluence of several factors: the deflating economy, the negative economic impact of the Vietnam War, high oil prices, ensuing inflation, increased unemployment, the decline of the U.S. heavy industrial base. This confluence has coupled with a diminished enthusiasm of U.S. citizens for government poverty programs. In the wake of these changes, the poverty rate then rose sharply to 15.2 percent in 1983, the highest level since 1965. The percentage of poor still remains as bad as when the War on Poverty began, or worse. Clearly the War on Poverty was not to blame for the unacceptable consequences for the poor.

One final note on the historical record found in *Fighting Poverty*. Writing in 1983, the authors anticipated that the economic recovery then gaining ground would reduce poverty. But, they argued, any decrease would not return the 1984-86 rate to the 11 and 12 percent levels of the 1953-55 period.[37] Their prophesy proved correct. The *Fighting Poverty* history is corroborated, at least at one point, by the 1986 Congressional Joint Economic Committee study. This ends its own picture of the poverty trend by stating that "in 1979, by any measure (official or one including other than cash income) poverty increased significantly."

Another method of tracking income of the poor may help in appreciating the direct impact of overall national economic performance on their status. This approach views poverty as a fraction of the nation's median income. By this measure the income of *poor* is conceived as keeping pace with that of the *median* U.S. income. According to such *Fighting Poverty* authors as Ellwood and Summers, median family income in real terms in 1980 was no higher than in 1969. Thus it is no surprise that poor families were not much better off than earlier. The same factors, in effect, account for the stagnation of the fortunes of both poor and non-poor.[38]

These same writers find the stagnation of the median family income difficult to explain in full, since real *per-person* disposable income *did* rise by about 27 percent in the same time period. One partial explanation of the anomaly is demographic changes. More of the income share was going to *unrelated individuals.*

Still, the decline in medium income per family was present. It is clearly etched in the decline of the median income of full-year, full-time workers between 1970 and 1980. True, some blame for this can be laid on declining productivity of the U.S. economic system. But more significant factors were declines in Federal programs and the failure of states to keep benefits in line with inflation, another key influence on the general economic situation. All of this shows that movements in average family incomes play their part, alongside the other economic factors enumerated, in affecting the fate of the poor.

It might be recalled here that Murray propounds the thesis that Federal programs have not aided the situation of the poor. He contends that as Federal cash for the needy increased from 1950 to 1980, more of the U.S. population became impoverished. As the Labor Department work and training programs grew, so did unemployment among the poor.[39] As money for education for the disadvantaged grew, test scores declined and urban crime, illegitimacy and families permanently on welfare increased.

The data presented here shows why so many scholars reject Murray's thesis. Yes, the poor are poorer and are a greater percentage of the population, as this chapter has demonstrated. And key to the increased poverty is unemployment. Murray's argument that poverty is to be blamed on welfare is simply wrong.

ENDNOTES FOR CHAPTER III

[1] From President Reagan's 1986 State of the Union Address, as quoted in *Up From Dependency*, Report to the President by the Domestic Policy Council on Low-income Opportunity (Washington, D.C., 1986).

[2] Charles Murray, *Losing Ground* (New York, Basic Books, 1984). This book was enormously influential among conservatives. Murray's views have been reiterated more recently, e.g., in *Gaining Ground* (Washington D.C.: Ethics and Public Policy Center, 1985). While I have been impressed by the sincerity of purpose of Murray, I have been considerably disillusioned by the evidence his challengers provide of sometimes incompetent, if not downright tendentious, use of statistics at critical points of his thesis.

[3] *The Growth of Poverty: 1979-1985* (Washington D.C.: Heritage Foundation, 1986), 2.

[4] The study makes extensive use of U.S. Bureau of the Census data, including that organization's "Current Population Reports." For additional overviews, see a major influential writer in the field of poverty, Michael Harrington. He spear-headed the 1960s "War on Poverty" with his monumental *The Other America* (1962). He returned to this theme in a 1984 update, *The New American Poverty* (New York: Holt, Rinehart and Winston, 1984). See also the series of helpful studies from the U.S. Catholic Bishops' Campaign for Human Development: *Poverty Profile*,

1972; *Poverty in American Democracy*, 1974; *Poverty in USA (*New York: Paulist Press, 1976); *Poverty Profile USA in the Eighties*. Except for the Paulist books, these studies are published in Washington D.C., by the United States Catholic Conference.

[5] *Current Population Reports*, Series P—66, no. 149, "Income and Poverty Status in the U.S." (Washington D.C.: Government Printing Office, 1985). And see Economic Justice for All, 16.

[6] The U.S. Department of Health and Human Services publishes the annual official revision of the poverty income guidelines reflecting changes in the Consumer Price Index. This figure is taken from a poverty study reported in January 1987 by the Democratic staff of the Joint Economic Committee of Congress. Data for 1985 are given in *The Impact of Federal Taxes on Poor Families* (Washington D.C.: Childrens' Defense League, 1985), 1, 4.

[7] A number of studies have investigated the impact of inflation, taxes, and the shift out of good-paying to poor-paying jobs. This impact is measured in terms of the consequent amount of wages that would be needed to provide the real-income equivalent of 1979. Bluestone and Harrison, *The Great American Job Machine*, p.10; Robert Greenstein, *End Results: The Impact of Federal Policies Since 1980 on Low-income Americans* (Washington, D.C.: Interfaith Action for Economic Justice, 1984), Part One, *Impact of Budget and Tax Policies on Low-income Americans*; Robert Reischaur, "Welfare Reform and the Working Poor," in *Work and Welfare*, pp. 38-41; and three essays in particular in Sheldon H. Danziger and David H. Weinberg, eds., *Fighting Poverty: What Works and What Doesn't* (Cambridge: Harvard University Press, 1986): Sheldon H. Danziger, Robert H. Havemann and Robert D. Plotnick, *Anti-Poverty Policy: Effects on the Poor and the Non-poor*; also David T. Ellwood and Lawrence H. Summers, *Poverty in America: Is Welfare the Answer or the Problem?*; also Rebecca M. Blank and Alan S. Blinder, *Macro-economics, Income Distribution and Poverty*.

[8] *Washington Post*, May 6, 1984.

[9] See the careful study of Ellwood and Summers in *Fighting Poverty*, 86-87. Here it is argued that the addition of in-kind benefits does not decrease poverty by very much. This is the position also of Danziger, Havemann and Plotnick in the same volume.

[10] *Smaller Slices of the Pie: the Growing Economic Vulnerability of Poor-and Moderate-Income Americans* (Washington D.C.: Center on

Budget and Policy Priorities, 1985). These issues are covered from a legislative perspective in *Hard Choices: Federal Budget Priorities in the Gramm-Rudman-Hollings Era* (Washington D.C.: Center on Budget and Policy Priorities, 1986).

[11] *Work and Welfare: The Case For New Directions in National Policy* (Washington D.C.: Urban Institute, 1987), 22.

[12] Ibid.

[13] Ibid.

[14] An excellent source of information on the effects of the war on poverty is *Fighting Poverty*. This volume contains papers originally prepared for a major review of welfare programs two decades after President Lyndon Johnson launched his War on Poverty. Sponsors were the University of Wisconsin's prestigious Institute for Research on Poverty together with the U.S. Department of Health and Human Services. A notable group of social scientists gathered in Williamsburg, Virginia to seek an unbiased assessment of the effects of the anti-poverty programs. Murray's *Losing Ground* had already appeared. It is noteworthy how scant attention was given this volume by the authors of the study papers. One of the contributors to *Fighting Poverty*, Christopher Jenks, has given his own account of the poverty picture in "How Poor Are the Poor?" *New York Review of Books*, May 9, 1985.

[15] "Poverty in America," in *Fighting Poverty*, 78-104.

[16] Ibid.

[17] Ibid.

[18] Ibid.

[19] Ibid.

[20] Relative poverty is noted by several writers as a significant factor. See Sawhill, op.cit., 22.

[21] Ellwood and Summers, op. cit., 81 ff.

[22] Ibid., 81.

[23] The non-entitlement programs are treated pretty much as here by a number of writers already mentioned, e.g., Isabel Sawhill, Robert Reischauer,

Robert Greenstein, and authors from the volume *Fighting Poverty*.

[24] Sawhill, op. cit., 24 and table 1. See under category "By employability status of head (1984)."

[25] Ibid., table 1.

[26] "Welfare Reform Revisited: New Consensus and Old Dilemmas," in *Work and Welfare*, 16 ff.

[27] "Welfare Reform and the Working Poor," in *Work and Welfare*, 36.

[28] Ibid.

[29] Ibid.

[30] Ibid.

[31] Ibid., 37

[32] Reischauer details the impossibility for several categories of the poor of getting out of poverty in 1984. The 1987 situation is comparable.

[33] Barry Bluestone and Bennett Harrison, op. cit., 4. Some critics dismiss the Bluestone and Harrison study. But strong confirmation for it comes from a study issued in January, 1988 by the William T. Grant Foundation Commission on Work, Family and Citizenship. That report, *The Forgotten Half: Non-College Youth in America*, focuses on youth. But it confirms the more general picture of joblessness of Bluestone and Harrison and the many others who note the strong trend away from good-paying jobs in manufacturing to far less remunerative jobs both for those remaining in smoke-stack industries and for those shifting into low-paid service jobs.

The Council on International and Public Affairs has extensively studied unemployment, giving particular attention to the increase in joblessness that arises once one ceases to count as employed (a) those employed for one hour a day--as is done in the Bureau of Labor Statistics surveys; (b) those seeking but lacking full-time employment; (c) especially those requiring but lacking work through the entire year. The Council also notes the uncounted many who have simply given up their unsuccessful search for work. See *Underbelly of the U.S. Economy: Joblessness and the Pauperization of Work in America*, Sixth Issue (New York: Council on International and Public Affairs, 1986). One factor that can and may work to stem, if not reverse, this trend is the ending of the baby-boom, a fact which will reduce the work-force.

[34] *Changing Distribution of Federal Taxes: 1975-1990* (Washington D.C.: Congressional Budget Office, 1987), xv ff.; passim. See also Rebecca M. Blank and Allen S. Blinder, "Macro-economics, Income Distribution and Poverty," in *Fighting Poverty*, 197-207. See also Mary Bourdette and Jim West, *Impact of Federal Taxes on Poor Families* (Washington D.C.: Childrens' Defense Fund, 1985), 8-20.

[35] For an overall view of the impact of federal policy on poverty since 1980, see the study by the Center on Budget and Policy Priorities, published by Interfaith Action for Economic Justice, Washington D.C., September 1984.

[36] *Growth in Poverty: 1979-85: Economic and Demographic Factors* (Washington D.C.: Joint Economic Commission of U.S. Congress, 1984), 2, 3ff. Blank and Blinder, loc.cit., 180 ff.; Ellwood and Summers, loc.cit., 83 ff.

[37] *Fighting Poverty*, 53-55.

[38] Ibid., 81-83.

[39] *Losing Ground*, 70 ff.

[40] Ibid. Chapter 7 argues Murray's thesis that federal dollars gave little return on the education investment or on the war against illegitimacy; chapter 9 presents his arguments on the family.

4

DOES WELFARE
DESTROY
THE FAMILY?

The preceding chapter looked at the charge that welfare produces poverty.[1] A second claim is that it destroys the family. As recently as
February, 1987, *Time* magazine unleased a ferocious attack against welfare ("a monstrous mess"), charging that it "breaks up families."[2] But
this indictment is not presently heard with the same intensity as in the
recent past. This change is due mainly to the serious research of able
scholars who have forced a reevaluation of these accusations.

If the attack on welfare with respect to families has been somewhat
muted, why raise the question? First, because many have heard only the
accusations and not the responses. Second, because the Bishops have
been attacked as "soft-headed" in ignoring in the Economic Pastoral the
supposedly destructive thrust of welfare against the family.[3]

It is therefore imperative in taking this look at the welfare debate to
relate some of the responses to this oft-cited charge that the U.S. welfare
system detrimentally affects family development. Both the charges and the
responses tell much about the state of the welfare system as well as the
state of the welfare debate in this country. They also shed additional light
on whether the charges against the Economic Pastoral are well founded.

I. SOME SPECIFIC CHARGES

The general charge about welfare and the family is specified in the contentions that welfare contributes to illegitimacy, encourages formation of
single-parent households to the detriment of the traditional two-parent
family, and destroys the incentive of young women heading households
to rise out of dependency by finding work.[4] Finally, this welfare system
is supposedly pernicious in another direction. It is passed on from one
generation to another.

Time's report added the charge that welfare—chiefly its central component of AFDC—is corrosively administered.[5] Moreover, President Reagan has frequently trotted out his anecdotes of the cheating "Welfare Queen." These last two charges about welfare's administration and the pervasiveness of cheaters seem to be utterly discounted by serious observers of welfare, and truly do not deserve further discussion.[6]

Charles Murray in his *Losing Ground* is usually cited as spearheading the attack on welfare as bringing a horrendous increase in illegitimacy.[7] But Murray recently has asserted that this is not a fair statement of his position.[8] He is not saying that young women are having babies so as to get on welfare. But, he says, welfare does provide an alternative to a woman's living with her parents (assuming that the father of the child is absent).

Murray adds that he has claimed only that the availability of welfare occasions marriage break-ups or discourages marriage formation, thus increasing poverty. He would say that AFDC has increased dependence upon welfare because it discourages its recipients from getting married and holding steady jobs. It is easier to get along without a job. A man, so the argument goes, can father a child without taking responsibility for its support. Also, a fact of life is that a woman can have a baby without a husband. Thus the cycle.

Before turning to the challenges of welfare's more extreme critics, it will be useful first to introduce a less extreme analysis, that of Blanche Bernstein, consultant on social welfare and author of the Twentieth Century Fund's *Saving a Generation*. Bernstein, unlike the harsher critics, is clear on her support, in principle, of AFDC. But as the title of one of her writings puts it, "Some Things are Wrong with the System."[9] The administration of the program, she charges, is too loose, yielding high levels of ineligibility and lengthy periods of dependency.

In particular, she attacks the failure over two decades to link welfare payments with a work requirement—something many welfare advocates have resisted.[10] Bernstein also criticizes AFDC for occasioning the deterioration of family structure through teenage pregnancies and for the abandonment of school by young AFDC recipients. Whatever may be the precise number of young women caught in long-term dependency—a theme shortly to be addressed—Bernstein acknowledges that they do need sympathetic help.

II. AN OVERVIEW OF THE EVIDENCE: AFDC AND FAMILIES

There is a considerable body of literature which has reviewed the evidence for these charges about the destructiveness of welfare for the family and youth. In the main, the evidence demonstrates that these charges are wanting.

Among the most recent reports is that of Gregory Duncan and Richard Coe, both of the University of Michigan's family research program. Reviewing Murray's *Losing Ground* they argue that there is no conclusive evidence of strong links between welfare and incidence of illegitimacy, divorce, or marriage breakup.[11] They support their position by noting agreement with their perspective from two other recognized researchers in the field, Mary Jo Bane and David Ellwood. These latter two, in a study completed after *Losing Ground* appeared, conclude that welfare does not seem to be an underlying cause of the admittedly dramatic changes in family structure that have occurred among recipient ages and classes.[12] Duncan and Coe defend the program against the accusation that it has worsened the plight of the poor and mired them in dependency.

The welfare program drawing the most fire is AFDC. This program makes cash contributions to aid children in families headed by unemployed parents, and these parents are overwhelmingly single females, the male parent being absent.[13] The cash contribution varies with eligibility standards, state contributions, age and number of children, and other factors. Of the many hundreds of thousands of parents in AFDC all but 250,000 are mothers without a husband in the household.

The first thing to be said about the program is that it represents, in terms of the overall federal budget, a relatively small amount of money compared to a program such as Social Security.[14] In proportionate spending, for one dollar spent on AFDC benefits currently, $20 are spent on Social Security. And as a fraction of the Federal budget itself, AFDC peaked in 1973 at 1.6 percent. Since then, this proportion has been declining. The reason is that whereas Social Security is indexed for inflation, AFDC is not. Senator Daniel Patrick Moynihan, a consistent observer of the welfare system who has critically reviewed its future, has calculated that since 1971 the value of AFDC payments has in real terms dropped by as much as a third.[15]

Ellwood and Summers, in the *Fighting Poverty* volume, highlight the concern over the value of welfare payments by noting that AFDC payments in real terms fell by almost 30 percent between 1971 and 1983. Concurring authorities are Sawhill as well as groups like the Center on Budget and Policy Priorities.[16] Also, while food stamps mitigate poverty, combined food stamps and AFDC payments have fallen by 22 percent in real terms in the median state.[17]

Ellwood and Summers note: "A smaller and smaller fraction of children in single-parent families were receiving AFDC for a very simple reason—benefit levels, and therefore eligibility of parents, were being sharply cut back."[18] Finally, they assert: "Family structure changes do not seem to mirror benefit level changes." They find this conclusion confirmed by another investigation of AFDC which examined whether differences in benefits from one state to another resulted in differences of illegitimacy or percentage of children in single parent families.[19]

Despite the very wide difference in benefits accorded by the states, "Variations in benefit levels across the states do not lead to corresponding variations in divorce rates, illegitimacy, or percentage of children living in a single-parent household. In fact, states with high welfare rates in general have less illegitimacy."[20] Yet, despite this evidence, the charge has consistently been made that there has been and is a welfare-induced explosion of children in out-of-wedlock households, subjecting more and more children to the "unnaturalness" of households headed by single females.

It is true that through the 1960s the number of families receiving AFDC transfers increased by 180 percent and the number of children in those families by 169 percent. But, as Moynihan has pointed out, in the next decade (the 1970s), AFDC families increased by only 68 percent and children in them by only 19 percent.[21]

Despite his somewhat negative appraisal of welfare in its current form, Moynihan appeals to the evidence of Ellwood and Summers. They have shown that, while the proportion of children living in female-headed households rose dramatically, from 14 percent in 1972 to almost 20 percent by the end of the decade, during the same period the proportion of children in homes collecting AFDC held almost constant at 12 percent.[22]

Senator Moynihan adds another point against Murray-type analysis—the sharp reduction in AFDC benefits themselves. Since 1970, these payments in constant dollars fell by 33 percent.[23] True, the impact of this drop was mitigated by the addition of in-kind contributions such as food stamps. But this does not militate against the implications for welfare of the cut in value of the transfers. The number of AFDC families increased, but the one-third reduction in value meant less funds for each child supported by the program.

Moynihan wonders how Murray could miss the fact that, contrary to his assertion that increased welfare funding accounts for more families in dependency, more families, for quite other reasons, became dependent on welfare even when its value was falling drastically. This situation is carefully documented by Ellwood and Summers.[24]

The recent, comprehensive work of Bane and Ellwood is also cited by Moynihan. They examined family patterns and the impact of AFDC across the 50 states as well as over time. That study conclusively demonstrated that differences in welfare benefit levels are not the primary cause of variations in family structures. Rather, factors more difficult to quantify—such as culture, attitudes, and personal expectations about home and family life—account for most differences in birth rates of unmarried women and in the divorce and separation patterns among families with children. "Welfare benefits are largely impotent as explanatory variables," they concluded.[25]

In further support of Moynihan's contention that welfare money does not lead to increase in children born out of wedlock or children in a household headed by a single female is the fact that welfare payments after the first child are in most states relatively small.[26] In some there is no benefit increase at all for additional children. There are even studies which show that with more children, female-headed families fell further below the poverty level than they already were. That economic incentive does not enter into child-bearing is also clear from the fact that, even though economic status with a second child worsens, most one-parent families nevertheless have a second child.[27]

With all of this, it must be noted that Senator Moynihan is especially concerned about the number of children "pocketed in dependency." He believes that 32 percent of children born in 1980 could expect to be on welfare before reaching 18 years of age. "A child born in Brooklyn to a 17 year-old mother is, you know, going to be on AFDC before it is very old."[28]

III. THE ISSUE OF LONG-TERM DEPENDENCY

Another charge against welfare must be addressed—that it promotes long-term dependency. This charge has been made by Charles Murray and others. It is their contention that poor people have come to rely on welfare payments and it thus becomes a way of life. The recipients lose all capacity or interest in finding gainful employment. Is this the case?

Duncan and Roe argue to the contrary, that AFDC statistics do not show long-term dependency.[29] According to Murray, 48 percent of all women receiving AFDC were off the rolls in two years, but 50 percent remained on them for eight years or more. This, Murray notes, adds up to 1.6 million families embracing more than 5 million people in a permanent dependency. Contrary to Murray's statistics, however, the proportion of women receiving AFDC for more than eight years is never cited by others as more than 25 percent; and, by important names in the field, as somewhat more like 15 percent.[30]

Ellwood, this time writing with Summers, refers back to his Bane and Ellwood study to say: "The evidence [on duration of AFDC] as analyzed by Bane and Ellwood, 1983, suggests two sides to the AFDC population. Most people who receive AFDC benefits leave within two years and 85 percent leave within eight years. Thus, most AFDC recipients do not seem to get trapped by it.

"At the same time, the minority who do stay on the program a long time accumulate and thus ultimately receive most of the benefits paid out. They also represent a large fraction of people on the program at any one point in time. The 15 percent of recipients who stay eight years or more on the program collect more than 50 percent of the benefits paid out."[31]

That language is clear enough. Even though only 15 percent remain on the AFDC rolls eight or more years, they cumulatively collect half the AFDC payments. Here is a dual situation: on the one side, it is a small fraction who constitute long-term dependency; and on the other side, this small fraction receives the lion's share of the AFDC payments.

But how is it possible that 15 percent receive up to 50 percent of the benefits paid out? Ellwood and Bane offer an analogy.[32] Consider a 13-bed hospital in which 12 beds are occupied for an entire year by 12 chronically-ill patients, while the remaining bed is used by 52 patients during the same year. Each of the latter group stays exactly one week. On any given day, a hospital census would find that about 92 percent of the patients were in long periods of hospitalization. Yet, viewed over the course of the year, short-term patients dominate the total patient count. Out of the 64 patients that would use the hospital services, about 81 percent (52 of the 64) spent only one week in the hospital. The remaining 19 percent occupy 12 of the 13 beds for the entire year. Similarly, the 15-20 percent who "occupy" AFDC for eight years or more account for half the funds paid out since they are carried eight years or more.

According to Ellwood and Summers, conservatives, in their exposition of this distribution according to years of occupancy, "throw the weight of their conclusion onto the caseload that the 15 percent represent." The distortion that represents is manifest in the illustration just given. Because the distortion is so triumphantly bandied about in the welfare debate, it is worth pursuing this point a bit further.

Three well-known researchers, Greg J. Duncan, Martha Hill, and Saul D. Hoffman, have examined the data between the mid-1960s and the late 1970s.[33] Their estimates reveal that about 30 percent of recipients received welfare for one or two years, and a similar proportion had eight or more years on the program. The median length of receiving benefits, however, was less than four years. For these authors, the dominating conclusion is that "long-term welfare usage characterizes only a minority of recipients." Nevertheless, nearly two-thirds are in long-term welfare usage at a given time.

Time (years)	Persons ever on AFDC (%)	Persons on AFDC at a given time (%)
1 to 2	30	7
3 to 7	40	28
8 or more	30	65

Like Ellwood and Bane, these authors point out that one's conclusion depends on which method of calculation is used: a count of all the people receiving welfare during the period observed, or a point-in-time count. The proportion in a given status—on welfare (or in the hospital)—at any given point is necessarily higher for individuals who occupy that status longer. It does not take into account the individuals who have left welfare—or left the hospital. Thus, they conclude, point-in-time examples of welfare recipients yield biased information on the typical experiences of welfare recipients.[34]

IV. A LOOK AT INTERGENERATIONAL DEPENDENCY

Turning to the related problem of intergenerational dependency, another way of stating the case of dependency is to say that welfare recipients transfer to their children their own dependency on welfare. Some hold that this intergenerational effect is due to culture—the culture of a family relying at length on welfare or the culture of a neighborhood of such households. The cultural experience socializes young children to enter the welfare mentality and then the welfare way of life.

Others hold that the intergenerational effect is not cultural but structural. The welfare mentality of the parent is acquired by children at the moment of encountering the same structural impediments their parents experienced. Examples of this situation are discrimination, persistent unemployment, poor educational systems, and extremely limited job opportunities.

Demonstrating such intergenerational causality would require data on values and attitudes, especially of children, over several different periods of their childhood. This data does not exist in any comprehensive form. But sampling has been done of the simple associations between the welfare dependence of parents and their grown children. This information can provide, many authors argue, a more accurate picture than frequently appears in the media of children and welfare. They point to a 19-year study of the economic fortunes of a large and representative sample of U.S. families, focusing on dependency of daughters.[35]

The study concluded that the majority of daughters who grew up in highly dependent homes did not share the fate of their parents. Only one out of five were themselves highly dependent on AFDC in their early twenties. More than three out of five received no AFDC during the period of the study. On the strength of their work, these authors feel able to affirm that the stereotype of heavy welfare dependence being routinely passed from mother to child is contradicted by the data.

There is, of course, the fact that the proportion of daughters of welfare homes who then turn to welfare is much higher than the proportion of daughters of non-welfare homes who become highly dependent on AFDC (20 percent to 3 percent). The parallel truth is that while it is so that more than three out of five daughters of welfare homes received AFDC themselves, the fraction of daughters of homes that had not relied on welfare who did not themselves later receive AFDC mounted to nine-tenths.

But one must also recognize that here other factors of parental behavior and environment affect the likelihood and length of welfare dependency. For instance, the facts are that children of welfare recipients often live in poorer neighborhoods, have parents who possess limited resources, go to inferior schools, and have a less promising vision of the future. Any of these factors could affect welfare dependency quite independently of the effect of their parents' having received AFDC.

There is also to be considered the fact that the fraction of daughters of non-recipients of welfare, who as adults come to depend upon welfare, jumps by half to 7 percent if the same demographic restrictions applying to daughters of welfare recipients are applied to them. This fraction doubles again to 14 percent if the sample is confined to daughters of welfare non-recipient families growing up in low-income and mother-only households. Clearly, the AFDC dependency of this latter group as adults is not linked to welfare dependency of their parents.

V. A REVIEW OF CONCLUSIONS ON WELFARE AND THE FAMILY

To conclude this review of welfare and family concerns, some additional time should be spent on an important earlier study by Greg J. Duncan and Saul D. Hoffman.[37] In this report, the two researchers review all pertinent research on alleged welfare impact—including their own. This study thus serves as a summary statement of the central points being made here.

The Duncan and Hoffman study advances the following observations on the basis of their investigations. The allegation that AFDC, by raising income available to single women with dependent children (but not to single women without children or—in most states—to intact families) encourages instability, illegitimate births, and independent households headed by unmarried mothers and discourages marriage and remarriage has plausibility. The supporting data is based on experimentation which, in accord with the experimenters' own expectations, disclosed substantially higher divorce or separation rates among the families studied in the experiment.

The results of the study, according to Duncan and Hoffman, are, though plausible, suspect on at least three counts: (1) individuals receiving the highest benefits showed lower rates of marriage disruption while the exact opposite should have been registered if the allegation were true; (2) the high rates of instability also were found among families without children and families receiving job counselling or education in addition to welfare payments, which is again the opposite of what should have been expected; and (3), a re-examination of the data confined to families with children revealed a much smaller and "statistically insignificant effect of the experiment on marital instability."

Still another study, this one non-experimental of a long list of family structure variables, using several sources of data, found that AFDC had no measurable impact on births to unmarried women, and only modest impact on divorce or separation or the proportion of female-headed families. Its biggest impact was on living arrangements. That is, single women without husbands, receiving AFDC, were more likely to live independently rather than with their parents.

Further, the main difficulty Duncan and Hoffman have with many of these studies (including Bane and Ellwood) is that they do not take into account the way in which individual behavior relates to the welfare system. Thus absence of good marriage prospects may have more to do with remaining on welfare. This non-welfare alternative is not measured in such studies. Consequently, the hypothesis can be advanced that "the generally small and often statistically insignificant estimates of AFDC effects are the consequences of flaws in research." And that being so, "unless welfare benefits have major impact on family structure decision, reduction in aid will only reduce the standard of living of the women and children involved."

As to the question that welfare causes dependence, these authors conclude that the patterns of welfare length of enrollment should "allay concerns that any brush with welfare necessarily leads to dependence." Still, they note that 30 percent of all who begin welfare will spend eight years or more of their prime working years on it. That adds up to some millions of women and children who live in families consistently dependent on welfare.

But, the same authors ask, is it welfare that explains the dependence? That is, does being on welfare generate a welfare trap—does the initial reception of welfare produce a change in the recipient making her more likely to stick to welfare? Or may it not be that other more "permanent" aspects of the individual and the environment account for the dependency? Examples would be disability status, education level, or other values and attitudes. If the latter, welfare might have little or no effect on the length of enrollment in the welfare program itself.

The authors are led to conclude that there is little evidence of program-induced dependence. They argue that "though the probability of leaving welfare is low for half the sample...still these long spells are neither created nor lengthened by the use of AFDC itself."

For Duncan and Hoffman, research shows nothing to indicate that experience with AFDC causes significant changes in personal efficacy. Or to put it slightly different, what evidence is available fails to support the notion that welfare would be reduced if potential or actual recipients were imbued with a greater sense of control or orientation toward the future. Moreover, as has been seen, there is little if any evidence of intergenerational transmission of welfare dependence.

It would appear, then, that the conservative charges concerning welfare's destruction of the family are not in large measure borne out. But liberals and supporters of welfare should not dismiss the disturbing evidence that some millions of young, unmarried mothers and their children live in dependence. In their Economic Pastoral, the U.S. Bishops recognize this. They are equally cognizant of irregularities in the impact of welfare on the family. The Pastoral consequently supports a more family-oriented welfare rather than an individualistic one.

The Bishops make every effort to make clear that, while welfare has a necessary role and function, its positive rather than its negative aspects should be the guide for future action on the prospects for welfare reform. The Bishops do not wish to perpetuate an unworkable or detrimental system any more than conservative critics do. The fact is, however, that welfare, even with respect to families, is neither unworkable nor has it been proved to be detrimental.

ENDNOTES FOR CHAPTER IV

[1] One other charge of a more explicit economic character is that welfare reduces the labor supply. Welfare programs like Aid to Families with Dependent Children (AFDC) are said to reduce the work availability of welfare recipients. This is assumed to happen because of two factors: AFDC provides income without work, and welfare recipients who do work even a few hours a week see their AFDC benefits reduced. So why work?

Duncan, Hill, and Hoffman say on this: "Evidence consistently indicates that income transfer programs do indeed reduce the labor supply, but estimates vary widely as to the size of the effect." They add: "One recent review of the evidence shows that AFDC reduces the average annual work effort among female heads of households by 180 hours." Greg J. Duncan, Martha S. Hill, Saul D. Hoffman, "Welfare Dependence Within and Across Generations," *Science* (vol. 239) January 1988.

This is surely not a severe loss to the nation's work effort. In another publication (*The Use and Effects of Welfare: A Survey of Recent Evidence*, November 1987; manuscript awaiting publication), Duncan and Hoffman give as figures of work reduction by recipients of AFDC 600 hours or 15 40-hour weeks. In this paper, the 180 hours figure includes alongside AFDC recipients other female-headed households. Duncan and Hoffman conclude: "The descriptive evidence provides substantial support for the view that the welfare system operates in a haphazard fashion."

[2] *Time*, February 17, 1987.

[3] The charges against the Bishops were addressed in Chapter I; they will be considered from another perspective in Chapter VIII.

[4] This and several other criticisms are examined and refuted in *Beyond The Myths: The Families Helped by the AFDC Program* (New York: Center on Social Welfare Policy and Law, 1985).

[5] *Time*, loc. cit.

[6] See the extensive discussions in Sheldon H. Danziger and Daniel H. Weinberg, eds., *Fighting Poverty: What Works and What Doesn't* (Cambridge: Harvard University Press, 1986).

[7] William Julius Wilson and Kathyrn M. Neckerman, "Poverty and Family Structures," in *Fighting Poverty*.

[8] *Society*, January/February 1986.

[9] *New York Times*, October 31, 1986.

[10] Ibid.

[11] Duncan and Coe cooperated in an 18-year study of poverty conducted by the University of Michigan. In an exchange with Murray they say of their study: "It reveals a picture of economic mobility and of generally benign welfare programs that differ dramatically from *Losing Ground*." More specifically to the point here, they add:"Mr. Murray's attack on the core social programs—AFDC and food stamps—is based on the premise that they foster dependency by discouraging work and marriage and reduce the stigma formerly attached to a life on the dole." *Wall Street Journal*, May 15, 1985.

A study written in the same vein as Murray's celebrated *Losing Ground* is *Up From Dependency*, a report to the President by the Domestic Policy Council on Low Income Opportunities, Washington, D.C., December 1986. This report relies greatly on a study by two renowned Harvard researchers, Mary Jo Bane and David Ellwood, *The Dynamics of Dependency: The Route to Self-sufficiency* (Cambridge: Harvard University Press, 1983). It seems to me that the Council report pulls the Bane-Ellwood study out of its contextual setting, neglecting in particular the studies to be referred to at the end of this chapter. The report argues that there is a sharp disagreement over whether welfare promotes family breakdown. But there is significant literature which challenges the impression thus given that sides are evenly divided over this issue.

The authors of the presidential report also feel enough confidence to assert a consensus on a somewhat related point: "Welfare surely enables mothers to raise their children without the help of a father or a job." Review Draft, 47. True. But how does that provide demonstration of their thrust that "Whatever the scholarly debates, the evidence of daily life in our cities and the first-hand testimony of families on welfare does implicate the welfare system." "Implicate" is a weasel word. What they really mean is "condemn." But does this testimony cited so implicate?

[12] Bane and Ellwood, op. cit. This instances the anomaly that Bane and Ellwood can be cited by writers in opposition to one another.

[13] For easy accessibility of relevant data, consult Ellwood and Summers, op. cit., 92 ff. They explain different kinds of cash outlays and in-kind benefits (86 ff). See also Sawhill, op. cit., 25 ff., and Center on Budget and Policy Studies, op. cit., 2, 31.

[14] Daniel Patrick Moynihan, *Challenge*, September/October 1985.

[15] Ibid.

[16] Ellwod and Summers, *Fighting Poverty*, 86; Sawhill, Work and Welfare, 23; Center on Budget and Policy Priorities, Smaller Slices of the Pie, 84.

[17] Ellwood and Summers add an alternative way of expressing the same reality: "If food stamps were treated as income in 1982, the number of non-elderly poor would have fallen from 30.6 to 29.1 millions." Obviously a negligible difference.

[18] Ibid., 86.

[19] Ibid., 95 ff.

[20] Bane and Ellwood, loc. cit., cited by William J. Wilson and Kathyrn Neckerman, in *Fighting Poverty*, 250.

[21] Moynihan, loc. cit.

[22] Ellwood and Summers, op. cit., 93 and table comparing children in female-headed households and in households receiving AFDC, 1960-1982.

[23] Ibid. Ellwood and Summers confirm the fall in terms of constant dollars, op. cit., 86.

[24] Moynihan, loc. cit.; Ellwood and Summers, "Poverty in America: Is Welfare the Answer or the Problem?" in *Fighting Poverty*, 78-105.

[25] Moynihan, loc. cit.

[26] Ibid.

[27] Study by Population-Environment Balance, reported in *Washington Post*, September 1, 1986.

[28] Moynihan, loc. cit.

[29] *Wall Street Journal*, review of Losing Ground, May 15, 1985.

[30] Ellwood and Summers in *Fighting Poverty* agree with the presentation of Bane and Ellwood.

[31] Sawhill, op. cit., 27.

[32] Quoted in *Up From Dependency* (review draft), 51.

[33] "Welfare Dependence Within and Across Generations," *Science* (vol. 239), January 1988, 467-71.

[34] Ibid., 468. The authors observe further that welfare experience differs markedly among AFDC recipients. They here contrast young women who first went on welfare at 25 but with high school education and previous work experience and young women going on welfare before 25 and without finishing high school and without work experience. Of the former fewer than one out of seven eventually receive AFDC for more than 9 years. In the case of the second group more than 40 percent will stay on welfare more than 9 years.

[35] Ibid., 469.

[36] It is of great significance that this highly reputed group of researchers have to date confirmed so many of the views on welfare's impact on the family held by more progressive analysts but rejected by conservatives.

[37] "The Use and Effects of Welfare: A Survey of Recent Evidence," forthcoming in *Social Service Review*.

5

DOES WELFARE
CREATE
A BLACK UNDERCLASS?

A third serious challenge raised to welfare must now be examined. This challenge raises an issue perhaps even more controversial than the question of welfare and the family. It finds detractors of welfare even among constituencies which might ordinarily be, in the political scheme of things, welfare supporters. The issue is the growth of what has been called the "black underclass" in the United States, and whether, or to what extent, welfare has contributed to it.

Black youths on street corners. Soaring school dropout rates. Rising teenage pregnancies. Large segments of black youth unemployed, under-educated, locked out of the system. Growing criminal activity. Tangible anger, wasted lives. The high unemployment and functional illiteracy rates among black urban youth are becoming common statistics, cited by liberals to support their call for more comprehensive public intervention, cited by conservatives to support their conclusions on the results of inept public meddling.

While both sides agree that the situation is distressing and dangerous to those involved as well as to the overall future of the country, there is sharp disagreement on effective approaches to the problem. And with respect to the role welfare has played in the development of this "black underclass," there is even sharper debate, some of which has resulted in splits within both conservative and liberal camps.

In responding to this central issue, the U.S. Catholic Bishops have taken a comprehensive approach in the Economic Pastoral to black unemployment and similar issues. They have been subject to criticism from both sides of the debate because, while shaping their own stance, they have not totally adopted the position of either. The debate itself is extremely important, for its outcome will shape the view of society and the role of government with respect to urban black youth for the next decade.

The young black American has been thrust to the fore in the welfare debate. Because of the concentration of black youths in hopeless and fearful urban slums, these young people are particularly visible. Indeed, statistics paint a grim picture of the young black, framed by the disturbing growth of illegitimacy and the worrisome number of households with children headed by teenage, single females. Yet it must be noted that experts point out that these manifestations of social deterioration are also present among young whites, if not in quite the same proportions.[1]

A chorus of critics, generally conservative, have proclaimed that this bleak situation is entirely due to welfare. Welfare, say Charles Murray, Mickey Kaus and many others, has created a black ghetto of social outcasts. Yet a careful review of welfare experiences indicates the need to examine these charges critically. The extent of the black underclass is exaggerated by some writers and—more important here—whatever amount of social disorganization does exist in poor black neighborhoods cannot be laid at the feet of the welfare program.

Instead, the evidence suggests two other main causes of this deterioration: changing U.S. family structures and the rapid transformation of the job market, particularly as this deterioration in employment options has affected young black males. Widespread unemployment among young black men also affects young black women, for it creates a pool of less eligible marriage prospects. Young black women are less likely to find a husband who can be counted on to help provide for the family's financial needs on a long-term, consistent, available basis. This situation has had its own affect on family cohesion and continuity.

I. A DISMAYING PICTURE

How can the situation of black youth in the United States be best described? One in two black youths lives in poverty and without a father present in the household. One in two black teenagers has no job. One in four black births is to a teenage woman. In 1950, 17 percent of black infants were born out of wedlock. The figure is now 50 percent.[2] Despite this high figure, one noted authority, Marian Wright Edelman, asserts that from 1978 to 1983 there has been a 5 percent drop of infants born to black, unmarried teenage mothers.[3] Nevertheless, the increased percentage of children living in female-headed families, a large part of the recipients of Aid to Families with Dependent Children, means that one-third of the black children born in 1980 are destined to be on welfare before adulthood.

Some authorities believe these dismaying aspects of young black life have, either in their sheer magnitude or coupled with other destructive effects, entered the bloodstream of the black poor, creating a veritable underclass in urban centers.

Twenty years ago, Daniel Patrick Moynihan wrote *The Negro Family: the Case for National Action*. Even then, Moynihan declared the situation to be pathological, with its poverty, brokenness of family life, fatherless families, illegitimacy, and welfare mentality. To these indicators he added the cultural phenomenon of black youth controlled by domineering mothers, resulting in youth growing up with no visual model of male authority.[4] This last characterization by Moynihan did raise some sharp criticism. His basic thesis—that the 1966 ghetto reflected earlier slave experience—had its supporters, but was widely challenged by white as well as black authorities.

Moynihan went further to say that a community facing this grim prospect, together with the unlikelihood of youth acquiring hopeful expectations about the future, is facing chaos, unrest, disorder, and violence. And in fact, in the 20 years since Moynihan's report, the overall situation of black youth has worsened. Not coincidentally, so has the level of violence and drug abuse in the urban ghettos.

Charles Murray, to whom is generally ascribed the view that welfare accounts for this underclass, has chosen to emphasize something which he regards as even more fundamental. The problem is not that young black males (or young poor males more generally) have stopped working altogether. It is rather that they have moved in and out of the labor force precisely at the points of their lives when it was most important that they acquire skills, work habits, and a work record. He adds that poor young women with children but no husband are consigned similarly to the economic margins of society.[5]

These black youths, according to Murray, become "decoupled from the mechanism whereby the poor of this country historically have worked their way out of poverty." Instead, these youths put together a combination of a little work, some underground income, and some welfare, and make do with that. In a debate with Rev. Jesse Jackson, Murray called for "dismantling the black ghetto," and the welfare system that supports it. He contended, "We have taught it's not your responsibility but the system's failure. We've said you can get along and survive without participation."[6] In a subsequent interview, Murray concluded that since the appearance in 1984 of his widely-discussed book *Losing Ground,* he feels more strongly than ever that either there will be non-welfare progress or a permanent welfare underclass.[7]

Some liberal voices echo Murray's general view. The well-known television commentator Bill Moyers, basing his comment on his own interviews in the black inner city, joins Murray: "Years ago liberals scoffed at the idea that welfare corrupts and that negative values had nothing to do with producing poor urban blacks."[8] Social economist Mickey Kaus give pretty much the same picture.[9]

Many blacks have joined in recognition of the existence of something of a black underclass—without, however, attributing its development to welfare. While these observers may oppose conservative analysis and proposals for the situations, they at least acknowledge a serious problem. Roger Wilkins, a noted black leader, says, "The hardest job is cultural arrest of moral deterioration and to reverse it."[10]

Among the most recent of these black-sponsored portrayals of the urban underclass is the 1987 study by the Joint Center for Political Studies entitled *Black Initiative and Governmental Responsibility*. The study states: "Most of the black poor are concentrated in badly deteriorated inner cities, are poorly educated and without the skills and experience acquired in today's workplace, are plagued by extremely high rates of unemployment and underemployment, and are strained by a rapidly deteriorating family structure. Many of these poor blacks are part of what a number of analysts call an urban underclass."[11] The condition of this underclass is stated in terms of "profound urban poverty among blacks—declining male labor force participation, very high rates of out-of-wedlock births, and female-headed households, a high level of welfare dependency, and high crime rates."[12]

Still another factor is proposed as an explanation of the presumed inner-city underclass—the flight from the inner city, with its dreary poverty and violence, by the growing number of middle-class blacks. Nicholas Lehman has popularized this thesis.[13] In essence, this perspective argues that flight in the 1960s was too rapid. Where before, doctors, merchants, entrepreneurs, teachers lived in the black community, holding it together, now all these community figures and role models were distant. The inner city blacks were left to their poverty and hopelessness.

True, a lot of hard-working fathers remained. But, says Lehman, there was a widespread absence of the father-provider model. There remained few visible examples to show that one can indeed work one's way out—that getting ahead is possible. Other studies agree with this diagnosis.[14]

It may be pertinent to point out, as did Rev. Jesse Jackson in his debate with Murray, that the black inner city is not devoid of virtue or of hard-working blacks. Rev. Jackson also observed that turning the spotlight of truth upon upper classes of our society would quickly reveal a high degree of vice in its own right.[15] "Contra-gate" is not a black phenomenon, nor is the economic entanglement of Wall Street.

The current debate here revolves around the legitimacy of the assumption that there is a huge black population permanently clustered in a run-down, poverty-locked quarter of the inner city. Liberal social economist Isabel Sawhill claims that on the contrary actually only 7 percent of the entire poverty population lives in a low-income area of a large city (low income area being defined as having a poverty rate of 40 percent of more)[16]. Although 70 percent of those living in urban low-income areas are black, blacks living in such areas comprise less than 5 percent of the total black population nationwide and only 15 percent of the black poverty population.[17]

Sawhill is joined by a considerable number of inner city observers. The key to reconciling their seeming rejection of the idea of a black underclass with those convinced that it does exist may be the word "pervasive." The black study, *Black Initiatives and Government Responsibility* turns on the words "many" and "most". Most of the black poor, the study contends, are concentrated in badly deteriorated inner cities and many of these poor blacks are part of an urban underclass.

For example, social economist David Ellwood, joining with William Julius Wilson and others in a symposium on Mickey Kaus, rejects an important supposition of Kaus on black migration.[18] Kaus, relying on other studies, says that black migrants moving from the South to Northern cities arrived there and wound up swelling the welfare rolls. On the contrary, retort Ellwood and Wilson, these migrants have lower records of both unemployment and of welfare than do blacks born in the North.

As for Kaus, both Ellwood and Wilson are prepared to concede that where migration is in fact an established pattern, the departure from the black inner-city by the upwardly mobile black professionals and other educated blacks is also deeply regrettable, as it does result in depriving young inner-city black youth of role models. But that result conceded, the authors consider this flight far less disastrous than the deterioration of the inner city schools, clear victims of economic stagnation.

This is not the place to explore further the pathology of an alleged black underclass. Nor is it possible to state definitively to what degree the very existence of such a population segment is factually founded. What is known is that there is a very disturbing rise of family instability, more prominent among young blacks than young whites. What must be taken up more directly is the allegation of welfare's responsibility for this situation.

II. IS WELFARE TO BLAME?

Much that is relevant to the question of welfare's negative impact on the family is also pertinent to the alleged deleterious effects of welfare on the inner-city black communities. Although welfare may be a contributing factor, it is hardly the sole or most prominent one. Thus, the support of welfare by the Bishops' Economic Pastoral is not a support of a continuation of the development of this black underclass.

There is very considerable family instability across the country, apparently more pronounced in the black communities than in white ones. But welfare has very little to do with this development. The fundamental causes are more related to family structure, along with the socio-economic factors affecting those structures, and joblessness.

1. The Role of AFDC

To begin with, Aid to Families with Dependent Children, or the prospect of it, has no measurable effect on out-of-wedlock birth rates among women likely to qualify for AFDC if they actually become single mothers.[19] Turning from welfare as affecting out-of-wedlock births to welfare as affecting black family instability, observers find the same negative results. AFDC benefits did not bring marital disruptions. The benefits did, however, make it more likely, as seen in the last chapter, that separated or divorced mothers would move into households of their own.

White women are far more likely than black women, especially young black women, to establish their own household as a result of divorce or separation. Young black women, however, are more likely to act from a desire to establish an independent home for themselves and their out-of-wedlock children. Thus, in the growth of female-headed families between 1940 and 1970, fully a third can be attributed to this desire to establish one's own home.

Viewing this phenomenon from the perspective of the children involved reveals that in 1969-73, of children born into single-parent families, 50 percent of the white and slightly more than 50 percent of the black children lived not in homes created by the caring parent but with the grandparents. But, in the next five-year period (1973-78), the figure for children living with grandparents dropped to 24 percent for whites but only 37 percent for blacks.[20]

It might be noted that young women mothering children, unlike older women with children, have tended to live with their parents as a sub-family. This arrangement is partly due to the less education and less work experience found among younger women than older women. But by the time their children have reached six years of age, even the younger single mothers will seek to move into separate housing arrangements. For blacks it is more likely that the situation will become an independent female-headed family.[21]

One other challenge is made to welfare's impact on the black underclass and on the family aspect of this situation. This charge is that AFDC makes it possible for women with children to leave non-poor homes to create independent poor homes. Since the public is reluctant to support a poverty that comes from such departures from a non-poor to a poor status, it is vital to sift through the evidence that is said to support this allegation.

Sociologist Mary Joe Bane devotes a chapter to this charge in the now-familiar book, *Fighting Poverty*.[22] Because of the reluctance of the public to support such poverty, she emphasizes the importance of having the facts. On this Bane writes, "less than half of the poverty of female-headed and single-person households and therefore only about a quarter to a fifth of all poverty, appears to have come about simultaneously with changes in household composition." Family composition changes in the early 1980s made only a trivial contribution to the increase in poverty. Most poverty, even of female-headed families, occurs because of job changes.

"It is also important," she continues, "that only about a fifth of the poverty among black female-headed and single person households appears to be driven by the event of household composition changes. Among blacks, poor female-headed and single-person households are much more likely to be formed from households that were already poor. They are also much more likely to fall into or back into poverty after the break-up, perhaps testifying to the chronic economic problems of black families and resultant intermittent poverty."

Bane emphasizes her point: "Although there has been a dramatic and shocking increase in female-headed families among blacks, and an equally dramatic feminization of black poverty, one cannot conclude that much of the poverty could have been avoided had families stayed together."

Her final conclusion is that "the problem of poverty should be addressed by devoting attention to employment, wages, and the development of skills necessary for productive participation in the workforce, rather than by handwringing about the decline of the family." Nevertheless, Bane recognizes that a fifth of all poverty occurs simultaneously with family break-up—again, not a welfare result.

Not addressed but also important is another situation. The young woman may have left her parents' home because of an intolerable living situation. Indeed, she may have been asked to leave. Thus the establishment of a new household is not always by choice and thus not always motivated by factors related to welfare.

2. Marital Dissolution

Two other researchers who have addressed the underclass question are William Julius Wilson and Kathryn Neckerman.[23] They begin by saying that their review of recent literature on welfare as encouraging out-of-wedlock births and welfare as affecting marital dissolution shows that the results are inconclusive.[24] For instance, they report one expert as showing in a 1983 study that "for blacks, the illegitimacy ratio in the South was only slightly lower than that in non-southern states, despite levels of AFDC payments that were less than half of those of the rest of the country."[25]

These researchers also reject tracing of the black female-headed family to slavery. Two-parent black families predominated in the 19th and 20th centuries. It is equally erroneous that migration from rural Southern communities to urban centers seriously affected the family structure. That stability continued to the 1960s, but concealed the beginnings of family break-up. Marriage dissolution was already on the rise. In 1960 only 22 percent of black families were female-headed, but by 1983 that figure had risen to 42 percent.[26] Of all black children under 18 in that same year of 1983, 48 percent lived in female-headed households.

Several factors of family structure are here at work: fertility rates, marital status, age, and living arrangements.[27] For observers Wilson and Neckerman, the unprecedented increase in the proportion of "birth out-of-wedlock" is a major contribution to the rise of female-headed families in the black community. In 1980, 68 percent of births to black women aged 15 to 24 were outside marriage (41 percent in 1955). The proportion has also risen for young white women, but not nearly to the same degree as for blacks.[28]

As to these high ratios: "Fertility rates of young, unmarried women have risen or declined moderately, while those of married women of these ages have fallen more substantially." Thus, out-of-wedlock births now constitute a far greater proportion of total births than in the past, particularly for black women. Wilson and Neckerman warn that the data must be used with caution. For this rise in black illegitimacy is not owing to any great increase in the rate of extra-marital births. It is explained by the decline in both percentage of women married and rates of marital fertility. On marital status itself, the researchers offer this observation. There has been a sharp rise in separation and divorce and a substantial increase of never-married women. The combined impact is particularly drastic for black women. The fraction living with a husband fell from 52 percent in 1947 to 34 percent in 1980.[29]

The editors of *Fighting Poverty* concur: the dramatic rise in the proportion of illegitimate births to blacks "is not because of a rising rate of out-of-wedlock births, but in large part because the rate of marital fertility and the percentage of women married and living with their husbands both declined significantly." The sharp reduction of the latter is due to the rise in black divorce and separation, black's lower percentage of remarriage, and an increase in the proportion of never-married women.[30]

3. The Cultural Factors

These authors also contend that cultural factors must be numbered among the causes other than welfare for the increase in out-of-wedlock births. First, while studies show that most of these births were unwanted and unplanned, they are unwanted less among young black women than among young white women. There is less of a social stigma attached in neighborhoods of young black women regarding out-of-wedlock childbearing. There are also fewer desirable options for a young black woman in the ghetto than for a young woman in a better position, be she black or white.

Next, in her limited situation, a young black woman may even derive some satisfaction in motherhood. She may feel that she has arrived at a woman's status and can seek to be treated as one. An analogous feeling has been identified also for young black men who pride themselves on fathering a child in a social environment that provides so few options and such limited opportunities for establishing pride and status.

Finally, studies show how home conditions of young blacks (or whites) affect child-bearing out-of-wedlock. Those living with both father and mother are less likely to bear illegitimate children than those living with only a separated or divorced mother; the former household is less conducive to out-of-wedlock child-bearing than the latter. Add to that the predictable effects of lack of supervision of young people when the responsibility falls entirely on one parent such as the mother.[31]

Still another factor is the difference in expectation between whites and blacks about timing of marriage and parenthood. While there is little attitudinal difference between the two groups on parenthood, on marriage a considerable difference has been noted. Blacks expect a later marriage. While whites also put off marriage, the reasons are more often education or career. Delaying marriage in the case of young black women is more often owing to the poor marriage prospects in her own social situation. In contrast, pushing for earlier marriages for young white women who do not choose a career or education are a combination of better economic situations and a larger pool of eligibile male partners. Young black women, in a word, have distinctly poorer marriage prospects.[32] True, this is not so much cultural as it is socio-economic: so many young black males are jobless—the image with which this discussion began.

A further cultural factor affecting whites as well as blacks is the prevalence of early sexual activity. This is true of middle-income youths as well as of lower-income and poor young people. That a disadvantaged background heightens sexual activity is not a strong conclusion to draw from the available evidence. Factors at least as strong appear to be youthful rebelliousness, availability of birth control, sophistication of youth in sexual matters, an ever-earlier effort to imitate adult behavior, and the effect of a very pervasive and sophisticated consumer marketplace which often uses sex as a powerful sales image—without the cautions that should accompany such images regarding the results of spontaneous, uncommitted, or irresponsible sexual activity.

Still another inner-city socio-economic factor operative in the black community's adolescent pregnancy is failure of the education system. Girls with poor basic skills are five times as likely to become mothers before age 16 as are those with average skills. Young women with poor or fair basic skills are three to four times as likely as those with average skills to have more than one child while in their teens. Low-skilled 18- and 19-year-olds are two-and-one-half to three times more likely than their average-skilled counterparts to become parents.[33]

Many disadvantaged youth sense that they have nothing to lose by being parents. They feel no door will be closed by teenage pregnancy because they believe from the outset that no doors are open.[34] The cause of female-headed households among black youth is, therefore, not the availability of welfare but the lack of opportunities for the disadvantaged and a host of other cultural and social factors. The explanation does not fully lie within the black community nor squarely with welfare. It must be seen as the result of a combination of other conditions, along with the movement in U.S. culture in general in the 1970s and 1980s to different forms of family structure.

III. THE IMPACT OF UNEMPLOYMENT

The conservative school's thesis is that welfare explains the high percentage of black (or white for that matter) families headed by a single, female parent. The response to that claim is that many other factors—not all of them quantifiable—account for the structure of the black female-headed family and for black poverty more generally. Thus far some family demographics and cultural factors related to the black teenage female-headed family have been examined.[35] It is necessary now to return to the specifically economic factor of joblessness among young blacks.

Young black joblessness has been studied by many experts. Most conclude that joblessness, not welfare or racial failures, is a major component in accounting for black female-headed families. Joblessness, in turn, stems from overall weak performance of the economy. The simple fact is that a lot of young black men are unable to support a family and for that reason are considered by young black women to be outside the most desirable marriage pool.

Edward Gramlich, an observer of this situation, has noted, "the rise in the number of single-parent families was related to the decline in employment of black young males." This phenomenon is known as "the marriage pool" or ratio of employed civilian men to women of the same race and age. Gramlich continues that some studies (Ellwood and Summers) found that black women, especially young, face a shrinking pool of potential mates—due to black males poor labor market prospects. So black women are more likely to delay marriage or to remain unmarried.[36]

A 1986 *U.S. News & World Report* article on blacks and employment gave a very grim picture.[37] One-half of the 8.8 million working-age blacks lack jobs. They are either unemployed, out of the labor force having given up the job search, or in correctional facilities. The unemployment rate for blacks is about twice what it is for whites.

In fact, blacks with jobs earned incomes far below those of whites. According to one estimate in 1984, the median income was 56 percent that of whites. Because black wives worked more often than white wives, they did gain slightly on median family income. Since then there has been a bit of progress, but not dramatic. In 1979, when good overall economic performance had lowered unemployment to 5.8 percent, the wage proportion to whites of black teenagers stood as low as 34 percent.

Unlike ethnic groups in the first half of this Century, unskilled blacks have not been able to shed poverty by taking manufacturing jobs offering decent wages. By 1970, that door was virtually closed to them. In the last 15 years, only 10 percent of the 23 million jobs created in the private sector were in manufacturing. The remaining 85 percent were in service industries, and even service industry jobs generally require educational levels beyond high school. Blacks usually do not get those service jobs that require relatively high education for the simple reason that many of them lack such education, another effect not due to welfare.

To this situation can be added the fact that such jobs are frequently available only in distant suburbs that are not serviced by public transportation. In both New York City and Philadelphia, 600,000 jobs in both manufacturing and service were lost from the central city areas. For most inner-city blacks new service jobs have not come near to compensating for loss of manufacturing job opportunities.

Many conservatives take the position that the reason young blacks are unemployed is that they refuse low-level jobs. Street life is more attractive, more lucrative, especially with the drug scene. Earning enough to get along can be achieved in the informal economy and is easier than an eight-hour grind at uninspiring toil—so the criticism runs. In supposed confirmation, some authors argue that young Asiatics here are willing to take on menial work even at below-minimum wage and forge ahead eventually out of poverty.[38]

Thus the allegation is made that black youths are widely unwilling to work for the minimum wage or even sub-minimum wage or at unattractive jobs. This is an hypothesis which deserves examination, but there does not appear to be any study that substantiates the charge in the sweeping fashion in which it is generally presented.

There is an argument that some welfare interventions send a signal to young blacks that there is little point in trying to escape a lifetime of welfare and crime. But this contention lacks the evidence needed to support it. In fact, this claim seems to fly in the face of earlier analysis which has demonstrated how little of welfare entitlements actually are available to males to begin with, and how many other factors account for under-employment and unemployment.

Glen Loury, of the Kennedy School of Government at Harvard, reminds us that "not all black problems are racial or solvable by legislation and courts."[39] By the word "racial" Loury seems here to mean the result of racial discrimination. Few could quarrel with that proposition, but its implications are that blacks are where they are because of basic racial flaws and welfare. Disagreeing with Loury is Elenor Holmes Norton, head of the Equal Opportunity Commission under former

President Jimmy Carter. She says, "permanent unemployment is at the heart of the black underclass today."[40]

What is available to young black males? According to Ellwood and Summers[41], if a single man is living alone, he is eligible only for food stamps worth $70 per month—hardly enough to live on. In 1982, if he earned any income beyond $85 per month, the food benefits would be reduced by 25 cents for every dollar earned. If he lives at home with parents, he brings in only $60 worth of stamps a month, the same as if he shares parenting in a household of his own. And once he is 18, he ceases to be counted in benefits for AFDC. If he found a full-time job at minimum wage, he would earn $560 a month (at least $450 after taxes and expenses). Earned income is far in excess of welfare benefits.

But do the structures of welfare create a culture of non-work? Ellwood and Summers respond by stating that in 1975, black youth holding jobs were in almost the same fraction whether in households with both parents (23 percent) or households with a single parent welfare recipient (20 percent). Welfare, clearly, is not the main operating factor here. Equally, job-holding for either "ghetto" or "out-of-the-inner-city" youth is not much different. Black youth with jobs in the latter is only 6 percentage points higher (38 percent) than that for the "ghetto" (32 percent). True, there are somewhat fewer jobs in the ghetto. But non-ghetto black youth fare just about as badly. Also, unemployment rates among black youth differ little from region to region even though welfare payments differ widely among the same regions. Once again, it is clear that something else than welfare is operating here.[42]

There is one set of statistics, however, which is cited in triumph by supporters of the thesis that welfare causes dependency. These figures show a changed correlation between joblessness and dependency. From the Great Depression through 1960, the correlation between black male unemployment and new AFDC cases was nearly one-to-one. As joblessness increased, so did AFDC cases, and vice-versa. In the early 1960s, however, this correlation diminished, only to vanish for the rest of the decade. So at the very moment that black male unemployment was declining, new cases of AFDC rose.[43] If, many argued, even with unemployment going down welfare rolls are expanding, this must mean that dependency was rising with increased availability of welfare.

Wilson and Neckerman explain the seeming shift by saying, "even though the rate of nonwhite male unemployment did drop during the 1960s, the percentage of nonwhite male civilian population in the labor force (labor force participation rate) rose steadily, thereby maintaining a positive relationship between joblessness and the number of new AFDC cases."[44] They highlight the gravity of this joblessness situation among blacks with this quotation from a 1984 study by the Center for the Study of Social Policy: "The persistent alienation and attrition of black men constitutes a formidable challenge…if we do nothing the turn of the

Century will see 70 percent of all black families headed by women and fewer than 30 percent of all black men employed."[45]

The situation of the black urban underclass is indeed one of the most vexing social problems in this country. It will certainly demand more attention in coming decades. The development of this situation, however, can be only partially attributed to welfare, and even that effect is only tangential. A variety of other factors have had an influence. It will take the foresight, cooperation, and persistence of many segments of U.S. political and economic life to truly have a long-range effect upon the situation.

ENDNOTES FOR CHAPTER V

[1] See, e.g., Eleanor Holmes Norton, in *New Perspectives Quarterly* (vol. 4, no. 1), Winter, 1987, 23. Norton is professor of law at Georgetown University and former chair of the Equal Employment Opportunity Commission under President Carter. Also Marion Wright Edelman, "What Can We Do?", *The Washington Post*, February 2, 1986; and Daniel Patrick Moynihan, *Family and Nation* (New York: Harcourt, Brace, Jovanovich, 1987). Constance A. Nathansan, Johns Hopkins School of Hygiene and Public Health, writing on alleged problem of black family's high rate of marital disruption, illegitimacy and teen-age pregnancy, says, "These changes have been more profound among whites than blacks." *New York Times*, February 17, 1986 letter to editor.

There are strong counter voices to this argument. Nicholas Lehmann strongly urges the thesis of a black underclass due in great measure from welfare in important articles in *The Atlantic*, June and July, 1986. For views of Mickey Kaus, see *The New Republic*, July 7, 1986 and "Welfare and Work," *The New Republic*, December 6, 1986.

[2] Charles S. Robb, in *New Perspectives Quarterly*, (Vol. 4, no. 1) Winter, 1987, 18.

[3] *New York Times*, February 2, 1986. Edelman is president of the Children's Defense Fund.

[4] See Moynihan's comments on his book, *Challenge*, September/October 1985.

[5] *Wall Street Journal*, May 15, 1985.

[6] *Harper's*, April/May 1986. Debate at Harvard Club, New York City.

[7] *Washington Monthly*, September, 1985.

[8] Moyers' 1986 television series on the black family stirred considerable interest and debate.

[9] *The New Republic*, July 7, 1986.

[10] *The New Republic*, March 17, 1986.

[11] Commission on Policy for Racial Justice (Washington D.C.: Joint Center for Political Studies, 1987), 1.

[12] Ibid., 3.

[13] *Atlantic*, June, 1986.

[14] Black Initiative and Governmental Responsibility, 5, 7.

[15] *New Perspectives*, Winter, 1987, 28-33.

[16] *Work and Welfare* (Washington D.C.: Center for National Policy), 23.

[17] Ibid, 25.

[18] See William Julius Wilson and also David Ellwood in "Welfare and Work: A Symposium" in *The New Republic*, October 6, 1986. See also Wilson's *The Truly Disadvantaged: The Inner City, the Underclass and Public Policy* (University of Chicago Press, 1987). This book accepts the fact of an underclass, but demonstrates that this is not caused by welfare but by the unavailability of employment options.

[19] See my discussion in Chapter IV on welfare and family.

[20] This increase in independent households does not imply an increase in the number of poor individuals. It is only a redistribution of them as the women—including unwed mothers—move out of their parental homes. This results in more poor families, not more poor people.

[21] Less than 10 percent of white children born into single-parent families will live out their childhood in that arrangement, but half of black children will remain in their single, female-headed families throughout their childhood.

[22] "Household Composition and Poverty," 230 ff.

[23] "Poverty and Family Structure" in *Fighting Poverty*.

[24] Ibid., 284.

[25] Ibid.

[26] Ibid., 234.

[27] Ibid., 236.

[28] Ibid., 234-237.

[29] Ibid., 237.

[30] *Fighting Poverty*, 11.

[31] Wilson and Neckerman, 242 ff.

[32] Ibid., 244 ff.

[33] See studies of the Washington-based Children's Defense Fund. William Raspberry, black columnist of *The Washington Post*, addressed this topic several times during 1987.

[34] Ibid.

[35] The last paragraphs did consider certain economic structures, but seen through the lens of their impact on the cultural setting of the young black. In what follows, the concern is for joblessness in itself.

[36] In his summary of the several authors addressing this theme in *Fighting Poverty*; for "marriage pool failure," 342, 344, 347.

[37] *U.S. News & World Report*, March 17, 1986, draws upon several studies, such as those issued by the Center for Study of Social Policy, the National Bureau of Economic Research, and U.S. Labor Statistics reports for 1984.

[38] Tensions between blacks and Asians have increased in several inner-city settings.

[39] A prominent black member of Harvard's Kennedy School of Government. He figures in a symposium "Regaining Ground" in *New Perspectives* (Vol. 4, no. 1) Winter, 1987, 20-22.

[40] Norton highlights today's "narrowing of the traditional and natural routes out of poverty" through jobs in her introduction to *Work and*

Welfare: The Case ofr New Directions in National Policy, Center for National Policy, Washington D.C. 1987, 11.

[41] *Fighting Poverty*, 100 ff.

[42] Ibid.

[43] *Challenge*, September/October, 1985.

[44] *Fighting Poverty*, "Poverty and Family Structures," 259.

[45] Ibid.

6

THE EMERGING
WELFARE CONSENSUS

The last three chapters have been devoted to three specific charges: welfare traps the poor in poverty, welfare destroys the family, and welfare creates a black underclass. The conclusion to be drawn from the review of these charges is that on the whole they cannot be sustained. Thus critiques on these grounds directed against the Bishops' support of welfare in the Economic Pastoral are not well founded.

But there is much more going on in welfare research on the positive side which supports the U.S. Catholic Bishops' defense of the system and their proposals for welfare reform. Indeed, this research constitutes a veritable consensus on the problems and the prospects of welfare. This positive consensus must now be examined. It will be seen that far from being out of line with the emerging majority view on welfare, the approach of the Economic Pastoral—while arrived at from Catholic social teaching—is fully within a wide consensus on the status, prospects, and desirable reforms of the welfare system in the United States.

In taking up this review of the positive welfare consensus, it is useful to note that the consensus reflects a definite shift in U.S. attitudes distrustful of and even openly hostile to welfare. Since the mid-1970s, the welfare system has come under almost constant criticism, building in the 1980s to calls for wholesale evisceration of some welfare programs and the near elimination of others.

Now, as the 1980s make way for the 1990s, and as political administrations change, much of U.S. public opinion—consonant with an impressive collection of studies, commissions, and special reports—is coming once again to the view that welfare has a positive contribution to make in the slow and laborious process of addressing the economic inequities of national life.

I. PUBLIC ATTITUDES ABOUT WELFARE

In November 1980, the U.S. Catholic Bishops first projected a Pastoral Letter on the U.S. economy. Four years of study and consultation went into preparation of the first draft, which appeared in November 1984. Two more years of work resulted in a second and then a third draft. The final version was approved at the annual meeting of the National Conference of Catholic Bishops in Washington, D.C., in November 1986, six years from the beginning of the process.

During this period the mood of the nation moved away widely from the established certainties about the destructiveness of the welfare program. In the early 1980s, conservative welfare critics, including Catholic critics, had little difficulty in finding wide support for their almost contemptuous dismissal of the Bishops' proposed defense of welfare. At that time, opinion was strongly with Ronald Reagan that welfare cheats abounded and that bungling characterized the administration of welfare programs. In this view, the system was beyond even drastic reform. It could only be wiped out. Those who then supported the position of the Economic Pastoral could only admire the Bishops' courage in taking such an unpopular and severely criticized stand. Hadn't they any sense in their heads? Were they seeking to be "laughed out of court"?

Now, quite surprisingly, the "foolish" Bishops have turned out rather to be on the side of the angels. There is a greater readiness today for a new thrust toward helping the poor and needy. It is important that Catholics, the largest single religious group in the nation, be open to give their Bishops a hearing on this important issue. It is also true that the Bishops have influence beyond their own community in laying issues before the nation. For this additional reason, support for the Bishops' economic positions, especially on welfare, is particularly important.

As already indicated in the Introduction, two articles in *Time* in early 1987 symbolized the shift in public attitudes toward welfare. The first report, an extremely critical treatment of welfare, surprised many, for it came at the exact moment when a dozen or more scientific studies were appearing, almost all in contradiction of the *Time* article.[1] One month later, a second *Time* article presented a more positive analysis of welfare programs and the public's view of them.[2]

In the first discussion of welfare, *Time* described the program as a monstrous mess. It breaks up families, traps the poor in degrading idleness, and breeds a self-perpetuating cycle of illegitimacy, poverty and dependency. *Time* even asserted that Senator Daniel Patrick Moynihan was in agreement with this view—despite the fact that Moynihan subsequently had almost the contrary to say: "It has become a belief bordering on prejudice that our present social ills are the consequences of misguided Democratic social policies."[3]

In its second article, *Time* admitted that it detected "a more active approach to deep-seated social problems." It perceived "new community values" and even dared to say that the "the Reagan era's battle cry that government is the problem, not the solution,is losing force." And "The swing is away from the...laissez-faire approach of Ronald Reagan to a more, active, compassionate approach."[4] *Time* discovered "a more public agenda" standing against a purely private morality. The national weekly then contrasted this changed perception with a time when people felt that the welfare state had grown almost unrestrained; when the public believed that welfare—that is, entitlement—meant getting something for nothing; when welfare was viewed as unfair to middle-class interests.

But now, according to *Time*, there is conviction that the Reagan Administration went too far in its attack on welfare, or, at least, wanted to go too far in cutting such programs as Aid to Families with Dependent Children and public housing. The U.S. public had discovered that we "need government after all." According to a recent poll, more than 70 percent said that funds should be increased for health care for the poor and elderly, for cleaning up the environment, and for aid to the homeless. Sixty percent were prepared to support such programs even if it meant tax increases.[5]

Time was correct, in its second analysis, to state the public's welfare perception. But supporters of welfare had suffered through a long drought before this significant—though not by any means universal—change finally arrived. With relief, those who had fought the uphill battle welcomed this change. One such was Marion Wright Edelman, president of the Children's Defense Fund, who was reported as saying, "It's been a long winter under Reagan but we've learned to survive...We've turned the corner."[6] Robert Greenstein, president of the Center for Budget and Policy Priorities, agreed: "Then it was a question of how far they [social service programs] would be cut. Now I think we may be heading to a growing national concern about poverty among children."[7]

II. CONSENSUS AMONG SCIENTISTS AND CONGRESS

This gathering consensus—already impressively contributed to by the important study referred to earlier, *Fighting Poverty*—was much enhanced by several scientific studies which appeared over the late months of 1986 and the early months of 1987. These studies themselves—several will be reviewed in this chapter—were triggered by the declaration of President Reagan in his 1986 State of the Union address that he intended to propose welfare reform in January of the following year. He subsequently set up a study body to advise him on welfare. That body reported in December 1986. Reagan, also in anticipation of announcing his reforms, had urged the states to make their own experiments with welfare changes. That led to testing of new approaches in some 30 states. Largely these turned on shifting from direct welfare payments to compelling welfare recipients to work.

Meanwhile, some members of Congress got into the act with statements which appeared at first immensely supportive of compassion regarding the needy—even to the enlargement in several forms of provisions for present AFDC recipients. But as will be seen, their subsequent legislative proposals several months later would bring the law to what some writers have appropriately dubbed *The Mean Season*.[8]

The concern here is how Congress was talking at the end of 1986, the year of the emerging consensus, the year the Economic Pastoral was approved. Then, Congressional liberals appeared to be rejecting the essentials of the Administration's programs. True, they were saying "yes" to Reagan's insistence that work is the ideal road out of poverty and dependency. They agreed that long-term dependency is of grave concern. They declared themselves prepared to look at an alternative to AFDC, provided the alternative was at least fair. Equally, they were prepared to go along with state experiments, free of federal direction—an attitude that would mean a major shift in the way that welfare is legislated and administered.[9]

At this point the Congressional liberals separated themselves from those colleagues who appeared to embrace the spirit of the "mean season." The liberals were at the moment more inclined to accept the experts whose studies cast strong doubt on the hitherto reigning myths about the consequences on welfare. They tended to oppose the harshness of terms the white House wanted for compelling young single women with children to get into "workfare" programs.

Many in Congress did profess a belief that moving women into work programs would not necessarily be harmful to their personhood. But they recognized that it would require federal financial support which the Administration, far from wanting increased, was doing its best to decrease. They acknowledged that a more humane welfare was going to cost more than legislators at any level—state, federal—were prepared to propose. A number of Congressional members, and most state Governors, continued to believe that the system will be financially viable only if the Federal government foots a large part of the bill.[10]

1. The Presidential Study

Into the discussion of consensus must now enter discussion of the Reagan Administration's own study, *Up from Dependency: A New National Public Assistance Strategy.*[11] According to its drafters, the welfare system contributes to poverty because the poor are provided no incentive for self-reliance. Charles Hobbs, chair of the study group, proposed Reagan's familiar brand of federalism which would turn over to the states most responsibility for the programs including financing. Also the states are to be "freed" from any federal determination of minimum welfare payments. This approach, the report argued, would emancipate the poor.[12]

Senator Moynihan, on reviewing the report, retorted that emancipation of the poor through removing or drastically reducing the federal role in the welfare system was no more likely to occur than Reagan's economics would balance the federal budget.[13] Robert Fersch of the Food Research and Action Center maintained the white House reform initiatives were "only platitudes and experiments with real pain."[14] The Hobbs report gives the assurance that the states would indeed take the appropriate steps to meet essential needs.[15] Several observers have asked how to reconcile meeting essential needs with the injunction to the states to freely set their own minimum of welfare, given that benefits provided by a number of states even now do not come to 15 percent of the poverty level.

So far as concerns the employment alternative to government outlays, *Up From Dependency* apparently has no question that adequately paying jobs are out there. There is nothing in the Administration's plans to provide further tax relief for the poor beyond the recently legislated increase of tax exemption, even though that exemption fails to lift the poor above the poverty level.

2. Some Scientific Studies

These views of the Reagan Administration, while hailed by some, received little support from a number of professional bodies studying the same question at the same time, in addition to several studies which had preceded the Presidential report.[16] A review of several of these more recent studies will reveal how close their thinking runs to that of the Bishops' Economic Pastoral.

One Child in Four: This title of a study from the American Public Welfare Association points to the fact that one in four children in the United States is born into poverty.[17] It calls for "investing" in poor families and their children. Notable about this report is the fact that it represents common ground found among both conservative and liberal members of the study group as they worked over the issues.[18] Once again, the focus is children and families--not just adult individuals. This also contains the familiar social contract: on the one side, responsibility on the part of citizens for self-sufficiency; on the other side, responsibility of the government for providing welfare.

For their part, citizens in need must accept mandatory participation in one or other program. And on the side of government, the commitment is to provide for the vulnerable: people would be guaranteed equal opportunity and support as they seek to move into self-sufficiency. The proposed aid will take the form of both setting norms and financing family living standards. Benefits from this program will replace AFDC, food stamps, low-cost housing and energy subsidies.

In the shift to self-dependency through schooling, job training, and employment, government would have its responsibilities even while the citizens, for their part, would have to participate—and accept penalties for non-compliance—in entering the school/training/job programs. Absent fathers who fail to support their offspring would to be pursued "relentlessly" by the legal system.

This plan recognizes that there will be costs in the short run. Three significant ones: (1) ensuring fathers the jobs that would enable them to support their dependents, (2) providing child care and other supports needed if AFDC women are to enter the alternative program, and (3) ensuring child support for children who, while above the poverty level, may depend on earnings of a parent in a precarious situation.[19]

To sum up this first part of the study: "We recommend that all physically and mentally capable adults in families receiving assistance, including those families with children three years or older, be required to work or participate in a job-training or education program that will prepare them for employment." Concerning two-parent families with children under three, "one parent will be required to meet the above obligation. The other parent will be required to follow the plan described below for single parents of children under three."[20]

For this latter group—and it is indeed a large number—the report recommends: "In single-parent households with children under three years old, parents must be required to complete high school and then engage in some part-time out-of-the-home activity, which could be work-related, community service, parenting—provided the program improves employability or promotes stable, strong family ties."[21]

Overall, the *One Child in Four* study focuses more on children and families than individuals. In these two key areas it proposes:

a) Quality Child Care: This is a prerequisite for a single parent whose goal is employment. The care should be such as to enrich the life and experience of the children. It must be a true equivalent to home care.[22] This will require substantial public as well as private investment.[23]

b) Family Living Standard: The study calls this approach a "Comprehensive Social Insurance Model."[24] Benefits are to be based on need, not simply on the level of deprivation, family composition, or even on deservedness. "Young persons in poverty who have never had the advantage of reliable gainful employment face just as many costs on behalf of their children as do auto-workers displaced by economic factors beyond their control. Government must help furnish the stable economic environment such families require if they are to move to self-sufficiency."

The Family Living Standard will cover basic necessities: housing, furnishings, food, clothing, transportation, utilities and other maintenance costs. The study urges that the United Sates commit itself to this comprehensive social insurance model. The Family Living Standard as replacement for current AFDC, food stamps, and low-income energy assistance will have to be phased in over some ten years. But from its very beginning it must maintain benefits at no less than the combined benefit level of AFDC, food stamps and energy assistance.

Trenchantly, against all the bland assurance given by the critics of welfare, the study here observes: "It is not useful to pretend that families can strive for self-sufficiency and support their children's development, and be active members of their communities if their economic survival is always in doubt."[25]

The Myth of Welfare A substantial exposé produced in 1985 by the Center on Social Welfare Policy and Law exposes the myths about AFDC.[26] While AFDC is only one component of U.S. welfare, it has been the main target of many critics of welfare policy. Thus it is worthwhile sketching out the myths addressed in this report and seeing how they are refuted:

Myth: Once on welfare, always on welfare.
Fact: The majority of AFDC cases are open for less than two years. Moreover, there is evidence that those who receive welfare as children are no more likely than other poor children to receive welfare as adults.

Myth: AFDC benefits are too high.
Fact: the combined benefit from food stamps and AFDC is below the poverty level in almost four-fifths of the states. This income falls far short of any standard of minimum income.

Myth: AFDC families receive benefits under a multitude of programs which fill any gaps left by inadequate AFDC benefits.
Fact: For families receiving benefits under other programs—and not all AFDC families are in such a position--benefits do not significantly increase the income available to meet other essential needs.

Myth: The AFDC rolls are full of able-bodied adults who are too lazy to work.
Fact: More than two-thirds of AFDC recipients are children, indirectly receiving through their mothers. The vast majority of adult recipients face multiple obstacles to employment. A significant number are employed at some point in the year.

Myth: Women receiving AFDC have lots of children and keep having more just to get more money.
Fact: Nearly three-fourths of all AFDC families include only one or two children. In many states the AFDC structure penalizes those with more.

Myth: Poor people migrate to states with high AFDC benefits.
Fact: The migration of poor people is not significantly different from that of the rest of the population.

Myth: Many AFDC recipients receive income to which they are not entitled.
Fact: Erroneous payments account for only 7 percent of benefits paid, and even this is a generous estimate.

Myth: Most recipients try to cheat the government.
Fact: Such fraud does not amount to more than 3 percent of AFDC payments. Contrast that with fraud among medicaid providers, or fraud concerning other government subsidies.

Myth: The federal government is faced with such a huge deficit because too much money is spent on programs like AFDC.
Fact: Federal expenditure for AFDC in 1984 represented less than 1 percent of the total federal budget.

These two studies demonstrate that the changing public attitudes about welfare do indeed have a scientific basis. What follows next is a more comprehensive description of this consensus. It includes a variety of studies and reports from both non-profit organizations and state-sponsored review committees. That consensus established, some attention will be devoted to the issues surrounding the notion of "workfare." Finally, a critique will be offered of a prominent book already introduced in this text, Charles Murray's *Losing Ground*. Murray's study is singled out because along with *Up from Dependency* it is a linchpin in that other, negative, consensus on welfare which here is being challenged.

III. THE POSITIVE CONSENSUS ON WELFARE

The best place to begin a comprehensive description of the consensus which supports welfare, elements of which have just been described, is with a book often cited before in these pages, *Fighting Poverty: What Does and What Does Not Work*.[27] Certain positive consensus themes clearly emerge from the book's studies (and other supporting work done by the authors).
These themes include:

1. Welfare works but it does not produce miracles

2. New policies must be built on what works and what does not.

3. Economic growth and decreased rate of unemployment are necessary to welfare.

4. Income transfers, necessary though they may be, cannot match income from work.

5. Work must not be imposed on single mothers with small children, and, in any case, there is the problem of finding jobs for all the low-skilled people looking for them.

That summary consensus statement is amplified by another report, described next.

1. Welfare Reform: A Coalition Statement of Principles

December, 1986 saw the release of a statement on welfare reform by a powerful coalition of 90 church and other organizations working on welfare issues together with former and current elected government officials.[28] These individuals and groups held one common concern: the fate of the one out of seven U.S. citizens trapped in poverty.

The coalition worked within the framework of the emerging positive welfare consensus. Before making its declaration of six principles of welfare, the statement maintains that the federal government, far from retreating from the field, should be much more responsive. This is so in part because poverty is owing much to macro-trends and both national and international policies. The signatory groups are opposed to "cashing-out" welfare benefits in favor of market-purchases. They are convinced that services on the market would be unaffordable for the poor.

The principles put forth by the coalition are as follows

1. Individuals who work should be rewarded for their efforts. They should receive income sufficient to support a family and provide access to necessary health care and child care. Barriers to the employment of low-income persons should be eliminated.

2. Job opportunities, job counseling, training, education and employment services should be widely available as primary tools to prevent and overcome poverty.

3. The federal government should assure a minimum standard of living—including sufficient food, clothing, shelter and medical care—to those in poverty.

4. Additional investments should be made in programs proved successful in preventing future poverty and its ill effects.

5. Welfare policies should aid both one- and two-parent families in need. Existing child support laws should be more effectively enforced.

6. In achieving the above objectives, the federal government should maintain a strong presence, setting minimum benefit standards, providing adequate resources for effective programs, and supporting appropriate and effective state and local initiatives.

2. Work and Welfare: The Case for New Directions in National Policy

This study, appearing in early 1987, was authored by the Washington, D.C.-based Center for National Policy.[29] One of the study's authors is Ben Heineman, former secretary in the planning and evaluation division of the Department of Health, Education and Welfare during the Carter Administration. He pulled together a synthesis on *Work and Welfare*, aligning it with the many other components of the growing national welfare consensus being reviewed here.[30]

In this synthesis, Heineman includes statements from Senator Daniel Patrick Moynihan, Governor Mario Cuomo of New York and Governor Bruce Babbitt of Arizona. He believes that the unstated U.S. "social compact" regarding welfare is now fixed: income through work wherever possible, rather than through direct cash transfers from any government source. For work—employed work—is at the heart of the answer to poverty in all its forms. In part that is because such work enhances human dignity. This may be true, but does no other form of human activity besides paid work have dignity associated with it? The consensus does allow for cash payments for the disabled and the elderly. But welfare and work programs entail responsibilities on the part of beneficiaries.

Heineman expounds the consensus in four broad categories: welfare recipients, the working poor, the children of poverty, and the need for income maintenance.[31]

a) Welfare Recipients: AFDC recipients must be provided education, training, assistance in job search, and placement in a decent job as transition to more permanent employment. If necessary the government must give them subsidized jobs. The effort must be to limit the time recipients remain on welfare in order to avoid their sinking into dependency.

For this approach there lurk recurring problems: training for and finding meaningful jobs is a proposition both difficult and expensive. When it comes to training and job-relocation, the consensus is not sure what welfare should or has to offer. A primary concern is the recognition that work for all those able to work is not—by itself—a solution. Also, the agreement that absent fathers must be made to support their offspring is not a total but only a partial solution. There will have to be a mixture of jobs and benefits in the form of cash and in-kind support. Jobs for mothers of pre-school children will have to be accompanied by child care. Moreover, state experiments must be made to comply with clearly stated and fully enforced federal standards.

b) Working Poor: These are persons just above the welfare poor. Moving them above the poverty level will require improved jobs, job placement, higher tax credits, and wage increases either through subsidies or by means of a higher minimum wage. To all of this should be added other options such as expanded health care, since the working poor are generally not eligible for Medicaid and are drastically under-served as a health care population.

c) Children of Poverty: To prevent children from sliding deeper into poverty and dependency, health measures are needed, early education (e.g., Headstart should be revived), and coordination of secondary school with the world of work should be initiated. The study notes how especially difficult it is for teenagers dropping out of school to avoid entering the ranks of the structurally unemployed.

d) Adequate Income Maintenance: Despite the emphasis on education and work for those in poverty, additional income maintenance may also be needed. Thus there must be a minimum national benefit in cash and food stamps which provides a higher percentage of the poverty line than is presently the case. According to Heineman's report, the experts agree on this basic framework. But again, he insists, there are hard questions: Will there be suitable work when welfare recipients have prepared them-selves? And what will wage subsidies to the people exiting from welfare do to the labor market? Will it end in supporting the employers as the exiters add to the pool of workers?

The study *Work and Welfare* is a crucial one for demonstrating the positive welfare consensus. Much of its central message is reflected in the U.S. Bishops' Economic Pastoral.

3. Black Initiative and Governmental Responsibility

Another 1987 study that enters the consensus comes from a research group associated with the black community, the Joint Center for Political Studies.[32] The study's title emphasizes self-sufficiency, but at the same time recognizes that government must assume its responsibilities. The focus is the disparity between black and white, and on black poverty taken by itself. According to the report: "We urge a concentrated effort by government to invest…in programs and strategies for human devel-opment that will facilitate economic independence and encourage the poor to take charge of their own lives." Proposals include recreating Headstart and welfare programs that stress education, training and work programs that require strong federal leadership.

On AFDC, this study seeks redesign of the basic program to encour-age the maintenance of intact families and the transformation of the cur-rent welfare approach to an approach of education, training, and employ-ment assistance. All this should be together with adequate support services such as those mentioned in several of the other studies exam-ined here. Moreover. the federal government must address structural unemployment. In consort with private industry, unions and universities, the government should re-train the permanently unemployed, among whom are an alarming number of black men.

In addition, there must be a comprehensive child development program.[33] Here again Headstart is mentioned. But other preschool programs are also stressed, to get poor children off to a good start with adequate health care. This report places heavy emphasis on quality education for black youth at all levels, with strategies to retain them in school.

4. Families in Peril: An Agenda for Social Change

Another important voice in the consensus is heard in Marian Wright Edelman's *Families In Peril: An Agenda for Social Change*.[34] On the occasion of appearance of this book, Edelman was quoted as saying that the poor prefer to work. They do not have babies in order to get welfare. But government, in order to remove people from poverty, must create at least eight million jobs.[35]

There is serious need, she added, for job training. And to pull the poor above the poverty line, government must raise the minimum wage, and guarantee health insurance for low-paid workers and dependents. Child-care for those mothers needing it must be of high quality and adequately subsidized. Finally, while she supports AFDC, Edelman is prepared to go along with New York Senator Moynihan to the extent of accepting his substitute as a "last resort"—provided the proposals afford an acceptable level of income. Edelman wants to see a suitable floor of income for all.

5. The Governors' Studies and Proposals

Among the other important reports and documentation to mention in describing the emerging welfare consensus are studies coming from individual state governors, or from committees of governors' associations. Here, too, are found statements on welfare, welfare programs, and welfare reform strikingly similar to those of the consensus. Yet it is still true, as will be seen in Chapter VII's account of legislative proposals, that most governors have given some support to a key Reagan demand—workfare, or compulsory work. First, a look at what they say collectively, and then a description of a few specific state plans and experiments.

National Governors Association: In a lengthy report, this body shares much of the positive consensus.[36] Income is to come from work rather than welfare payments. Dependency must be avoided. AFDC women with children above three will be compelled to take work. Absent fathers must be forced to support their children.

The governors would extend AFDC benefits to households where the father is present along with the mother. The study proposes that the federal government fix a minimum support level for all the states to adhere to. While it talks the language of social compact, the Governors' study wants the combination of cash transfers and food stamps to significantly exceed present levels. On this point, too, the governors in the subsequent federal legislation proposals yielded—as did the Congress—to "fiscal exigencies." Finally, the study suggests that the federal government eventually move toward a minimum assistance payment, adjusted for regional differences in the cost of living. This would be designed to take the poor out of poverty.

The Mario Cuomo Commission: The governors have as a body supported quite liberal positions on welfare but have subsequently yielded to conservative preoccupations. It is still useful to see how their most important study enters—if somewhat on the margin—into the growing welfare consensus. In 1983, chaired by Governor Mario Cuomo of New York, the National Association received a task force report on welfare.[37] It is interesting to compare it to the Reagan-sponsored Presidential study reviewed earlier.

While agreeing with the President's goal of reducing dependency and developing self-sufficiency, the report differed sharply with the *Up from Dependency* study on several key points. The President's strong insistence on leaving so much responsibility for welfare to the states is considered simply an evasion of responsibility. According to the task force, what the Administration in effect wants is to shift its revenue problem to local authorities. (A coalition of big-city mayors, meeting at the same time, came to the same conclusion.)

Cuomo's task force also believes that welfare policy must not focus only on the destitute. It must also embrace all the working poor, who often are only a few dollars away from dropping into dependency. Because of the characteristics of these two poverties, the real remedy is not a narrow welfare reform but an economic progress which will generate high productivity and better-paying jobs. Training must be provided to enhance the productivity of those seeking to leave the roles of AFDC.

Turning to the problem of teenage mothers, the Cuomo study proposes that teenage mothers receiving AFDC should be required to finish high school even while receiving aid. Older recipients would participate in transitional programs such as receiving counselling and special training. Once placed in jobs in the private sector, they would receive supporting services such as child-care and transportation. And if there is no private sector job available? The task force states that recipients of aid must accept a public job in the form of guaranteed employment in exchange for benefits. Here reappears the language of social contract: government agreeing to open up the economic mainstream to as many as possible, while aid recipients agree to prepare themselves for self-sufficiency.

6. State Level Experiments and Studies

Among the studies and programs that appeared at the end of 1986, one from the State of Washington is particularly notable, mostly because the proposal raised great consternation among local welfare directors, even though they saw at least some merit in the plan. The Washington State plan was titled the Family Independence Program (FIP).[38] This plan, as in the Moynihan proposal and others, would replace AFDC. Government contributions of AFDC and food stamps would be put into FIP. That fund would in turn require all able-bodied recipients of welfare to enter work-training and job placement programs. During the first two years participation would be voluntary, then would change to compulsory. Only women with very small children would be exempt.

According to the proposal, subsidies and other support would motivate young mothers on welfare to greet FIP with enthusiasm. Those unable to enroll or awaiting employment within the program or still in training for work would get from FIP the equivalent of current welfare payments plus food stamps. These women would then receive more as they participated more fully in FIP. Those refusing to enter FIP's programs after two months would receive only 80 percent of the benchmark of dollars and food. After that, they would be cut off from AFDC. Children, however, will continue to receive assistance.[39]

For one critical group, the Coalition for Fair Work, the proposed Washington State program presents certain disquieting features.[40] This coalition brings together many of Washington's welfare advocates, churches and community organizations.[41] They fear the potential loss of federal entitlement. Shifting AFDC into FIP appears to be the equivalent of a block grant (i.e., all federal funding for welfare put at the disposition of states according to their own discretion). Rather than leave the allocation of these funds to the discretion of the state, the welfare supporters would much prefer to retain federal assurance that programs will not get lost. Thus, the coalition would keep the present AFDC payments and food stamps. Only within the framework of AFDC and food stamps would it move to FIP's desired removal of some work disincentives perceived in AFDC and to FIP's help for training programs and for child support for working mothers.

The Coalition notes that the compulsory character of the Washington State program is more severe than California's. Moreover, FIP compares badly in this respect with that of Massachusetts, which remains voluntary. That state's experience is that they can draw more volunteers into the program than they can handle and hence have no need of compulsion. The Coalition equally rejects forcing women with children to work if the mothers believe they should be at home nurturing their children.

In general, the Coalition feels that the state hopes to get by on the cheap. But child-care, for example, cannot be had at the low-level funding the state proposes. Jobs leading to freedom from dependency are also going to cost much more than the state program allows for in its budgeting. Critics charge that the program moves AFDC parents into the ranks of the working poor, into dead-end jobs that won't lift them out of poverty.

IV. WORKFARE: PROPOSALS AND POLICIES

Another proposal about welfare that has produced much attention is workfare. The very name of this program—"workfare"—is intended to be a statement against welfare. Most observers agree that the word workfare connotes compulsion. Few think in terms of the poorhouses of old but they are convinced that society ought to get a quid pro quo, an obligatory service through work. The idea is workfare also makes its appearance in some of the consensus studies analyzed above, but in an attenuated form. This attenuation occurs in the emphasis on not undoing what is most useful and needed in the present welfare scheme, and on the need of funding to make workfare humane, e.g., providing childcare.

Other scholars such as Lawrence Mead, author of *Beyond Entitlement: The Social Obligations of Citizenship*, argue in defense of an uncompromising workfare that the welfare system violates a fundamental norm of the national ethos: people should, if they are able-bodied, be required to work for benefits.[42]

Many welfare administrators agree. As noted, certain liberals in Congress, intimidated by the conservative charge that they were "bleeding hearts" on this issue, have moved over to supporting workfare. But others in Congress, pulled to the left by colleagues who reject the arguments that people on welfare owe something to society and that society has no obligation to welfare mothers, have felt compelled to downplay the social obligation of welfare beneficiaries. In its place, they appeal to the benefits derived by welfare recipients from being compelled to work. Instead of asserting that "welfare recipients are getting a free ride," these Members of Congress prefer to urge that welfare recipients move into job programs on the grounds that this would contribute to their overall development.

The question is whether workfare, so widely acclaimed, can in any shape or form be fitted into the positive welfare consensus. Another question is whether workfare in any form is superior to welfare as presently administered. Before a final judgement can be made on these questions, there is a need to explore a few more state experiences. There are presently over twenty such state experiments or programs. The plan of Washington State, as seen, calls for mandatory participation. Plans of both California and Massachusetts have less of a mandatory character.

1. California
As president, Ronald Reagan has been critical of welfare programs and has called for reform and new approaches. But when he was Governor of California, Reagan experimented with a different plan. The state's Auditor General called on a University of Maryland expert to prepare a special review of the Reagan program. That appraiser has gone on public record as characterizing the Reagan experiment as "inefficient and ineffective."[43]

California's current Governor, George Deukmejian, followed up the Reagan program with "better proposals." According to these, California's counties were required to provide training, education, job counselling and job placement. Eligible welfare recipients were obligated to participate in one or other. If the county failed to place an eligible AFDC family in the workforce, it would be required to substitute a six month or one-year workforce opportunity that would not be make-work but real service to the community.

Some exemption to mandatory participation was granted mothers with children under six years old. For working welfare mothers, child care was assured during work hours. The program's limits on obligations helped liberal members of California's State Assembly to go along with conservatives. However, many students of welfare widely question the remaining degree of compulsoriness of the program, as will be seen below.

2. Massachusetts

Many components of the California and Washington State programs are present in the Massachusetts program. Because of widespread national publicity accorded to Governor Michael Dukakis, the Massachusetts workfare plan has received considerable attention. Dukakis does not wish to see welfare people forcibly moved into public service jobs. According to the Governor, "the question is how to help people lift themselves out of poverty where they are overwhelmingly young mothers with small children. Working off your welfare check in some public service is just not going to do it."[44] Dukakis insists that his program of moving welfare people into private sector jobs is not compulsory.

The issue is seen primarily as one of volunteers accepting placement in education, training for work, or a job. Only one parent in two-parent families and parents of teenagers are required to work. As in other programs, the young mothers receive counseling and help in finding the right kind of work. While training or on the job, they get child care and other supporting services.

Questions that have already been posed above are also relevant here. If it is truly non-compulsory, is this program a model for others? And has it really been the success the Welfare Department of Massachusetts claims? That department says that in its first three years caseloads of AFDC dropped by 8.6 percent at a cost of only $30 million. It also resulted in a saving of $107 million from no longer having to disburse cash, food stamps, and medicaid to AFDC mothers. And earnings from their paid work mean increased tax revenues.

But the widely touted success story of Massachusetts has had its serious challengers. Two important critics were a task force of the American Friends Service Committee on the Massachusetts Employment and Training program,[45] and the liberal economic magazine, *Dollars and Sense*.[46] The sum of these two critical appraisals is that under political pressure to show results, officials of the Employment and Training program (ET) emphasized moving people into employment over job training that might have eventually led to a better job.

During the program's first twenty months, more than 40 percent of the participants were active job-seekers without further training or schooling. About 30 percent took courses at state-funded colleges or took other general training needed to prepare them for work. Only 15 percent received short term training to provide skill for specific jobs. Seven percent got on-the-job training through supported work.

The Friends task force also states that success in transferring people into jobs largely reflects the state's very low rate of unemployment—half the national average. ET is marketed to businesses with low-level, low-wage job offerings, of which there is an abundance in the state. One woman interviewed by the Friends for the study indicated that ET just takes women on welfare and serves them on a silver platter to the private sector.

The economic magazine *Dollars and Sense* agrees, especially on the point of the Massachusetts program's propensity simply to move welfare recipients from low-paying welfare benefits to low-paying jobs. The program is designed for "people who have minimum work experience or are disabled. It essentially diverts welfare benefits to employers." The magazine adds that it is from this transfer of welfare benefits that employers pay the subsidy component of the check. The Friends conclude their critique by pointing out that the income gain in the transfer to work means for most job-takers very little increase in income. Besides, they still have to pay for transportation and work clothes. Also, medicaid terminates four months after getting a job. With whatever increase in income they experience, food stamp benefits drop and public housing goes up.

3. General Appraisals of State Programs

Blanche Bernstein claims that workfare has shown itself effective in implementing the principle that those who can should work.[47] Also, it is her belief that the programs would be more effective were it not for the negative mentality of welfare beneficiaries.

The most noted research on these state programs has been done by the Manpower Demonstration Research Center (MDRC) of Manhattan.[48] After an initial study of eight state programs, MDRC president, Judith Gueron, felt able to proclaim them a success.[49] In making their tests, MDRC compared two groups: (1) those on state welfare roles who chose not to enter the work programs, and (2) those who accepted entry into the workfare effort. The latter were selected on the basis of work-experience and job search received by participation in the state's preparatory program. The jobs they took on were regular, non-subsidized ones.

The program entrees registered a three to nine point success in the employment search over the woman who chose not to enter it. That difference is admittedly positive, but certainly not very striking. This is especially true if, as several critics charge, the programmers skimmed off the top in choosing those to work with. Reflecting on that MDRC report, *The Washington Post's* welfare expert, Spencer Rich, argued that "hopes for huge cuts in welfare resulting from training and workfare are a fantasy."[50]

The coordinator of social services at AFSCME expressed skepticism in more detail.[51] If workfare really works MDRC should produce facts on three matters: (1) the number of participants in workfare who were moved directly from such workfare assignment into full-time, unsubsidized jobs as compared to the number of non-participants who found jobs of their own; (2) what kind of job did the two groups move into and at what entry-level salary and did they get jobs that lifted them out of poverty; and (3) how many recipients in both groups no longer needed public assistance.

Another cautionary note is added by a study conducted by the Washington-based Coalition on Human Needs. Its interviews indicate that, contrary to the supposition on which workfare programs are built, people on welfare expressed a genuine interest in participating in work-oriented programs. This was provided that they are given such supports as child care, transportation and health care. Those interviewed gave the typical description that AFDC and food stamps run out well before the end of the month.[52] The Medicaid they receive would have to be continued in a job providing a decent living.

The question arises, then, in the light of these and similar criticisms, why there is support for workfare in its more compulsory forms. It is not even clear that welfare caseloads are significantly less in workfare states than in states that have not yet begun workfare programs. One is left to wonder whether support for workfare may not rest largely on the experience of job-taking by non-welfare women with children. That seems to make it less intolerable to demand the same from welfare beneficiaries. But there is a sharp distinction between these two groups of women. The non-welfare mothers have voluntarily chosen to enter the workforce. Welfare mothers—and many are definitely prepared to seek work—do not want to do so as long as that choice would leave them and their children too vulnerable.

An added observation emerges from these critical studies: workfare programs may simply cost much more than the nation is prepared to face up to. This is alluded to in testimony in late 1987 before the Senate Finance Committee by Judith Gueron, MDRC President.[53]

In early summer, 1988, MDRC reported additional state workfare experiments, specifically in Arkansas, Virginia, Maryland and Maine. Notable in these studies is that they were extended to a full three years. Gueron reported these gave "new confidence about the cost effectiveness of a key part of this system." She added on the positive side that the find-

ings "confirm that a range of strategies can be effective in moving welfare recipients into paid employment." Despite this positive evaluation,
Gueron also does warn that "gains are still relatively small" and that it
"doesn't move a large percentage of people out of poverty." Finally, she
observes that we should be "careful in drawing general conclusions about
the relative effectiveness of voluntary versus mandatory" programs.[54]

Reflecting on the MDRC reports, Joanna Weinberg, University of
California expert on mandatory workfare, adds still another warning: "The
workfare proposals will create a permanent class of partially employed
people. As marginal jobs cease to exist, these workers will return to public assistance until the next marginal job becomes available."[55]

V. THE BISHOPS AND THE ETHICS
OF COMPULSION

Because compulsion is central in the notion of workfare, a brief discussion of its morality (which might have been deferred to the chapter on
the Bishops and welfare) is appropriate here. None of the ethical aspects
to follow derive simply from a priori speculation. All derive from asking
what relationship human dignity, the good of the family and the nature
of society have to the proposed compulsion.

In their Economic Pastoral, the U.S. Bishops argue that "Public assistance programs should be designed to assist recipients, wherever possible, to become self-sufficient through gainful employment" (211). Since
adults in AFDC are overwhelmingly women, this suggests that the
Bishops view as desirable helping young mothers on to the road of independence through work for welfare. The catch is "wherever possible,"
because the normal situation is one of a woman with very young children who need their mother's continued care in the home.

This real-life situation leads the Bishops to say: "We affirm the principle enunciated by John Paul II that society's institutions and policies
should be structured so that mothers of young children are not forced by
economic necessity to leave their children for jobs outside the home"
(207). The Bishops' strong opposition to compulsion, is shared by many
welfare-concerned groups within the Catholic Church and many other
faith communities. The Bishops believe that welfare mothers should have
the option to care for their young children at home. Compulsory exit from
welfare into jobs gives scant evidence that its proponents sense the value
of the family for society. The Bishops note, as do many others, that in the
main these young mothers would—all things being equal—prefer work.
It seems clear, therefore, that there can be a large number of entries into
good work/training programs without using compulsion.

This position of the U.S. Bishops was presented in testimony by Bishop James P. Lyke of Cleveland.[56] His testimony was given in the name also of Catholic Charities U.S.A., the national association of local Catholic charities. Bishop Lyke used as the unifying theme of his testimony the question: "What is the message our welfare programs are giving poor children whose families must resort to welfare?"

The first of these messages is that fathers do not count for much, since in most states welfare payments are not made to a family if the father is present. The second message is that a mother's work at home, nurturing and teaching her little children, is of no value to society. The only work that counts is that done out of the home for a wage. The scandously low level of benefits suggests that society places no value on home-work and that dignity comes only from paid work. According to Lyke, current efforts in many areas to push mothers of very young children out of the home into unpaid workfare programs is further evidence that care for one's children is not sufficiently respected.

Shifting from child care at home to work outside the home as the area of achievement does not always improve the situation of welfare mothers. In general workfare programs prepare mothers for only the lowest paying jobs, which feature frequent lay-offs, few if any benefits, and very little opportunity for advancement. These situations are even worse when these mothers are put in unpaid jobs without training and with none of the status, self-respect, or benefits of a real job.

Bishop Lyke concluded his testimony by saying that government should not be in the position of forcing welfare mothers to put their children in day care. "We support voluntary programs for such mothers, but the decision to leave young children should lie with the mother, not the government."[57]

In keeping with this Catholic statement are the views of several welfare observers in a symposium on compulsory workfare drawn together by *The New Republic*.[58] This article pursued a theme earlier introduced in the journal by Micky Kaus.[59] In the symposium, two writers, Lawrence Mead and Charles Murray, supported workfare in its most compulsory form. But opposed to compulsory workfare, in varying degrees, were several notable welfare experts: Barbara Ehrenreich, Frances Fox Piven, Robert Kuttner, Sylvia Ann Hewlett, William Julius Wilson, and David Ellwood (most of these writers have been introduced earlier in these chapters). Their statements supported the same general direction as Bishop Lyke's testimony given in the name of the U.S. Catholic Bishops.

VI. A CRITIQUE OF *LOSING GROUND*

Charles Murray's *Losing Ground* has been proclaimed Ronald Reagan's bible against welfare. Because of the centrality of Murray's attacks against the positive welfare consensus, his analysis deserves to be given more thorough-going analysis in this chapter. Robert Greenstein, Director of the Wasington-based Center for Budget and Policy Priorities, offers an extensive, substantive critique of Murray, one that is worth examining in some detail.

Greenstein opened his attack in *The New Republic*, and Murray responded in a subsequent issue of that publication. Greenstein replied, and then returned to the attack once again in later Congressional testimony.[60] The charges and counter-charges illuminate some of the weaknesses of the welfare opposition. Greenstein's assesment substantially supports the basic premise offered here that welfare has a viable and valuable role to play in addressing the economic needs of a significant number of people in our society.

1. Welfare, Family, and Illegitimacy

According to Greenstein, Murray advocates elimination of every federal program for the non-elderly poor with the sole exception of unemployment insurance. Murray, in defense of his position, reduces his list of programs to be cut to what he describes the "failed welfare programs." But of Murray's "endless recital of statistics," Greenstein says they rest on numbers juggling. Consistently omitted or concealed are critical facts and research (some of which has been already noted in prior discussions above).

One case which Murray makes much of is, according to Greenstein, "flatly wrong." It is a history of a hypothetical couple—Phyllis and Harold—that demonstrates for Murray that social programs have led to unemployment and illegitimacy among blacks. These programs, Murray argues, encouraged this couple to live off welfare rather than go to work. The couple faces a choice: either he works or she draws on welfare. The question supposedly is solved by Phyllis' accepting welfare payments. But this choice is presented as occuring in 1970. Had it come in 1961, when weak welfare benefits favored work, Harold might well have gone to work, Greenstein points out.

Greenstein also notes a devastating fact which he discovered only after reading through a mass of citations in *Losing Ground* The family budgets in Murray's hypothetical case are based on one state, Pennsylvania. There welfare benefits during 1970 grew twice as fast as for the nation as a whole. The supposed incentive shift in favor of welfare over work was nation-wide very much less than Murray asserts.

Another error shows up in Murray's hypothetical welfare analysis. He assumes that if Phyllis and Harold went to work they would be ineligible for food stamps. But that was not so. In order to establish the monetary superiority of welfare over work in 1981, Murray puts into the welfare program the food stamps he had denied the working couple.

Contrary to Murray, and considering the nation as a whole, it was not true in 1981 that Phyllis and Harold would have done better financially in welfare than in work. In all states except Pennsylvania, Harold and Phyllis would have been one-third better off working. Also, there is no pattern to sustain Murray's thesis that illegitimacy is higher where welfare payments are higher. In fact, illegitimacy turns out to be higher in states with lower welfare benefits.

What is more, if Murray had gone beyond 1970 into the 1971 decade—and the subtitle of his book, *Social Policy: 1950 to 1980*, leads one to suppose that that would have been his intent—he would have discovered that whatever incentive shifts there were moved in the direction from welfare to work. This is true because most states failed to adjust welfare payments to inflationary losses. Also, the work side of the alternatives was further strengthened as government increased the earned income tax credit.

By the same token, supposing it were true that illegitimacy grew as the monetary advantage of welfare grew, then illegitimacy should have dropped in the decade of the 1970s when work gave much more reward incentives than did welfare. But that in fact did not happen. The plain fact is that welfare had nothing to do with the problem.

2. Welfare and Poverty

Turning to Murray's poverty equation—the more welfare, the more poverty—it would follow from this view that as the economy improved it should have provided more jobs. Thus poverty should have receded. Greenstein notes, however, that during the 1970s employment opportunities were not growing as fast as needed to pull a significant number out of poverty. He adds that the fact that poverty at that time was no higher than it was evidences that the welfare programs were helping people who otherwise would have been impoverished by the sluggish job growth. The unemployment rate of the 1980s recession was double that of 1968.

In 1965 before poverty programs were expanded, federal benefits lifted out of poverty less than one-half those under the poverty line. By the late 1970s a broader program lifted 70 percent out. In effect, the slowing of the economy between 1968 and 1980 dropped people into poverty, while broadening welfare benefits lifted them out.

Murray denies that poor economic performance kept poverty high. He states that the Gross National Product rose more in the 1970s than in the 1950s. But Greenstein claims that Murray misses a crucial point. The economy was too slow in the 1970s to create jobs enough to match the baby-boomers then entering the labor market. Greenstein supplies economic data which he contends pokes another hole in the Murray theses.

3. Welfare and Unemployment

Murray moves his attack on welfare to another point. He asserts that between 1965 and 1980, as welfare programs were growing, the number of black men in the labor force diminished and the employment gap between young whites and blacks widened. But for Greenstein, research points in the exactly the opposite direction. Employment among black teenagers actually declined more in the 1950s before there were any significant welfare programs than it declined later when more welfare was available. Greenstein cites authorities showing that virtually all of the decline in black teenage employment occurred in the South as Southern agricultural technology displaced workers.

Contrary to Murray's assertion, in the North, where welfare benefits were higher and welfare participation grew faster than in the South, black youth employment did not drop off; however in the South where welfare benefits are low, black teenage employment fell drastically. One curious phenomenon was that even after mechanization of agriculture had been completed, black employment in the South continued to fall. This appears to be accounted for by the fact of competition for low-paying jobs in the South by older women (and also Asiatics). This competition pushed young blacks to the end of the job queue.

4. Welfare's Positive Contribution

Murray's contentions against welfare also include a denial of any positive contribution welfare may have made to the situation of the poor. In effect he asks: admitting for the sake of argument that welfare did not cause poverty, did it in any way produce any positive results? According to Greenstein, Murray cites as evidence only the case of some improvements among welfare recipients in the city of Oakland (and even there he overstates his case since careful evaluation shows mixed results).

But there has been, says Greenstein, increased life expectancy and a 50 percent decrease in infant mortality. Murray persists: a variety of indicators show continued deterioration in the condition of the poor. For Greenstein, the story for blacks and other poor is exactly the opposite. He notes a study by the Department of Agriculture of improvement in nutrition among the lower income people as a result of welfare payments including food stamps.

The attack shifts ground again. Supposing that the welfare programs did decrease poverty and increase health, did they also create jobs or increase earnings for the poor? If that indeed is the goal of welfare, it is a very difficult goal to achieve in an economy which in fact is not generating enough jobs to prevent unemployment from rising and real wages from stagnating. Nevertheless, generating a higher level of employment does stand as a goal that welfare supporters also seek.

In summary, Charles Murray's *Losing Ground* may have been a clarion call for conservatives and those who have a fundamental philosophical difficulty with welfare. But its main charges against welfare simply do not stand up to close examination. The support of welfare found in the U.S. Bishops' Economic Pastoral, then, cannot be attacked on the basis of the contentions made by Murray. The positive welfare consensus is based on the very substantial grounds of well-researched experience of recent years.

ENDNOTES FOR CHAPTER VI

1 *Time*, February 16, 1987.

2 *Time*, March 30, 1987.

3 Daniel Patrick Moynihan in *New Perspective Quarterly* (vol. 4, no. 1), Winter, 1987, 16-8.

4 *Time*, March 30, 1987

5 Ibid.

6 *The Washington Post*, February, 1987.

7 Ibid. As the next chapter shows, the political change has turned out-- at least for the present--to be less promising than hoped for concerning pending federal welfare legislation.

8 Fred Block, Richard A. Cloward, Barbara Ehrenreich, Francis Fox Pliven, *The Mean Season: The Attack on the Welfare State* (New York: Pantheon Books, 1987).

9 Spencer Rich of *The Washington Post*, through the early months of 1987, tracked the record of this liberal Congressional stance of going along with several welfare reforms of Reagan, while opposing the worst of the "mean season." See his columns of, e.g., February 23, March 30, April 3. *The New York Times* also frequently ran columns in the same vein, e.g., February 24, April 3.

10 Ibid.

11 Report for the President by the Domestic Policy Council Low

Income Opportunity Working Group, Washington, D.C., December 1986. The group was chaired by Charles Hobbs of the White House Office of Policy Development. In this Chapter, I have used the "for review" draft; the study has since appeared in book form.

12 Ibid., 80 ff.

13 Reagan's federalism in other public policy areas has also come under strong fire.

14 Washington D.C.: Food Research and Action Center.

15 *Up From Dependency*, 80. Here is the full statement of goals of the report:
   1. To ensure that public assistance is an adequate supplement for other resources in meeting essential needs;
   2. To focus public assistance resource on efforts to reduce future dependency on public assistance itself;
   3. To individualize determinations of need for public assistance, and to make such determinations to the extent possible, through local decisions;
   4. To provide public assistance only to those in need and only to the extent of that need;
   5. To make work more rewarding than welfare;
   6. To require that those who are able to work do so for their public assistance benefits;
   7. To encourage the formation and maintenance of economically self-reliant families;
   8. To require public assistance recipients to take greater responsibility for managing their own resources, and to encourage community-based administration of public assistance;
   9. To create opportunities for self-reliance through education and enterprise;
   10. To reduce future costs of public assistance by reducing the need for it.

16 Several of those studies have already been explored in earlier chapters.

17 Subtitle, *Investing in Poor Families and Their Children: A Matter of Commitment* (Washington, D.C.: The American Public Welfare Association, 1986).

18 Ibid., 11. Also, *Report to the Press* by the study chair, Stephen Heintz, Commissioner of the Commission on Income Maintenance.

[19] Ibid., 31.

[20] Ibid., 19.

[21] Ibid., 19

[22] Ibid., 19

[23] Ibid., 22.

[24] Ibid., 22, ff.

[25] Ibid., 22.

[26] Barbara Leyser, Adele M. Blong, and Judith Riggs, eds., *Beyond the Myths: The Families Helped by the AFDC Program*, 2nd Ed. (New York: Center on Social Welfare Policy and Law, 1985).

[27] Sheldon H. Danziger and David H. Weinberg, eds. (Cambridge: Harvard University Press, 1986).

[28] Reported in news releases by Food Research Action Center, (FRAC), Washington, D.C., December 1986. The core group working on the preparation of this statement included Robert Fersh, director of FRAC, and Sharon Daly, director of Domestic Social Development, the United States Catholic Conference. Catholic organization signers were the United States Catholic Conference, and the National Conference of Catholic Women. In addition, several Protestant churches signed, as also the American Jewish Congress, the National Association of Social Workers, and the National Center for Policy Studies.

[29] Well-known names in welfare studies who collaborated with this statement included Ben W. Heineman, Jr., Isabel Sawhill, Robert Reischaur, Stuart Eizenstat, and Robert Greenstein.

[30] Heineman published this synthesis and consensus statement in *The Washington Post*, February 15, 1987.

[31] Ibid.

[32] *Black Initiative and Government Responsibility* (Washington D.C.: Joint Center for Political Studies' Committee on Policy for Racial Justice, 1987).

[33] Ibid., 12.

[34] Cambridge: Harvard University Press, 1987. Edelman, a black scholar, is president of the Children's Defense Fund.

[35] *The Washington Post*, February 26, 1987.

[36] *The Washington Post*, February 24, 1987.

[37] *1933-1983—Never Again: A Report to the National Governor's Association Task Force on the Homeless*, chaired by Mario Cuomo, Governor of New York, July, 1983.

[38] Washington State Family Independence Program, presented to the Honorable Booth Gardner, Governor of the State of Washington, by Jule M. Sugerman, Secretary of Department of Social and Health Service and by Isaiah Turner, Commissioner of Employment and Security Department, November 12, 1986.

[39] This study has much more to say about specifics of the Washington State program. For our purpose the above suffices.

[40] "Position Papers on Governor's Welfare Proposals."

[41] These include the Fair Budget Action Campaign and the Welfare Rights Organization Coalition.

[42] *Society*, January/February 1986.

[43] *The Washington Post*, February 13, 1986.

[44] Ibid.

[45] American Friends Service Committee, Philadelphia.

[46] *Dollars and Sense*, July/August 1986.

[47] Bernstein is a welfare administrator in New York.

[48] *The Washington Post*, February 24, 1986.

[49] Ibid.

[50] *The Washington Post*, December 11, 1986.

[51] AFSCME (American Federation of State, County, and Municipal Employees). For an extensive probe of these work-welfare programs, see

Demetra Smith Nightingale and Lynn C. Burbridge, *The Status of State Work-Welfare Programs in 1986: Implications for Welfare* (Washington D.C.: The Urban Institute, 1987).

[52] All those interviewed lived in the Washington D.C. area.

[53] Testimony of October 28, 1987 released by MDRC. The findings on program effectiveness are based on studies of women with school-aged children. But there is no solid evidence that mandatory employment and education services will work for younger mothers, nor—given the cost of the child care that will be required—that it would be cost effective to run such programs on a large scale.

[54] Manpower Demonstration Research Center, New York, Press Release, June 22, 1988.

[55] *New York Times*, August, 1988.

[56] Testimony of the Most Reverend James P. Lyke, Auxiliary Bishop of Cleveland, Ohio, on welfare reform, before the Advisory Committee on Intergovernmental Relations, Washington, D.C., September 11, 1986.

[57] Ibid.

[58] October 6, 1986.

[59] July 7, 1986.

[60] *The New Republic*, March 25, 1985. Murray replied in the April 8, 1985 issue of the same publication and in that same issue Greenstein rebuts decisively Murray's attempted replies. Greenstein followed again in June, 1985 with testimony before the Subcommittee on Fiscal and Monetary Policy of the Joint Economic Committee of Congress.

7

CONGRESS AND
WELFARE PROPOSALS

This examination of the welfare consensus and the role of the U.S. Catholic Bishops' Economic Pastoral in shaping public attitudes about welfare also requires some brief review of the current Congressional proposals regarding welfare. As will be evident, the positive welfare consensus described in this study stands rather at arms-length from the legislation emerging in mid-1988. True, it comes close—with varying degrees of closeness—to some Congressional statements on workfare and social compact which are more akin to earlier philosophical explorations than to present, 1988, legislative intent. It also recognizes fiscal needs. But it repudiates the meanness that these fiscal needs—unfairly and unnecessarily—entail.

Congressional legislative proposals may have been treated previously in the discussion of the early 1987 Congressional attitudes. These attitudes manifested more sharing in the positive welfare consensus than does present political intent. However, there are advantages to examining these subsequent legislative ideas on welfare in light of the consensus. That consensus was forged antecedently to the 1988 Congressional efforts. Moreover, since workfare seems to figure in all present House and Senate legislative proposals, Congressional thinking on this and perhaps on other programs can be better understood in light of the review made in the previous chapter of the state workfare experiments. It will also be helpful to reflect on House and Senate alternatives in light of the Bishops' strong rejection of compulsion and their equally strong insistence that welfare reform must not be injurious to the family.

It is not necessary here to enter into the intricacies of the process by which Congressional welfare measures move to a floor vote and then on to a compromise consultation by the two chambers. At this writing (mid-1988), there are several committees in the House alone working on one or another welfare proposal. The Republican minority in the House has its own proposal (H.R.3200) which it hopes will get a hearing if the House Democratic bill (H.R.1720) fails to get a floor majority. Meanwhile, Senator Daniel Patrick Moynihan has gained wide Senatorial support for his bill (S.1511).

It is sufficient for purposes here to set out the basics of the three Congressional proposals and the critiques which have been made of them. Additionally, some attention will be paid to where each stands with reference to the welfare consensus outlined previously.

Earlier, Congress used language that separated all but the most conservative spokesperson from much of President Reagan's proposed welfare program. There was a mood of understanding and compassion for the poor. The need was felt for more responsiveness to them. Nevertheless, by the fickle fate of national politics, Congress's current proposed legislation, in one degree or another, now puts many national legislators in the camp of those who have brought about what many observers still call the "Mean Season".

One understands that budgetary constraints appear to many in Congress to make it impossible to forward to Reagan legislative proposals he is sure to veto. Still, there is on the part of some members of Congress a surprising and perhaps unwarranted enthusiasm for compulsory work—quite apart from the value questions that such proposals raise. In some degree or other the main proposals of this legislation seem to justify the title the "Mean Season."

For this presentation of the Congressional proposals as well as for their critique, three major sources are heavily relied upon:

1. Legislative updates of the Department of Social Development and World Peace of the United States Catholic Conference (USCC)[1] and conversations with Sharon Daly, Director of the USCC office of Social Development;[2]

2. *Network*, a quarterly publication of NETWORK (Catholic social justice lobby) devoted entirely to this subject;[3]

3. The many very well-researched publications of the Washington-based Children's Defense Fund.[4]

Specific details of the various Congressional plans and the critiques of them can be drawn from all three of these sources in virtually the same vein.

I. THE SENATE PROPOSAL OF MOYNIHAN

Starting with the Senate, one main proposal is on the floor. This is the "Security Act of 1987" (S.1511), presented by Senator Daniel Patrick Moynihan (D-N.Y.). The Moynihan bill plans to substitute for AFDC a program oriented more to Child Security Supplement and to the family.

Two positive features give some justification for this proposal. The first extends assistance to all families on the basis of need. No longer will aid be extended only to households where the mother alone is present. It will be given also those households in which both parents are present. The second feature requires fathers to contribute to the support of their children, even if this necessitates withholding wages.

But the Moynihan plan does not involve any increase in child care benefits. There is also no guarantee that the states provide child care at all. Indeed, the plan seems to pull the rug from under state responsibility in its approval of "waiver authority," whereby ten states will be permitted to experiment as they choose with child support and welfare, free from any federal guidance. This is a concept that can eventually be extended to other states. The federal government's role in this "waiver" experiment will be to make a block grant. Block grants permit the states to put all federal funding—food stamps, AFDC, Medicaid, low-cost housing—into a single fund from which disbursements would be made as the state administering the program saw fit and in areas the state decided require support. Federal rules which presently provide funding guidelines could be swept away.

The workfare program—linchpin of the plan—would be compulsory for parents with children over three years. It could be extended, according to the various states' inclinations, even to parents with children under that age. Also, the proposed legislation carries no requirement of meeting minimum funding standards. For their workfare program, the Senate offers no proposal for adequate federal or state funding for either child care or for supplying the financial resources needed to move parents from welfare into workfare. Workfare is given the euphemous title of "Community Work Experience."

Critique of the Moynihan welfare proposal:
A good number of critical reflections on the plan have appeared. As for the Children's Defense Fund, NETWORK, and the USCC, all three have grave concern over the block grant or "waiver approval" provision. This does not mean that the ten states to be involved in the program have to reduce (or alternatively cannot increase) welfare benefits. But given the reluctance many states show of expressing any generosity on welfare, the worst can not easily be dismissed.

The USCC regarded as positive in Senator Moynihan's S.1511 the proposal that states be required to implement the AFDC program for two-parent families 15 months earlier than the date proposed in the House Democratic bill (H.R.1720). Another element viewed favorably was requiring states to strengthen their efforts to determine paternity of children born out of wedlock, as well as to strengthen the system for collecting adequate child support for children living with only one parent.

Problems USCC has with S.1511 are:

1. states could compel welfare mothers to "work off" benefits without offering them alternatives such as education, job training, or subsidized jobs;

2. states are not obliged to set minimum health and safety standards for day care for young children whose parents would be compelled to participate in work or training programs

3. there is no provision (present in H.R.1720) to permit employed welfare recipients to keep more of their earnings without becoming ineligible for AFDC;

4. families that go off AFDC when a parent gets a job would lose Medicaid benefits after 9 months (after 2 years in the H.R.170); and

5. pregnant and parenting mothers under 18 and living apart from their own families would not receive AFDC.

The USCC, in addition to these objections, presses Congress on two other provisions that it seeks: (1) all states must provide benefits for two-parent families, and (2) Medicare must be continued for two years after families go off welfare as a result of a parent finding work.

Similarly, for NETWORK and the Children's Defense Fund (as also for the consensus studies), welfare must be more generous. Hence, the Children's Defense Fund is dismayed to report that "Prospects for moving any incremental improvements on behalf of poor children and families in...this Congressional session are uncertain." Consequently, "much work must be done to secure needed changes in Senator Daniel P. Moynihan's Family Security Act...before it is acceptable."

NETWORK calls on its members to urge Senators to consider the following with regard to the Moynihan proposal:

1. there is no national minimum benefit standards and no increase in benefits;

2. the jobs program has inadequate funding;

3. there is lack of child care guarantee; and

4. there must be revision in the proposal for mandatory participation in the work and training programs.

The Children Defense Fund's "essential modifications" of the Moynihan bill are in line with NETWORK's. The Fund would like to see the compulsory job-acceptance provision dropped. Priority must be given to recipients of welfare who actively seek education, employment and training services. In effect, this means priority to volunteers. While it would be ideal to eliminate Community Work Experience, i.e., workfare, at least the program should limit the length of assignment and require a training/education component. In addition, there must be adequate funding, an opportunity for high school education, and a minimum set of education, employment and training activities to be made available by the state. Quality child care must be required of the states. The Fund also urges improvements to be made in Medicaid.

Sad to say, this Senate welfare "reform" proposal sounds nothing like the generous response one would have anticipated from Senator Moynihan's 1986 calls for reform. There are the two positive features noted above, and there is at least nominally the advance of putting welfare within the framework of the family. But in the view of the criticisms, there is too much wrong with S.1511 to have any hope it will turn out to be a truly family-oriented welfare alternative.

II. THE HOUSE DEMOCRATIC WELFARE PROPOSAL

The major legislative vehicle for welfare proposals in the House of Representatives is H.R.1720. Its provisions, often stated with alternative individual proposals from different House committees, are also not very generous. The House Democrats would extend AFDC for unemployed parents to the father when he is living with the mother of his children, and where the principal wage-earner is unemployed. This is all to the good.

But turning to workfare—referred to as CWEP (Community Work Experience Program)—it is, in effect, the same workfare program as offered in S.1511 discussed above. For the House, this requires that recipients work off their welfare grants at the minimum wage, even when other workers are receiving higher pay for the same work. Will such work lead to long-term employability? And will it not end up in displacement of already-working people as a result of the new competition for jobs generated by this law?

Here, too, appears mandatory participation of mothers of small children in education, training and work programs. Parents of a child three years or older will be required to enter these work programs, provided day care is guaranteed by the state and state resources permit. Also included in this qualified provision are mothers of children of under three years, provided day care can be established. (The House Education and Labor Committee wants to exclude from mandatory participation mothers with children one to three.)

There is a strong component of compulsion in the program. In this connection, it should be noted that the House Ways and Means Committee would deny benefits to pregnant and parenting teenagers under 18 who live apart from their parents. Apparently, proponents of this severe measure will deny benefits only if the state can demonstrate that the young woman could in fact live at home.

The House Democratic welfare proposal would increase slightly federal disbursement for a child. The Ways and Means Committee, in its approach, would provide higher "earned income disregards". This is the money families can disregard when calculating their eligibility for welfare. Health care—a very important element—gets different treatment from different House committees. Under the Ways and Means version health care is limited to six months, whereas Energy and Commerce would permit such health care for twenty-four months.

Critique of the House Democratic welfare proposal

The USCC notes that, while H.R.1720 is very much preferable to H.R.3200 (House Republican bill), and to the Senate's bill, the Bishops' Conference would not endorse the bill because of its unalterable opposition to Congress' permitting states (and federal authorities) to require mothers of preschoolers to leave their children in the care of others. The USCC did approve several portions of H.R.1720:

1. requiring states to continue Medicaid for two years to families going off welfare as a result of one parent finding work;

2. states' feeding their programs into the National Education, Training and Work (NETwork) programs;

3. requiring participants without high school education to participate in some educational program, such as remedial education or learning English as a second language; and

4. states' no longer offering only job search and workfare.

The USCC went on to approve still other measures on wage standards and on transitional help. It believes that it is proper to require the states to be specific about their responsibilities as well as the client's in NETwork participation. It strongly supports H.R.1720's extending AFDC not just to single-parent families but also to two-parent families.

On other provisions, however, the judgement of the USCC is negative. The report remarks that the USCC had argued before Congress in favor of higher reimbursement for child care. Further, it insists that parents who are minors must not be forced to re-enter their parental households where such re-entry would neither be safe nor appropriate.

NETWORK also considers most troubling the absence of a national minimum standard for benefits, and denial of aid to pregnant and parenting teenagers who live apart from their families. Moreover, it rejects mandatory participation in workfare.

The Children's Defense Fund parallels these two critiques of H.R.1720. On mandatory participation, it nuances the positions of the USCC and NETWORK. That is, instead of an absolute "no" to compulsion, the Fund does allow for mandatory participation, but only after volunteer participation is provided for and exhausted. Also, instead of straight-out elimination of Community Work Experience, the Fund accepts "establishing a clearer link with training and the imposition of certain preconditions on who can be required to participate in such programs."

III. THE HOUSE REPUBLICAN WELFARE PROPOSAL

If the House Democratic bill leaves very much to be desired from the viewpoint of the consensus, and the Moynihan Senate bill requires thorough redoing if it is to be acceptable, the House Republican welfare proposal (H.R.3200) is quite beyond redemption. This legislation was proposed by 104 House members including Robert Michel, minority leader.

The Republican bill incorporates many of the Administration's proposals to impose quite stringent requirements on AFDC recipients. It concedes broad authority to the states to redesign basic federal assistance programs. The Michel bill has received approval of the Administration. With the introduction of the Administration's proposals in the Senate by that body's minority leader, Robert Dole—who has promised a legislative proposal of his own—there is strong concern that Michel's bill will be offered on the House floor as a Republican (white House) substitute for the House Democratic proposals.

There are two main platforms in H.R.3200: to get more people off the welfare rolls and to make welfare less expensive for the government. On the latter, several estimates of the relative costs of the three programs, over five years, concur that the House Democratic bill will cost in the neighborhood of $5 billion, the Moynihan Senate bill $3 billion, and the House Republican bill $1.5 billion. The savings, of course, are made at the expense of what the welfare consensus group would consider a basic minimum of welfare—one that indeed needs by all accounts to be increased, not decreased.

Unlike the two bills previously considered, H.R.3200 contains no increase in benefits at all for any category. Nor does it, as do the two others, ask that welfare be extended to two-parent families. Like the Administration, this bill would make strong demands on AFDC recipients, while conceding to states wide powers to do pretty much what they choose about welfare. Despite these limitations, sponsors of H.R.3200 appear to believe that the Moynihan proposals are not very different from their own.

On work requirements, H.R.3200 provides: mandatory participation for all mothers with children above six months, no provision for part-time work for mothers with preschool children, and no request that states include in their employment programs any education and training service. States must over a time period put that percentage of minors in work/education programs stipulated in this bill.

The Michel bill falls very short of providing child care services and caps reimbursement for welfare children at $160—far short of needs. It requires participants to take jobs which would result in a loss of income and imposes sanctions on participants in educational programs if they fail to maintain satisfactory progress. Moreover, it does not, as do the House Democratic and the Senate bills, allow for child care benefits in the transition from AFDC to education/work.

Another sanction is imposed by H.R.3200 on pregnant and parenting females under 18 who refuse to accept living with their parents. The two preceding bills allow for other possibilities: minors living in foster homes or in maternity houses. This bill would also force child care to compete against work or education for the money of a common fund, whereas the two preceding bills allow for special funding for child care.

In criticizing the House Republican welfare proposal, NETWORK calls upon its members to urge Representatives to vote against H.R.3200 because it does little to improve the situation for welfare recipients in this country. The Children's Defense Fund concludes that it is critical to voice unconditional opposition to this legislation to members of both houses.

Finally, where do Congressional welfare proposals fit into the positive welfare consensus described earlier? Some would argue that the House Republican bill is straight-out Reaganism, that the Moynihan Senate bill embodies too much of the Administration's proposals, and that the House Democratic bill is not boldly enough anti-Reagan and indeed may fall more into the Administration camp as amendments are voted. The current national legislative consensus on welfare turns out to be, on the whole, supportive of Reagan. As the law-making goes on, it will be possible to see better to what degree the final product that emerges from Congress stands outside or perhaps approximates—even at a distance—the positive welfare consensus.

ENDNOTES FOR CHAPTER VII

[1] See, in particular, the United States Catholic Conference *Legislative Updates* of July and November, 1987.

[2] Ms. Daly is one of the drafters of the "Coalition of the 90s Welfare Principles."

[3] See NETWORK, September/October, 1987, devoted entirely to pending Congressional legislation on welfare. In its March/April, 1987 issue, NETWORK set forth its own ideas on welfare reform, or, in its view, what is more accurately referred to as the war on poverty.

[4] Children's Defense Fund study, mimeographed, August 21, 1987.

8

CATHOLIC SOCIAL THOUGHT AND WELFARE

It has often been said that the great body of modern Catholic social teaching developed since nearly a century ago is the Church's "best kept secret."[1] Indeed, much of the misunderstanding about the role of the Church in society, the need of the Church to speak on social issues, the Church's perspective on social issues, the specific proposals based on that perspective, and the importance of action on them, comes from a lack of familiarity with this social teaching.

A wide variety of papal encyclicals, Vatican Council documents, Bishops' Synod declarations, Bishops' Conference pastorals, and papal statements have formed this Church social teaching for nearly 100 years. Very important has been the social teaching developed from the 1960s on. Two important documents are central to this teaching: John XXIII's encyclical *Peace on Earth* and Vatican II's document *The Church and the Modern World*.

The U.S. Catholic Bishops' Economic Pastoral is developed from a solid foundation in this social teaching. And much of the misunderstanding about the Pastoral, in turn, comes from a basic unfamiliarity with or a tendency to misinterpret this Church teaching. A basic review of this social teaching is imperative if the Bishops' Pastoral is to be understood more clearly and its message more fully observed.

In this brief review, attention will be paid to the core Church documents which make up this modern social teaching, to the major principles of those documents—especially as they relate to the principles found in the Pastoral, and to the primary concepts that run through this still-developing body of Church commentary on the social, political, and moral challenges of the modern world.

I. CATHOLIC SOCIAL TEACHING:
IMMUTABLE PRINCIPLES?

A preliminary question must be raised. Can there be said to be an organic whole of Catholic social teaching? That is, is there an official and unchanging body of tenets about social life that are valid for all times and which must be upheld by Catholics everywhere? Is there a Catholic social doctrine bearing the character of universality? The question is more than semantics. That there is a single set of principles which must be always and everywhere applied was the prevailing view up to the Second Vatican Council. One social encyclical after another pronounced the existence of such an organic body of social teaching, valid for all and for all times. This universal validity was seen as stemming from two sources: the Scriptures and natural law, the latter in turn a reflection of divine law.

However, in the years just preceding the Second Vatican Council there was a major shift away from the notion of such universal validity and the deductive method supportive of it. This shift, an important one for the overall impact of the documents themselves, was signified in 1961 by John XXIII's encyclical, *Christianity and Social Progress*[2], commemorating Leo XIII's 1891 major encyclical, *The Condition of Labor*.[3]

Though Pope John's encyclical gives the traditional nod to the organic link of his document with his predecessor's statements, in fact *Christianity and Social Progress* excised the central model of socio-economic organization proposed by other encyclicals, notably Pius XI's 1931 *The Reconstruction of the Social Order*[4]. That encyclical had proposed, among other things, a return to or a revival of the medieval guilds. These were called in the encyclical's Latin, "ordines" (a cognate to the English word "order") They were perhaps similar to such present social organizations as "The Ancient Order of Hibernians" or "The Order of Elks." But whereas these modern groups are purely voluntary, Pius's "corporative orders" were said to be "if not of natural law, as if they were (quasi) of natural law" and therefore obligatory. Church teaching could only reflect this unchanging "natural law" or "divine law"—not restate it or re-interpret it.

John XXIII, 30 years later, unceremoniously discarded this notion of "corporative orders" in favor of a more fluid approach to Catholic social teaching on economic organization. This new approach would be a more dynamic response, borrowing from the ideas of the day, adapting the teaching to current conditions and analysis, and insisting that Catholic social teaching was more than a *pro forma* pronouncement of universal principles. This view, a shock to the proponents of the theory of organicity, has by and large prevailed.

In the theory of a complete and unchanging body of teaching, the notions of "Catholic" and "social" modified the substantive "doctrine" and implied a certain irrevocability. But with the arrival of the historic Second Vatican Council (1963-65), there was a certain unease with this idea and more interest in other approaches. This situation was typified by a short essay by one of the greatest authorities in Catholic social teaching, the French Dominican, M.D. Chenu, entitled "La Doctrine Sociale de l'Eglise Comme Ideologie."[5] Chenu both summarized and advanced the emerging approaches toward the Church's social teaching. He stated that a principal source of Catholic social thinking is reason and imagination. These qualities are shared not only with those who join in shared religious symbols, but also with the entire human race.

It is noteworthy that John XXIII, confident that all people of good will everywhere could and would respond to the reasoning of a peace encyclical, deliberately addressed his 1963 *Peace on Earth* not to Catholics only but to all people of good will. Despite all this commonality of reason and imagination, there are of course manifest differences in shaping social thought which will emerge later in this chapter.

In keeping with the shift in Catholic social thought from organicity to a looser body of thought is an accompanying change in method. Before, Catholic social thinking was seen to be highly deductive and speculative. Its principles worked from top, down: from the natural law inscribed in human condition as derived from the divine law itself, to the concrete applications in the social order. As such, this view considered Catholic social doctrine to be an almost infallible source of knowing.

Today, following new approaches that preceded and were in fact embraced in considerable degree by the Second Vatican Council, the development and application of Catholic social thought proceeds more empirically, more inductively. Modern Catholic social thought certainly is concerned with the foundations of the social that are derived from being human. But it places more reliance on the concreteness of the specific situations in which the human experience is imbedded. Catholic social teaching today also relies much more on the imagination of communities, confronted by their differing realities, to fashion their particular responses to the challenges of human life.

It remains now to state some of the concepts in Church social teaching and then to examine in very limited fashion the major documents. The main focus here will be on the approach of social teaching with respect to welfare.

II. SOCIAL HUMAN NATURE AND HUMAN RIGHTS

1. The Human As a Social Being

To consider Catholic social teaching as it relates to welfare, it is necessary to set forth some basic statements with respect to the human experience in general. The starting point is the core existence of each individual as a person, essentially linked to the existence of all other persons and to the whole of creation.[6]

One classic statement on the human person is that of John XXIII's *Peace on Earth*: "Any well-regulated and profitable association of [people] in society demands the acceptance of one fundamental principle: that each individual is truly a person, that is, endowed with intelligence and free-will. Men and women possess rights and duties that are universal and inviolable, and therefore inalienable."[7] Vatican II, borrowing from another John XXIII encyclical, *Christianity and Social Progress*, adds: "The beginning, the subject and the goal of all social institutions is and must be the human person." This thought prominently appears in the Vatican II document, *The Church in the Modern World*.[8] This emphasis on the centrality of the person connotes innate dignity and worth. The focus must be on the person in evaluating all institutions: social, political, economic and religious.

2. Person and Society

The human person is essentially social. Inter-personal relations do not exhaust this reality. Beyond is a community sense of being. Hence Vatican II states that human social nature "makes it evident that the progress of the human person and the advance of society hinge on each other." Social life "is not something added on" to human life. Hence, "through dealings with others, through reciprocal duties, and through fraternal dialogue," individuals develop all their gifts and rise to their destinies.[9]

Vatican II went further and, for the first time, the Church recognized as part of its teaching that the social nature of the human person is derived, not only from reason, but also from revelation. Jesus, when he prayed "that all may be one...even as we are one" opened up "vistas closed to human reason, for he implied a certain likeness between the union of the Divine Persons and the unity" of all people.[10]

The individual, and then the social collection of individuals, each has a place and a purpose in the human experience. Therefore the various systems—political, economic, religious, etc.—which develop from the social collectivity of individuals must have a social purpose and a reason. They must be evaluated according to how they serve the rights, duties, and interests of the individual and individual social groups.

3. Economic Rights

Each person, as a social being, has certain basic rights. Among these are rights of a socio-economic nature. Conservative Catholics in the United States strongly resisted the introduction into the Economic Pastoral of such economic rights. According to these conservatives, there are no rights except of a political and civic nature: the right to freedom of speech and of assembly, the right to be free of unreasonable government searches, the right to elect officials of our own choosing, and so on. These are, of course, classic freedoms enshrined in the U.S. Constitution's Bill of Rights. For Catholic conservatives, a suggestion of economic rights is too close to the idea of "economic democracy." It suggests that the state is given the right and responsibility, under whatever circumstance, to provide everyone a living. That—according to the conservatives—is socialism. (Further discussion of the conservative critique of economic rights will be taken up in Chapter X.)

Nevertheless, Catholic social teaching had already, long before the Bishops' Economic Pastoral, recognized the importance of economic rights. A classic enshrinement in Church social teaching of socio-economic rights alongside the civic and political is found in John XXIII's *Peace on Earth*. And the same central themes reappear vigorously in John Paul II's 1981 *On Human Work*.[12] These economic rights are more than the rights to participate in a certain economic system, such as the right to engage in contractual arrangements or the right to become employed. Economic rights in the sense noted here are rights that relate specifically to the economic well-being of the individual.

These rights include the right to life, to bodily integrity, and to the means necessary to sustain these. In addition, there is a right to the means necessary for the development of a proper life. Economic rights therefore include the right to food, clothing, shelter, medical care, and to "necessary social services." A recognition of these rights also later appears in Vatican II's *The Church in the Modern World*.[13]

The "necessary social services" are those things which a state is expected to provide for its citizens to ensure a proper and adequate life. Such social services include security in event of sickness or of inability to work, or widowhood, old-age and unemployment. Still other economic rights are: the right to work, to suitable working conditions, to a wage in accord with justice. Finally, there are those economic rights more readily recognized by conservatives: rights to freedom of initiative, to private property, to enter freely into contractual relationships. And all these "human rights" which flow from work are part of the broader context of the fundamental rights of the person.[14]

The enshrinement of social and economic rights alongside civic and political rights appears also in documents of the United Nations which have been recognized and praised in Church social teaching. There are two instruments of the United Nations' approach to rights. The first is the 1948 Universal Declaration of Human Rights, adopted by the UN General Assembly. This Declaration is not a binding treaty but a standard by which the nations of the world can measure their sensitiveness about rights. The United States is a signatory to the Universal Declaration.

The other UN instrument is in fact two Covenants: one on civil and
political rights, and the other on economic, social, and cultural rights. The
United States has not signed either Covenant. Among the economic, social
and cultural rights enumerated by the UN Covenant are the following:

—the right of everyone to an adequate standard of living for themselves and their family, including adequate food, clothing, and housing (Article 11)

—the right of everyone to form trade unions and to join in the trade
union of their own choosing (Article 8)

—the right of everyone to social security, including social insurance
(Article 9)

—the fundamental right of everyone to be free of hunger (Article 11)

—the right of everyone to enjoy the highest attainable standard of
physical and mental health (Article 12)

—the right of everyone to education (Art. 13)

Within the social systems that emerge from the collection of individuals,
then, there must be a recognition and guarantee of these human rights.
Church social teaching seeks to address the development of human systems from this perspective, with the additional consideration, to be
detailed later, of the option for the poor. Thus there is a fundamental difference between the approach taken by Church social teaching in evaluating social systems from the moral perspective and the approach taken
from a purely political perspective.

The above discussion of rights has avoided using the word "entitlement." This term can be the equivalent of right conferred by nature or
nature's Creator. But for many, entitlement is some title specifically conferred by the state. The position taken here is that basic rights—those
described above—are inherent in human nature. It is true that their
implementation may require state initiative. For instance, certain
inequalities deriving from the market may need to be corrected by the
redistributive actions of the state, prompted by distributive justice. But
entitlements thus achieved may appear to many to be wholly state-origi-
nated. This leads the more conservative to express the fear that the state
will be pulled to meeting whatever entitlement a liberal can think up.
Catholic social thought, however, precludes that position. Moreover,
this body of thought equally insists that the rights/entitlements of the
middle class—indeed all classes—must be prompted by the state.

4. Society as an Institution: The Common Good
As the social interiority of persons expresses itself in public forum, the
common good is brought into existence. The common good is not something apart from people, something pre-existent to social life. It is both

the fruit of human cooperation and the guarantor of the fruitfulness of further cooperation. The common good is the total of the conditions of social living—economic, social, political, cultural, even religious—which render possible the opportunities for each person to achieve the fullness of common humanity.

In fact, this concept relates closely to the "General Welfare" which the preamble of the constitution of the United States asserts is one of the reasons for people's banding together: "We the people of the United States of America, in order to form a more perfect union,...promote the general welfare..."

This common good is itself the matrix of rights. Rights, however personal they may be, do not exist outside a common framework which is the good of the whole. The common good nurtures personal rights, frames their exercise, and lays social claims of sharing on the individual good embodied in personal rights. The common good in no way detracts from individual rights or from the total respect that individual rights deserve.

The concern for the rights within the common good is in direct opposition to the notion of an adversarial society which pits one individual against another, one person's rights against another's. The common good unites individual rights in sharing, cooperation, bonding. The Catholic teaching notion of common good thus carries with it the implication of solidarity and the joyous and self-fulfilling work for the good of society in a communal sense of living. It is a notion quite directly opposed to the individualist, consumerism philosophy that drives much of U.S. social thought, a narrow philosophy of "me-tooism."

As a brief review of these four major points demonstrates, the social teaching of the Catholic Church has very clear starting points in its evaluation of social systems. Church social teaching is concerned with how the system respects persons as individuals and as social beings, how they protect individuals and collective rights, both political and economic, and how they promote the common good of all society. The Church therefore has much to say about contemporary social institutions such as welfare which will be very different from an evaluation based simply on political considerations.

III. SOCIAL INSTITUTIONS, RIGHTS, AND ROLES

1. People and Institutions

According to Church social teaching, the social person lives in a matrix of institutions and cultures. These should serve to express and develop the person and will be the conduits of rights and responsibilities. Of these societal organizations proper to the individual, some are more cultural in character. They are the traditional ways in which children in nearly all cultures are "socialized," that is, ways in which memory is evoked, a deity worshipped, rules passed down, traditions expressed, ancestors honored.[15] Other institutions are of a more structural character. These are institutions of a "folk," many constituting their way of expressing social and political participation and of organizing work.

The family—both as a cultural and as a structural institution—has always been seen in Catholic social thought as a fundamental social institution. The family is the basic cell of society. (Certainly there could be an immoral "familialism"—an attitude that says only our family counts and we will not bother about the rest of society.) Contemporary societies, especially those experiencing a growing number of singles, will have to learn how to avoid turning family priority into a tool of oppression or how to regard the legitimate roles and concerns of singles.

Traditionally, Catholic social thought's consideration of the institutions proper to human life has moved on from the family to the state. However, the state does not have only one characteristic. Church teaching sees two sides to the state. On the one side is the polis, the body of people, recognizing that people are, as Aristotle argued, political animals made for public and political life. On the other side is the state authority, necessarily created in some form to uphold law, order and structure. In Catholic social thought, the state is regarded as the necessary guarantor—but not the sole producer—of the common good and of all rights.

"To safeguard the inviolable rights of the human person...should be the essential office of every public authority," states John XXIII in *Peace on Earth*.[16] This safeguarding of rights by the state is in the name of the common good. "The very nature of the common good requires that all members of the political community be entitled to share in it." For this reason, "every civil authority must take pains to promote the common good."[17] "The common good", the encyclical continues, "of all without preference for any single citizen or civic group." The reason for this principle is that the civil power was "established for the common good of all."

In today's political debate, this caution against preference might be interpreted to exclude welfare considerations which favor some groups over others. But to preclude such an interpretation, John XXIII immediately adds that "considerations of justice and equity can at times demand that those involved in civil government give more attention to the less fortunate members of the community."[18] *Peace on Earth* goes on to reinforce the grounds for this special attention: "unless these authorities take suitable action with regard to economic, political and cultural matters, inequalities between citizens tend today more than ever to become more and more widespread."[19]

Politicians and others demanding today that work for welfare be mandatory have a different conception of the reciprocity that lies between making an individual contribution to the common good and being a beneficiary of that common good. In Catholic social thought, there surely must be contributions to the common good on the part of all. But they are not on a strict contractual basis of quid pro quo. They are proportionate and the proportion is arrived at by a number of factors—not all of them of the purely economic order.

Thus it is depressing that proponents of a conservative welfare policy see economically productive results as the sole social contributions a person can make to the common good. This has policy consequences such as the demand that teenage women with very young children work off their AFDC benefits. Such a narrow view totally ignores the important good these women do socially by bringing up their children at home. It is for this reason that the justice that lies between individual and the state is called distributive.

2. Social Institutions and the International Dimension
Alongside the family and the (nation) state, there is a third form of social life: the international. Catholic social thought emphasizes that individuals are born into the family of humankind before they are born into any particular nation. The rich tradition on this need not be of concern here since international affairs do not enter very directly into welfare considerations. However, it should be mentioned that the Economic Pastoral does discuss very substantially the international situation in economics. It notes, for example, the responsibility that U.S. citizens have to those within the entire human family who happen to live in other nations.

3. Other Social Institutions and Cultural Factors
But what about other forms of societal life between individual/family and state? What about community? Political and cultural communities? Work community? Surely all of these have implications for welfare. As noted earlier, John XXIII rejected the attempt to install between individual and state the "orders" or guild system of Pius XI's "The Reconstruction of the Social Order." But if that formula is not acceptable, are there no other imaginable forms of economic social organization between the individual or family and the state?

John XXIII, in his *Christianity and Social Progress*, suggested a formula of worker-owner cooperation through some arrangement of joint management or of workers' sharing in stocks or profits.[20] This proposal was repeated by the Second Vatican Council and reappears once again in John Paul II's *On Human Work*.[21] This approach has significant implications for the relationship between Capital and Labor that will be returned to in Chapter IX under the discussion of "economic democracy."

It must be acknowledged that official Catholic social thought has not done much thinking about community, various forms of community living, or bodies intermediary to state and individual. Today there are new experiences, Catholic and other, that are influencing thinking about community. This is true in Africa, where there is often a vibrant community life, and in Latin America, where base Christian communities abound. This new thinking often echoes U.S. thinking on community and on other locally-based social-economic forms of organization. The U.S. Catholic Bishops thus devote much more space to this theme in their Economic Pastoral than is traditional in Church social documents.

IV. THE MEANING OF JUSTICE

What impels people to live out the societal impulse inherent in our humanity? Catholic social teaching holds as primary two virtues that should form the motivation for human action in the social context: love and justice. Of course, it is a natural progression from the concepts like "the social context" and "love and justice" to another primary concept: "social justice." Catholic social teaching is first and foremost a teaching about social justice, in turn derived from principles embedded in Scripture and exemplified in the life and ministry of Jesus.

1. Development of "Social Justice"

Up to the latter part of the 19th Century, the justice that impelled people to live their social obligations had been designated as "legal", presumably because the obligations of social living tended to become concretized in law. But that was precisely the difficulty with it. It tended to make justice nothing but observing laws. There was little to be said about how laws originate and for whose benefit the laws are made and enforced. The term no longer conveyed—as it did for Thomas Aquinas, one of its originators—the idea of a general virtue ordering relationships in society toward the common good. A new name was sought for the notion of justice that Church teaching contended should impel persons to live out their social obligations.

It was at this juncture that the term "social justice" became enshrined in Catholic papal teaching, especially by Pius XI in his 1931 *The Reconstruction of the Social Order* and his 1937 *The Divine Redeemer.* In fact, the earlier encyclical became known as *The Social Justice Encyclical* for its bold (at that time) use of the term. The question that entered the debate among observers and theologians following these documents was whether this was a new name for general or legal justice, or whether this was some new form of specific justice.[22] Those interested in this question would do well to read the two encyclicals just mentioned and through them the continuing tradition including Vatican II.

For present purposes, it is necessary only to direct attention to certain key texts of what justice is and how it relates to welfare. For instance,

The Divine Redeemer states, "there is also social justice with its own set of obligations."[23] And it continues, "the distribution of created goods...must be effectively brought into conformity with the common good, i.e., social justice."[24] Productive human effort "cannot yield its fruits unless a truly organic body exists, unless a social and juridical order watches over the exercise of work..."[25] Thus, all institutions of social life "ought to be penetrated with this justice."[26]

Several characteristics of social justice emerge from these papal encyclicals.[27] Social justice:

1. Is the equivalent of the earlier general or legal justice, for its object is the common good;

2. Commands, in the name of that common good, more specific acts of justice—at a minimum, exchanges between individuals and groups and the acts of justice that lie between individuals (and intermediary groups) and the state;

3. Is given some central thrust toward organizing the institutions of a social and legal order; from this organized and productive society social benefits will be distributed to all individuals of the society; and

4. Commands individuals, organizations and the state to structure their behaviors, policies, and activities in conformance with its principles and goals.

2. What Sort of Justice is True Social Justice?

One other element in a somewhat fluid tradition needs to be noted before trying to say a final word on social justice. The first draft of what was to become John XXIII's *Christianity and Social Progress* attempted extensively to resolve the debate over the nature and form of social justice for purposes of Catholic social teaching. The final draft of the encyclical, in contrast with the first draft, in fact uses the term only twice—without any definition or elaboration. It turns with seeming indifference to such equivalents as "justice and equity" or "justice and love." Yet that document in its final version and other related encyclicals clearly establish social justice as central in the moral evaluation of human institutions according to Catholic social thought.

The following components of the current consensus over the use of the term social justice offer insight into this key theme in Catholic tradition.[28]

1. Doing justice—not naming it—is what is important.

2. Nothing in recent times has so commanded the Catholic conscience as the historic document of the 1971 Synod of Bishops, *Justice in the World* with its reliance on the plain, unmodified word—justice.

3. Worked out from social nature and the common good, social justice

has established itself as at least a replacement for legal or general justice, the notion of justice found in earlier development of Catholic social thought.

4. Justice requires acts of justice in the individual and hence in some way becomes also a particular form of justice—of the part to the whole.

5. In this latter function, social justice especially requires acts of organizing of such institutions (e.g., welfare) as may be called for in the name of the common good.

6. Social justice must be motivated by and be exercised under the guidance and influence of human love and compassion.

In deciding how to apply the term "justice" in current Catholic social thought, the biblically inclined will probably stick with "Justice in the World"in confining themselves simply to plain justice. "Justice demands..." Those attracted to the power of the symbol of social justice may divide up: some confining its use as a substitute for legal or general justice; others, even if it be ambiguous, using the term also to describe the call on all to organize towards a just society.

3. Justice and Love and "Charity"

A time-honored distinction among the virtues assigns primacy to love. Love informs, that is, exists within and motivates all other virtues. It gives them life; it is their soul force. Thus love transforms justice from within. More fundamentally, the doing of justice stems from the fundamental option for God who loves me and wants me to love others as God loves them. Out of this love one is to give others all that is their due as part of the human community. Still another priority of love over justice is the Christian conviction that owing to human sinfulness the motive-force of justice may not be adequate to the job of getting justice done. On occasion the power of love may have to reinforce a sense of justice. If one shifts perspective from motive-force to acts, love gets expressed as acts of charity and acts of justice. It is recognized that there can be charitable acts congenial to, if not absolutely required by, social living that lie in boundaries beyond the call of justice. That creates no problem. What does pose problems is the equating of charitable works with—and limiting them to—works of "counsel" or supererogation. This equation is a device used by those who want to narrow the field of moral obligation: what is of obligation is only what results from contract. All else is charitable work and not of obligation. If one pays a worker the contracted wage in a free market, one's obligation to the worker is dissolved.

However, papal social teaching has repeatedly challenged this view. First, charitable works put in place to supply needs not met by the market must be perceived as merely provisional to a fuller justice. Second, social justice calls upon each person to create the institutions which will ensure the required justice, thereby reducing the need to do charitable deeds. The Catholic tradition will never say that deeds of free giving are nobler than bestowing what is owed in justice as an expression of a loving concern for the good of society and for individuals and groups within that communal life.

Social justice, therefore, grows out of the rights and responsibility of individuals both collectively and individually, and becomes a motivating factor that should drive human activity, form human associations, and shape human institutions. Social justice is a primary principle of Catholic social thought. There are still other primary principles in this social thought that bear even more directly on the situation of welfare and on how the Economic Pastoral comes to the evaluations that it does concerning welfare. Three key principles are the option for the poor, subsidiarity, and socialization.

V. THE OPTION FOR THE POOR

The primary principle of the option for the poor is another characteristic which sharply differentiates Church social teaching from other forms of analysis of political or economic systems. "Option for the poor" may only be new language for the Church's two thousand year-old special concern and compassion for the poor and the needy. It links the justice of God and the justice of the Christian community. This concern for the poor is powerfully expressed in the Hebrew Scriptures, significantly featured in the Jesus story, and deeply imbedded in the early writers of the Church. The tradition moves forward so persistently on this principle that theologian Donal Dorr can title his recent study of Catholic social tradition from Leo XIII to current times: *One Hundred Years of Vatican Social Teaching: Option for the Poor.*[29]

The primary document of the 1971 Synod of Bishops, *Justice in the World,* a document which powerfully moved the Catholic community across the world, has this to say of the teaching of the Old Testament: in the Hebrew Testament God reveals himself as the "liberator of the oppressed and defender of the poor, demanding faith in him and justice toward one's neighbor. It is only in the observation of duties of justice that God is truly recognized as liberator of the oppressed."[30] This statement sums up the wealth of verification of the definition of God that runs through Exodus, Deuteronomy, prophets like Amos and Deutero-Isaiah, and the Psalms. The Covenant God, in a word, is a God of Justice. God's own righteousness demands justice toward all in need.

Turning to the New Testament, the Synod avers that "In his preaching

Jesus proclaimed...the intervention of God's justice on behalf of the needy and the oppressed." Further, Jesus identified himself with the least—named as the poor, the needy, the imprisoned: "Insofar as you did this to my least sisters and brothers, you did this to me."(Mt. 25:40)

The Synod had its own way of linking love of God and of neighbor. "Love and justice cannot be separated. For love implies the absolute demand for justice, recognition of the dignity and rights of one's neighbor." And it is because "everyone is the visible image of the invisible God and brothers and sisters of Christ that the Christian finds in everyone God..." The final consequence is clear: Whoever loves must commit self to liberating from injustice, economic, social, political at national and international levels.

Notable statements of this option for the poor appear in the writings of Liberation Theology.[31] It has its origins in the Second Conference of Latin American Bishops, held in Medellin, Colombia in 1968.[32] There were bishops and others who, subsequent to Medellin and the 1971 Synod, wanted to weaken this option for the poor. Certain Latin American bishops made an attempt at the Third Conference, held in Puebla, Mexico in 1979, to dilute the strength and the impact of this message. But Puebla imbedded the principle into the social teaching and pastoral action of the Latin American Church.[33]

Further, the option for the poor was reaffirmed by John Paul II in an address the following year to the bishops of Brazil. "You know the preferential option for the poor was strongly proclaimed at Puebla. It is a profession which, while not exclusive, is a call to a special oneness with the small and weak, the humiliated, those left on the margin of life and society."

The U.S. Catholic Bishops Economic Pastoral contributes to this theme and reaffirms it strongly, in spite of the fact that the "preferential option for the poor" raises critical questions among some in the U.S. community. First, how does one square the option for the poor with the option of all members of society for the good of all society—for the common good? Second, does seeking the option for the poor pit the poor against the middle class with their own proper concerns and worries? Some of these questions have answers for a particular time and place, but others will be the focus of continuing discussion on how the option for the poor is to be recognized and realized. (These are discussed further in Chapter X.)

The option for the poor is clearly a functional and primary concept for Catholic social thought that forms a base for the evaluation of human systems. It is linked powerfully to the notions of social justice and of human rights.

VI. SUBSIDIARITY AND THE ROLE OF THE STATE

Since "subsidiarity" is a notion absolutely key to the Catholic social thought and the discussion of welfare, it must be examined at length. This concept links strongly to the Church teaching on the role of the state and on the common good. It seeks to spell out the implications of the bipolarity that relates the state to individuals and to groups lesser than the state. (Question: is the state higher and these individuals and groups lower in status, as the concept of subsidiarity is sometimes formulated? Obviously, not. "Higher" is strictly a functional term.)

1. Meaning of Subsidiarity
Subsidiarity, to begin with, is based on the Latin word for "helping"—subsidium (as in subsidizing). It is unfortunate that a principle so crucial to expressing the welfare relation of state to individual has to bear the freight of that Latinity.

There is the additional inconvenience that for people in the United States and for many others a "subsidiary" relationship conjures up corporate business images. One thinks of a smaller, subordinate part of a company and its relationship to the larger parent company. But this image has no relationship to the ideas embodied in the Catholic teaching on subsidiarity. This false image would present subsidiarity as a principle that, just as the smaller company serves to support the purposes of the parent corporation, so individuals and small groups serve the purpose of the state. This of course stands the Catholic principle of subsidiarity on its head! Subsidiarity assigns to the state a role, indeed a very large one, in promoting the common good. The principle of subsidiarity makes the state the ultimate guarantor of the common good. The principle is in fact a remarkable statement of how the state's functions are held in workable and creative tension with individual and intermediary groups, each making its contribution to social living.

2. Subsidiarity in Church Social Teaching
John XXIII made the principle of subsidiarity a cornerstone of his social teaching and makes his classical statement of it in *Christianity and Social Progress* He prefaces the quotation by stating that primacy in economic affairs must be given to individuals. But, "it is necessary that public authorities take active interest, the better to increase output of goods and services and to further social progress for the benefit of all citizens."[34] The encyclical continues, "This intervention of public authorities that encourages, stimulates, regulates, supplements and complements, is based on the principle of subsidiarity."

John then quotes that principle as it appears in Pius XI's *Reconstruction of the Social Order:* "It is a fundamental principle of social philosophy, fixed and unchangeable, that one should not withdraw from individuals and commit to the community what they can accomplish by their own enterprise and industry. So, too, it is an injustice and a great evil to transfer to the larger and higher collectivity functions which can be performed and provided for by lesser and subordinate bodies. Inasmuch as every social activity should, by its very nature, prove a help to members of the social body, it should never destroy or absorb them."[35]

What precise measures the state should take to further the general welfare is not a matter for the Church to say. It is sufficient that Church teaching advances certain principles relevant to the discernment and judgment of practical programs. Beyond that (or below it) lies the area of what Thomas Aquinas called political prudence. This is the exercise of practical reason and imagination working with ethical principles creatively within the context of a given historical situation or of a specific community's experience. Catholic social teaching does not pretend to say how the two poles of political action—that of the state on the one hand and that of individual and intermediary groups on the other—should interrelate. What it does contend is that this is a dialectical relationship, in inevitable tension. They must operate together and in a mutual, symbiotic fashion.

3. Bi-Polar Relationships

This duality-in-tension was first noted by Pius XI in the passage quoted above from his 1931 *Reconstruction of the Social Order*. John XXIII, in his 1963 *Peace on Earth*, addresses the bi-polar relationships in the context of international society. He moves to that from the original application of subsidiarity at the national level: "Just as within each political community the relations between individuals, families, intermediate associations and public authority are governed by the principle of subsidiarity, so too are the relations between the public authority of each political community and the public authority of the world community."[36]

In brief, the world community must tackle problems of an economic, social and political character posed by the demand to meet the needs of the international common good. These problems are so vast and complex that the public authority of the individual states cannot cope with them. When the world community acts in some organized fashion (e.g., through the United Nations), it is not to limit action by individual nations. Rather, it is to create the environment conducive to carrying out the proper tasks of each political community, its citizens and intermediate associations.[37]

Returning to the functions appropriate to the national authority with respect to its own citizens, Pius XI in *Reconstruction of the Social Order* lists several such functions: "directing, watching, urging, restraining."[38] John XXIII extends this list in his *Christianity and Social Progress* by adding the functions of "supplementing and complementing."

It is important to note that in speaking of the bi-polar relationships these terms surely connote a substantially activist role for the state. John XXIII does note that the pole of the individual's responsibility must be respected and that enterprises of the state should be entrusted only to people of integrity ("less in the administration of the state itself there develop an economic imperialism"). But he nevertheless is able to say of the state's role that the common good will require the state "to exercise ever greater responsibilities."[40]

In still further explanation of the principle of subsidiarity towards the direction of proper state concern, John XXIII introduces the supplemental principle of intervention.[41] As to be expected, these interventions are parallel to those earlier enumerated in *Peace on Earth* where that document, in leading up to the discussion of subsidiarity, lists rightful functions of the state. One function is worth citing here because of its immediate relation to welfare: "Insurance systems are made available to citizens so that in the event of misfortune or increased family responsibilities no person will be without the necessary means to maintain a decent standard of living."[42]

VII. THE PROCESS OF SOCIALIZATION

Long before the U.S. Catholic debate over the Economic Pastoral, more conservative Catholics in Europe had sought to swing the pendulum between the poles of subsidiarity more securely over to the side of individuals. They sought sharply to diminish the role of the state. It was this situation that persuaded John XXIII to reinforce the subsidiarity of Pius XI's *Reconstruction of the Social Order* by introducing the supportive principle of intervention.

John's concern that the problems of today's economic society are so complex and interdependent that public authorities would have to assume still more responsibilities led him to further address the phenomenon of "socialization." This socialization arises from modern society's complexity and interdependence and in itself is not to be dismissed as evil. Quite the contrary, it is, however ambiguous, only a new manifestation of the evolving social thrust of humankind.[43]

The phenomenon of socialization is seen in the patterns of social life that give rise to new social institutions. John XXIII speaks of a "wide range of groups, associations, institutions having economic, cultural and political ends." Socialization is the "effect and cause of growing state intervention."[44] Add the complexity of social problems like health care, rehabilitation of those physically or mentally handicapped, education, and still further state intervention in the social fabric is involved.

Controversy arose over the use of the word "socialization" in John XXIII's encyclical. This is because the official Vatican Latin text reads "rationum incrementa socialium."[45] That translates as "multiplication of social relationships," and the Paulist Press edition in English opted for that literal translation. America Press translated the term as "socialization," following the version used by the Vatican Press Office. The Vatican Italian text read "socializzazione;" their Spanish, "socializacion;" their French, "socialisation." At least one German text followed with "socialierung."[46]

It has been alleged that the word "socialisation" suggests to many socialism. This is perhaps understandable. Some argue that the real reason why the Vatican Latinists came up with their unwieldy (and uninformative) phrase was to avoid any confusion. At any rate, there can be little doubt that the Pope's helping hand in writing the original text had in mind--contrary to the subsequent Latinists--the phenomenon delineated in the encyclical itself.

Dangers of Socialization

Of course there is always in the process of socialization, as in those of subsidiarity and intervention, the chance that the freedom of the individual will suffer. John XXIII recognizes this: "...an atmosphere develops where in it becomes difficult to...do anything on one's own initiative."[47] But even while recognizing that potential, he is confident that such abuse will not be the normal case. He puts the question: "Will people perhaps cease to be personally responsible?" He answers negatively: "This socialization is the creation of free people who are so disposed to act by nature as to be responsible for what they do."[48]

Perhaps a more fundamental answer is also found in a statement by John XXIII: "This trend also indicates and in part follows from that human and natural inclination...whereby people are impelled voluntarily to enter into association in order to attain objectives which each one desires but which exceed the capacity of single individuals."[49] Socialization is also the process by which small children are inducted into the mores and customs of their society.[50]

All this section of John's *Christianity and Social Progress* is replete with statements on both the good and the possible evil of socialization. There is expressed a desirable return to individual, small groupings: "The various intermediary bodies and the numerous social undertakings wherein an expanded social structure primarily finds expression, must be ruled by their own laws..."[51] "Within these intermediary grouping individuals must be considered persons and be encouraged to participate in the affairs of the group." Yet just one paragraph later, Pope John XXIII returns to a reassuring note about the state's role in the process: "If this norm is observed socialization will enable people not only to develop…but also lead to an appropriate structuring of the human community."[52]

Socialization must be recognized as a process running through subsidiarity. It begins with those impulses of human nature to confront the complexities of social life through social organization in order to achieve the common good. Note too its link to social justice, for that is the virtue supportive of these same impulses. The process then moves forward by other actors entering the picture—e.g., the state with its proper role. The same bi-polarity is at work in socialization as in subsidiarity. And it has consequences for the promotion of welfare, as the Bishops' Economic Pastoral makes evident.

ENDNOTES FOR CHAPTER VIII

¹ See Peter J. Henriot, Michael J.. Schultheis, and Edward P. DeBerri, *Catholic Social Teaching: Our Best Kept Secret* (Maryknoll, NY: Orbis Books, and Washington: Center of Concern, 1988).

² This encyclical is known in Latin as *Mater et Magistra*. While declaring itself in the line of previous social encyclicals, it broke new ground with the principle of socialization and paid scant attention to the definitions of the various kinds of justice, especially social justice, elaborated in the sixty years since *The Condition of Labor*.

³ Rerum Novarum is its Latin title. While there was much social thought preceding this—the Scriptures, the Fathers of the Church, St. Thomas Aquinas, etc.—this document represented the first attempt to organize a systematic body of thought on a social question. That question for Leo XIII could only be the struggle between capital and labor. This theme largely remained central to the rest of the great social encyclicals, though the social question was finally perceived by Paul VI in his 1971 *Call to Action* to be worldwide.

⁴ Known in Latin as *Quadragesimo Anno* (commemorating the 40th anniversary of Leo XIII's *Rerum Novarum*), this encyclical introduced into Catholic social thought the organizing principle of social justice. Text is available from the United States Catholic Conference, Washington, D.C.

⁵ Paris: Les Editions Du Cerf, 1979. Not available in English.

⁶ One of the great modern philosophers of the human person is the German Jesuit Karl Rahner. For an introduction to this thought on this subject, see Ann Carr's essay in Leo O'Donovan, ed., *A World of Grace* (New York: Seabury, 1980).

⁷ *Peace on Earth*, 9.

⁸ *The Church in the Modern World*, 25.

⁹ Ibid.

¹⁰ Ibid., 24. This same Vatican II statement says that all things were created for the use of the human. The human is the pinnacle of creation with all other things subservient to human need. Such "anthropocentricity" is resisted by today's ecological philosophy/theology which prefers

to see the human more in continuity and communion with the totality of God's creation, all of which, with the human, renders God praise.

[11] *Peace on Earth*, 11-34. An excellent discussion of Catholic teaching on rights is found in David Hollenbach, S.J., *Claims in Conflict: Retrieving the Catholic Human Rights Tradition* (New York: Paulist, 1979). Hollenbach, a major ethicist in this field, served on the committee of consultants in the drafting of the Economic Pastoral.

[12] Latin title, *Laborem Exercens*. Text in Origins (vol. 11, no. 15), September, 1981. Chapter 4 is entitled, "Rights of Workers Within the Broad Context of Human Rights."

[13] *The Church in the Modern World*, 67-71.

[14] *On Human Work*, 16.

[15] Peter L. Berger and Thomas Luckmann, *The Social Reconstruction of Reality* (New York: Doubleday, 1966). See, for example, their discussions of "Institutionalization," 37-92.

[16] *Peace on Earth*, 60.

[17] Ibid., 56.

[18] Ibid.

[19] Ibid., 63.

[20] Treated in several places in *Christianity and Social Progress*; e.g., 77 ff., 91-96, 111.

[21] *On Human Work*, 14.

[22] See Philip S. Land, "Justice," in Joseph A. Komonchak, Mary Collins, Dermot A. Lane, eds. (Wilmington, DE: Michael Glazier, Inc. 1987).

[23] *Divine Redeemer*, 51.

[24] Ibid., 57, 58.

[25] Ibid., 69.

26 Ibid., 88; cf. also 110.

27 Land, loc. cit.

28 Ibid.

29 Maryknoll, N.Y: Orbis Books, 1983.

30 All quotations following are from *Justice in the World*, 13-15.

31 See e.g., Jon Sobrino, *The True Church of the Poor* (Maryknoll, N.Y.: 1984). Also Donal Door, op. cit., 157-162.

32 The Medellin documents are translated in *The Church in the Present-Day Transformation of Latin America in the Light of the Council*, Vol. 2, Conclusions, ed., L.N. Colonnesse (Washington, D.C.: United States Catholic Conference, 1970).

33 See John Eagleson and Philip Scharper, eds., *Puebla and Beyond: Documentation and Commentary* (Maryknoll, N.Y.: Orbis Books, 1979). For a discussion of Puebla and the option for the poor, see Donal Door, op. cit., 207-17.

34 *Christianity and Social Progress*, 52.

35 Ibid., 53.

36 *Peace on Earth*, 140.

37 Ibid., 53.

38 *Reconstruction of the Social Order*, 80.

39 *Christianity and Social Progress*, 53; also 117, 152.

40 Ibid., 117 ff.

41 Ibid., 53.

42 *Peace on Earth*, 64.

43 *Christianity and Social Progress*, 59-62.

44 Ibid.

[45] The Encyclical was originally written in Italian, and then translated into Latin for its official promulgation.

[46] I was in Rome at the time and recall that the reason given for translating the original Italian text's "socializzazione" into "rationum incremtum socialium" was that the Vatican Latinists knew no Latin word for the original Italian word. They would not corrupt the Latin language by attempting to create a new word.

[47] *Christianity and Social Progress*, 62.

[48] Ibid.

[49] Ibid.

[50] Berger and Luckmann, op. cit.

[51] *Christianity and Social Progress*, 64.

9

ECONOMIC PASTORAL

AND

WELFARE CONSENSUS

Before situating the teaching on welfare of the U.S. Catholic Bishops within the context of the emerging positive welfare consensus, it has been necessary to establish several points of clarification. In the preceding chapters, the general critiques of the Pastoral were reviewed and the philosophical and political positions of both sides of the welfare debate were laid out. Then the major criticisms against welfare were examined from the point of view of recent scholarly research. What is here called the positive welfare consensus has been described in detail, and then a review made of current Congressional welfare proposals. Finally, Church social teaching was outlined with particular reference to teaching which bears on welfare and the role of the state.

In this present chapter the task will be to compare the teaching of the Pastoral to the consensus. In the next chapter, more in-depth analysis will be offered of the theological/philosophical foundations of the Pastoral's teaching in view of attacks made on these. In sum the following points will emerge:

1. The Bishops hold a middle ground between conservatives and liberals on the welfare function of the state. But it is a proper ground of its own, and not simply a picking of ideas from one side and the other.

2. The Pastoral is thoroughly in accord with the proposals that comprise the welfare consenus, although the Bishops do express some significant reservations.

3. Quite apart from the Bishops' position within the consensus on welfare reform, the Pastoral holds foundational views about welfare. While being the objects of severe attack from within and outside the Catholic community, these views are both defensible and a powerful contribution to welfare policy in general.

I. THE PASTORAL'S MIDDLE GROUND

It must first be said that the Pastoral is in agreement with the conservative perspective in that it clings tenaciously to the proper role of the individual and to the importance of small, local group intermediaries between the individual and the state. Yet, in agreement with the liberal position, the Pastoral makes very clear that the state has a positive role in bringing about economic good. This view the Bishops adhere to even while rejecting the liberal's Utilitarian narrowing of the state's role to that of serving the interests of the individual.

This middle position in the Pastoral is not at all a waffling or a compromise fraught with innate ambiguity. Rather, it evolves out of a fundamental social philosophy. Two basic principles guide this philosophy. The first principle joins the dignity of the individual and the expression of that dignity in intermediary societies with the common good which grounds all individual goods together. The second principle states the need for properly constituted political authority to guide, complement, and supplement individual and intermediary group contributions. These principles are part and parcel of the Church's social teaching on which the Pastoral is based and they form the Pastoral's own specific perspective. In short, the Pastoral lives out of its own truth.

This "middle ground" with its own philosophy is, of course, not unique to Catholics. Others can and do come to the same foundations of social welfare. But the Pastoral has added a new dimension to the welfare debate by showing the significant role that theological and biblical principles play in this complex question of modern social policy. (This, of course, other faith traditions have also done.)

Besides appearing in the Pastoral's section on biblical images and social ethics (30-126), the topic of welfare is treated in three major policy sections: (1) employment (136-169); (2) poverty (170-215); and (3) a "the New American Experiment" (295-325). The Pastoral makes use of generic language, e.g.: "welfare system" (215), "welfare programs" (212), "public assistance" (211), "income-support programs" (210), and "social policies."[1]

Welfare, to be sure, can be as widely conceived as one chooses. For example, even Social Security can be viewed as securing the elderly from poverty and hence be seen as a form of welfare. Medicare, apart from its health promotion aspects, can be thought of as preventing older people from falling into poverty because of medical bills. And while government efforts to seek full employment does protect the dignity of citizens through employment, it also has the welfare function of helping people to escape poverty. Welfare thus can have the additional aim of securing people against the debilitating experience of being unable, though willing and able-bodied, to take care of themselves and their families.

(There is even a form of "reverse welfare." This reverse welfare involves all the measures a free enterprise-oriented government is prepared to take—even while cutting aid for the poor—to bail out troubled industries, banks, and loan institutions.)

The Economic Pastoral's welfare policy recommendations speak strongly about the need for the nation to continue the fight against poverty. Among those recommendations specifically mentioned are the following: Aid to Families with Dependent Children (AFDC), food stamps, child nutrition, medical care, programs which have an impact on the family and on child well being. In addition, the document mentions the need for programs for the disabled and the chronically ill.

1. Attitudes Toward Welfare Programs

The Bishops begin their specific discussion of welfare by noting both the successes and shortcomings of social welfare programs. (They also include Social Security and Medicare). Reviewing the record, the Bishops argue first that there have been splendid successes, e.g., Social Security (190-91). But the Bishops also speak forthrightly about the failures of the welfare system: some programs have been "ill-designed, ineffective and wasteful" (192).

In totalling up the balance sheet, the Bishops say: "Where programs have failed, we should discard them, learn from our mistakes and fashion a better alternative. Where programs have succeeded, we should acknowledge that fact and build on those successes" (192).

This judgement reads very much like the conclusion arrived at by the several authorities of the very highly regarded research volume, *Fighting Poverty*, used extensively in earlier discussions in this study. The editors of this important volume conclude that their authors "reject the view that government programs do not work."[2] Further: "Although it is clear in each of these areas that significant problems remain, ...these authors...[do not] advocate abandonment of public efforts to reduce poverty." Rather, they conclude that new policies must build on what works and must abandon what does not. This statement sounds almost as if it were written from the Pastoral.

2. Welfare "Cheating"

On the very sensitive and highly politicized question of welfare cheating and frauds, the Bishops have been charged with "soft-headedness." This charge has already been examined and found wanting.[3] In fact, it is most striking that the many studies that go to make up the newly-emerging welfare consensus give little or no attention to the charges of fraud and waste. Not that some problems are not present. But the plain fact is that the charges have been vastly exaggerated. In short, there simply are not many of Ronald Reagan's "Welfare Queens" around today. Consonant with their view of promoting human dignity, the Bishops ask the public to "refrain from actions, words or attitudes that stigmatize the poor, that exaggerate the benefits received by the poor and that inflate the amount of fraud in welfare payments" (194).

The Bishops go further. Prompted by the compassion for the poor that characterizes the entire document, they call upon the U.S. community to realize the need for fairness. They urge avoidance of steoreotypical and punitive attitudes toward the poor. Such attitudes include the view that the poor are mostly racial minorities and are in poverty by choice or through laziness, that anyone can escape poverty by hard work, and that welfare programs make it easier for people to avoid work (193-194).[4] With strong indignation, the Bishops contrast these views with the attitude toward hand-outs for the rich: "Some of the most generous subsidies for individuals and corporations are taken for granted and are not called benefits, but entitlements" (194). Those who thus claim or support such "entitlements" are the very same ones who condemn labelling welfare payments as entitlements, insisting that these payments are benefits to be handed out only on a *quid pro quo* basis—i.e., one must work to receive them.[5]

II. THE CONSENSUS POSITION

The task is now to examine the Bishops' welfare positions by juxtaposing them with the positions of the welfare consensus outlined in Chapter VI.[6] A helpful statement of the overall positive consensus has been referred to earlier, the elaboration offered by Ben W. Heineman, Jr.[7] (It is worth recalling that Heineman is a considerable authority in this area, having served in the Carter Administration as Assistant Secretary for Planning and Evaluation in the Department of Health, Education and Welfare.) He divides his approach to reviewing the consensus into themes and policies.[8]

The procedure here will be first to state the consensus and then in the next section to unfold the parallels in the Bishops' positions.

1. CONSENSUS THEMES

a) Work Rather than Cash

There is a growing conviction that holds that meeting the needs of people on AFDC should ideally be through paid employment. The strong emphasis on work has a two-fold base. First, it is felt that paid employment as a way of gaining livelihood carries with it dignity. (But does not non-paid work also carry dignity?) Second, it is now so common to see women in the work force that it seems less unacceptable to urge young teenage unmarried mothers to join the work force. However—and this is a strongly stated reservation in the consensus—there will still be those who need cash transfers because they are unable for one reason or another to work (or are legitimately unwilling). Thus, there emerges the need for a mix of jobs, cash, benefits, and in-kind help.

b) Experiments by States

These are approved, all the more because there is concern that not too much is to be anticipated from the Federal government in the way of increased benefits.

c) Federal standards

There should be national standards to govern state programs. For example, there should be minimum levels of welfare and humane eligibility guides.

2. CONSENSUS POLICIES

a) Programs for Welfare Recipients

The first objective is to complete high school (with at least a general diploma). This policy is founded on the belief that education is crucial to life in modern U.S. society. The second objective is to train for a job that holds a future of advancement in work experience. If jobs are not available in private industry, then subsidized employment must be provided. As needed, day care must be provided for small children. Absent fathers will be required to contribute more to the support of their children. To prevent long-term welfare dependency, a time limit is to be set on receiving welfare benefits. Prominent in the consensus is that benefits should be given to both spouses maintaining a household with children. Most see the absurdity of a system wherein half the states deny welfare to a household in which both parents are present.

b) The Working Poor

Moving beyond the more narrow purview of welfare, these, it will be remembered, are people who have jobs—even full-time, year-round—but do not receive enough income to lift them and their families above the poverty line. The consensus here is that these individuals must be helped. Help will come by upgrading available jobs, by providing higher pay (e.g., reform of minimum wage), by providing health benefits, by reducing the still-heavy burden of taxes paid by the poor. According to Heineman, Reagan Administration policies have been particularly oppressive toward the working poor.

c) Children of the Poor

Regarding poor children, concern grows into a serious fear that present indifference to their plight will result in their reaching adulthood without being able to suitably care for themselves. To rectify this situation, there is need for increased health benefits and improved education. Imperative is keeping teenagers in school

d) Adequate Income

The programs for welfare recipients described above may be inadequate to lift the poor above the poverty level. To remedy that gap, the consensus speaks for a national minimum benefit in cash, in-kind benefits, and medical care.

III. THE BISHOPS' POSITION

Those who had been unduly concerned by the critics of the Economic Pastoral should be relieved that there is much agreement between the Bishops and the welfare experts. So true is this that it is difficult to understand the near-contempt with which many Catholic conservatives have widely viewed the document. The following categories present the Bishops' positions on welfare.

1. Employment (136-155)

There is a "right to employment" given the fact that in today's society most income comes through work. For that reason, the U.S. must not be content with accepting six to seven percent unemployment as "normal." It is necessary to strive for "full employment" at averages well below the present unemployment levels (152), and at decent paying jobs.

2. General Economic Policies (156-169)

After the call for full employment, there is a call for targeting programs to fit specific requirements for such employment, e.g., job training (159), especially in view of our constant technological change (160). There must be direct job creation achieved through a partnership of business and government (162). Supporting services are needed (164). To spread the work more widely, job sharing, flex-time and a reduced work week are suggested (167). The section ends with the call for moving away from so much military expenditure toward conversion to more productive and useful industrial or research activity (168).

3. Poverty (170-182)

Here the Bishops recognize that there are different kinds of poor. They point first to the working poor, already described (174). It is noted that often people above the poverty line can be impoverished by an illness or a loss of job. A household thus afflicted, even with two incomes, may be able only to keep the family's head barely above water. Second, children in poverty deserve serious attention—a problem especially severe among female-headed households and among black families (176). Many poor families have no assistance or health benefits (177).

A third category of poor is women. "The past twenty years have witnessed a dramatic increase in the number of women in poverty. This includes women raising children alone as well as women with inadequate income following divorce, widowhood or retirement. More than one-third of all female-headed families are poor. Among minority families headed by women the poverty rate is over 50 percent" (178). In part, the special poverty of women is owing to their receiving a wage only 61 percent of male workers (179).

The Pastoral pays special attention to the injustice experienced by racial minorities, reduced to deeper poverty than whites (181). The Bishops are concerned with the particularly negative effect of some aspects of the economy when it comes to minorities and to the continuing consequences of racism (182).

4. Economic Inequality (183-185)
According to the Bishops, the distribution of wealth in the U.S. is very uneven (183). The distribution of income is somewhat less uneven but still quite striking. In 1984, the bottom 20 percent of U.S. families received only 4.7 percent of the total income in the nation; the bottom 40 percent received only 15.7 percent—the lowest share on record in U.S. history. In contrast, the highest one-fifth of the population receive 42.9 percent of total income, the highest share since 1948. This is one of the most unequal distributions of income among the industrial nations. What is worse: "The gap between rich and poor in our nation has increased during the last decade"(184).

Gar Alperovitz, president of the National Center for Economic Alternatives in Washington, D.C., was brought in for several consultations by the committee drafting the Pastoral. In two articles, he offers other startling statistics on U.S. inequality.[9] During most of the 40-year postwar period, the percentage of the nation's total resources allocated directly to the poor—for income maintenance, food stamps, welfare, etc.—has varied roughly between 7/10th of one percent and two percent of the Gross National Product. If indirect programs (e.g., Medicaid) are included, a reasonable estimate of the upper limit would reach three and four percent of GNP.

Says Alperovitz, "In what's left of the 'war' on poverty, politicians and the press regularly dramatize what in fact are pitifully small skirmishes."[10] He adds the "revealing truths" that: (1) at any point in time, the fight is over a tiny fraction of much less than one percent of GNP; (2) the overall struggle is essentially stalemated and moving up or down very slightly relative to GNP (currently down); and (3) at best, 96 to 97 percent of our national resources (and, in direct terms, fully 98 to 99 percent) are simply excluded from the debate for all practical purposes.

On income inequality, the Bishops state that Catholic social teaching does not require an absolute equality, but can accept a degree of inequality if it is productive of the general welfare ("incentives and rewards for greater risk")(185). But, they add, such inequality must be framed by two other principles: the priority of meeting the basic needs of the poor, and the need to increase participation by all members of society in national economic life. "These norms establish a strong presumption against extreme inequality of income and wealth as long as there are poor, hungry and homeless people in our midst. They also suggest that extreme inequalities are detrimental to the development of social solidarity and community"(185).

IV. ACTION RECOMMENDATIONS

The Pastoral now moves into a set of specific "Guidelines for Action" (186-215). But before offering their proposals for dealing with poverty in the United States, the Bishops remind readers of the Pastoral Letter that their recommendations are built upon several moral principles developed in the Pastoral's earlier section on social ethics. In particular, these principles include human dignity and the option for the poor (186), social solidarity (187), participation (188), and moral responsibility (189).

The Pastoral is fully within the welfare consensus view in its treatment of the need for a national strategy to combat poverty. Although this may sound to some like simply a return to the somewhat discredited (although unfairly so) "war on poverty" programs, the Pastoral's discussion is a strong combination of current consensus views, its own unique perspectives, and principles applied from Catholic social teaching.

1. Remedies
A healthy economy with expanded employment heads the list of strategies to deal with poverty (196). Congress is asked to raise the minimum wage since through inflation it has lost nearly one-quarter of its value since 1981 (197). Turning to remedies for specific causes of poverty, the Pastoral calls for elimination of barriers against equal treatment for women and minorities (199). It adds job training for these as well as affirmative action (199). As for the poor, the Bishops emphasize self-help programs at the local level (200) and urge that the poor "be empowered to take charge of their own futures and become responsible for their own economic advancement" (201).

2. Taxes
The Economic Pastoral is clear in asserting that "the tax system should raise adequate revenues to pay for the public needs of society, especially to meet the basic needs of the poor" (202). Because neither politicians nor the public in general appear to be in a mood for more taxes to meet welfare needs, it is good that the Bishops have had the courage to raise a prophetic voice. Agreeing with the consensus, the Bishops insist that welfare reform and other poverty programs including employment

efforts are going to cost more, not less. The Bishops also urge that taxes be more progressive, proportionate to the ability to pay, taking into account income, assests, and tax bracket. A single percentage tax, and "flat taxes" such as sales taxes, have a greater impact upon those with less income.

3. Education

It is clear that any effective strategy to provide a long-term solution to U.S. poverty "must pay serious attention to education, public and private, in school and out of school" (203). The Pastoral lays great stress on improving the educational programs for the poor. It praises Catholic school efforts, especially in inner-cities (204), and also affirms strong support for the public school system (205).

4. Families

The Pastoral focuses on families, declaring: "Policies and programs at all levels should support the strength and stability of families, especially those adversely affected by the economy" (206). In support of this principle, the Bishops say, "Employment practices, health insurance policies, income-security programs, tax policy and service programs can either support or undermine the abilities of families to fulfill their roles in nuturing children and caring for infirm and dependent family members" (206). This echoes a paragraph in the introduction of the Pastoral: "The lack of a mutually supported relation between family life and economic life is one of the most serious problems facing the United States today. The economic and cultural strength of the nation is directly linked to the stability and health of its families." (18).

It is in this context that the Pastoral reiterates its position against pulling mothers of young children out of their homes into the workplace. "The nation's social welfare and tax policies should support parents' decisions to care for their own children and should recognize the work of parents in the home because of its value for the family and for society" (207). For children whose parents do work outside the home, affordable, quality day care is seriously lacking (208). According to the Bishops, the high rates of teenage pregnancy and of divorce are distressing signs of the breakdown of traditional family values. The Pastoral calls for "a revived sense of personal responsibility and commitment to family values" (209).

5. Taxes and the Family

In its earlier discussion of taxes, the Pastoral suggests that families below the offical poverty line should not be required to pay income taxes: "Such families are by definition without sufficient resources to care for their basic needs" (202). It should be noted that after the Bishops made that recommendation, Congress did exempt a very sizeable dollar amount from poor families taxability. Despite that, very many families still need further tax exemption to meet their basic needs.

Senator Moynihan, highly regarded for his studies on welfare and the family, supports the Bishops on this point. He notes that in the 1940s families under the poverty level were exempt from federal income taxes. By the early 1980s less than one-third of these poor families were exempt. In 1983, the poverty line for a family of four was $10,166. But federal tax in that year began at $8,783. Personal income exemption in 1948 was $600. Moynihan says that indexing that 1948 figure according to today's Consumer Price Index would require that the exemption be in the neighborhood of $2,500, rather that the $2,000 recently accepted in legislation. The Senator adds a sobering reflection to that statistic. The Department of the Treasury states that raising the exemption that high would cost $40 billion in revenue, the measure of the support the government has actually been siphoning off from raising children.[11]

6. Welfare Reform

The Pastoral judges that the current programs are not serving the needs of the poor adequately and with dignity. Nothing short of "a thorough reform of the nation's welfare and income support programs" is urged (210). Among the immediate, short-term improvement that can be made are the following:

—Programs should be designed to help beneficiaries become self-sufficient through gainful employment (211). Individuals should not be worse off economically when they obtain jobs than when they rely only on public assistance.

—Public assistance programs should work in tandem with job-creation programs that provide fair compensation along with training, counseling, placement and child care (211).

—Adequate levels of support for welfare beneficiaries should be provided, covering basic needs in food, clothing, shelter, health care and other essentials. Here the Bishops note that at present four percent of poor families receive enough cash welfare benefits to lift them out of poverty. The combined benefits of AFDC and food stamps typically comes to less than three-fourths of the offical poverty line (212)

—Agreeing strongly with the consensus view, the Bishops call for national eligibility standards and national minimum-benefit level (213).

—Again in accordance with the welfare consensus view, the Bishops urge that welfare programs be available to two-parent families as well as single-parent families. The father who is unemployed or poorly paid should not have to leave home so that his children can receive help (214).

7. Welfare Alternatives

After discussing welfare reforms, the Pastoral closes this section calling for "serious discussion of more fundamental alternatives to the existing welfare system" (215). Only hints are given of what the Bishops want entered into such public discussion. These include the following: family allowance, children's allowance, "negative income tax." More generally, they urge that there ought to be discussion of measures to be taken to meet the continuing problem of long-term poverty.

The Bishops express once again their strong sensitivity as to how welfare and poverty programs affect the family. Earlier drafts of the Economic Pastoral had been criticized for lack of attention to the possible negative impact of welfare on the family. But the final document remedied that deficiency.

Siding with the Bishops in their emphasis on family and alternatives is Senator Moynihan.[12] Moynihan's fundamental point is that the welfare program has been based on the U.S. culture of individualism. Individuals in destress are cared for; the distressed family is ignored. Moreover, in the concern shown for the individual, the family is often harmed or destroyed.

Moynihan notes (as do the Bishops and the consensus view) that welfare frequently does not provide aid to the two-parent family. It is given to the broken family and after the enforced break-up. In 1960 nearly nine out of ten families were wife/husband-headed; in 1986 only three out of four are such. Moynihan has estimated that by the year 2000 the number of female-headed families will have increased more than five-times the rate of two-parent-headed families. He suggests that the U.S. consult European experience, where family is a prime concern in social policy. For the sake of a healthy society, family allowances are given. But among industrial nations, the U.S. is the only nation without such a program. (One could have hoped to see more evidence of this sensitive approach in the welfare reform legislation Moynihan subsequently sponsored in Congress.)

8. Mandatory Work Programs

This is the place to repeat one strong demurral on the part of the Bishops to the welfare consensus position. That consensus—though with due caution on the part of many—generally accepts mandatory work programs for teenage single mothers on welfare. But the Bishops are equally insistent that these young women with their children not be forced to enter the workforce or to live in the household of their parents. The United States Catholic Conference (USCC) is on record as not opposing incentives to induce these young women to work and/or to join their parents. But the USCC, along with the Pastoral, recognizes that they may have good reasons for not doing so. The mandatory work program on which the consensus mainly focuses is that of forcing these teenage mothers to take a job in exchange for welfare benefits and to move more quickly out of welfare itself.

Expressing the views of the USCC and the Pastoral on mandatory work, Father J. Bryan Hehir, then-director of the USCC Department of Social Development and World Peace, testified before Congress.[13] He argued: "We are troubled at the way the problem is posed." The majority view appears to be that only paid work outside the home confers dignity and contributes to society. But "caring for children at home is a contribution to society." Moreover, Hehir added, there is no need for mandatory programs. In most states, not enough jobs are available for those on AFDC programs who voluntarily seek work. Hehir said further that "it is discouraging to hear policy-makers argue for mandatory work for mothers of preschool children without any real effort being made to help mothers of older children."

This testimony sheds further light on the Economic Pastoral's treatment of poverty and welfare. In one summary statement, Hehir said that the Bishops' message remains: improvements in AFDC, adequate AFDC benefits, full employment strategy, rejection of welfare rules that weaken the family, and adminstration of welfare that favors dignity, equity and self-determination. While his statement does use the language that "it is not unreasonable to expect young mothers to work," the rest of the testimony makes clear that this does not apply to mothers of very young children. Incentives to take a job include those already seen: adequate income, a job that establishes future possibilities, child care, medical support. Any such program must in the view of the Bishops be one that rewards, not punishes, recipients who try to be self-supporting.

Hehir's testimony ends on the note that the Pastoral had strongly stressed: there is more needed than these short-term reforms. There must be a commitment to develop "fundamental alternatives." In this connection, he urges careful examination of family allowances and/or child allowances.

This concludes the parelleling of the welfare position of the Economic Pastoral and the position of the positive consensus on welfare propounded by various social experts. From this it is possible to derive a sense of the wholeness of the Bishops' approach and of its strong affinities with the body of thought which makes up the consensus. The paralleling has been largely programmatic, but an effort has been made to point also to the philosophical underpinnings of both consensus and Pastoral. Central to the exposition here is that the U.S. Bishops' teaching in their Economic Pastoral both reflects and reinforces the best of the positive welfare consensus.

ENDNOTES FOR CHAPTER IX

[1] Numbers within parentheses refer to the paragraph number in the final document. The text of those sections of the Pastoral which deal with welfare can be found in the Appendix to this study.

[2] Sheldon Danziger and Daniel Weinberg, eds. (Cambridge: Harvard University Press, 1986), 15.

[3] See Chapter I for examples.

[4] For a thorough look at the question of whether or not welfare creates a disincentive to work, see the study published by the General Accounting Office, *Issues to Consider in Assessing Proposals for Reform* (Washington: General Accounting Office, 1987). The GAO argues that extensive research does not substantiate the charge that welfare provides a notable disincentive.

[5] See discussion of "workfare" in Chapter IV.

[6] The Economic Pastoral, of course, contains major elements of the Bishops' positions on welfare. But this has been supplemented by other statements, e.g., Congressional testimony, as will be noted.

[7] "Welfare Reforms Revisited: New Consensus and Old Dilemmas," in *Work and Welfare: The Case for New Directions* (Washington, D.C.: Center for National Policy, 1987).

[8] Ibid., 13-20.

[9] *Sojourners*, November 20, 1985; *Christianity and Crisis*, March 3, 1986.

[10] *Christianity and Crisis*, loc. cit.

[11] *Challenge*, September-October, 1985.

[12] "The Family and the Nation," *America*, March 22, 1986. Also, "We Do Not Have Children to Waste," statement before Subcommittee on Social Security and Family Policy, Senate Committee on Finance, February 2, 1987; and "Making Welfare Work," statement before Subcommitee on Social Security and Family Policy, Febrruary 23, 1987.

[13] Testimony before Subcommittee on Social Security and Family Policy of the Committee on Finance, U.S. Senate, February 2, 1987.

FOUR FINAL CHALLENGES

The U.S. Bishops ground their teaching on welfare—and hence their location of it within the welfare consensus—on solid philosophical and theological foundations. These foundations are derived from Church social on the dignity of the human person and the structures of community. But within the Catholic community and wider in the United States, these principles have been challenged as have the programmatic recommendations derived therefrom. Thus it is important in concluding this study to carefully examine these challenges and evaluate their seriousness.

In many circles the Bishops have been taken to task for: (1) placing emphasis on a preferential option for the poor; (2) supposedly failing to understand and follow papal teaching on the role of the state and subsidiarity; (3) supporting "economic rights," viewed by many as a "sell-out" to "socialism," and (4) approving of "economic democracy" in deed if not in word, equally viewed as endorsing socialism.

I. OPTION FOR THE POOR

As indicated in Chapter VIII on Catholic social teaching, the preferential option for the poor is fundamental to the Catholic perspective on welfare. There is no doubt that the U.S. Bishops have made this fundamental option key to their Economic Pastoral. Recalling Vatican II, the Bishops say that the griefs and anxieties, especially of the poor, are the griefs and anxieties of the followers of Christ (2). The poor, the Pastoral adds, "have the single most urgent economic claim on the conscience of the nation" (86). "As individuals and as a nation, therefore, we are called to make a fundamental option for the poor" (87). Again, "The fulfillment of the basic needs of the poor is of the highest priority" (90).

Making this option for the poor will call on the citizens of the United States to examine their way of living in light of the needs of the poor (75). The entire thrust of the Pastoral's sections on poverty (170-215) is a consequence of putting this option into practice in society today. Even investment decisions ought scrupulously to be worked out in this perspective. According to the Bishops, policies governing the investment of wealth, talent and human energy "should be specially directed to benefit those who are poor or economically insecure" (92). (Quite opposite to this perspective is columnist Charles Krauthammer's derisive retort: "Capitalism is the option for the poor.")

The option for the poor goes beyond national boundaries. There are poor in lands distant from the United States and towards whom this country bears responsibilities (4). In international economic relations, "The preferential option for the poor is the central priority for policy choice" (260). The Pastoral makes specific applications of this option in addressing trade's impact upon the poor (267) and the consequences of the burden of debt (274).

Several strong objections have been raised against this option. There exist a whole school of business-oriented thinkers who dismiss the Bishops outright as woolly-headed do-gooders. The working supposition of these critics seems to be: "Leave the capitalist system alone and it will effectively take care of the poor." But that easy supposition is of course precisely what the Bishops, in union with many of today's best economic thinkers, are challenging. It is also alleged that the Bishops want to eliminate any and all inequality, ignorant that in so doing they would kill the goose that lays the golden egg. But in truth the Bishops, as noted earlier, clearly recognize that some degree of inequality may be productive. What they object to are the sharp extremes in society (183-185).

Of more substance are two other related questions which have been raised by critics of the Pastoral's option for the poor. The first is that the fundamental option ought to be for the common good—not for one particular segment of society. The second is that the Pastoral seems to be written as if there were only the marginalized poor exploited by the rich. But what about that vast body of the middle class? What about their economic problems? And are they to be considered, alongside the rich, responsible for the poor?

It is important to look seriously at both of these objections since they touch on major points in the message of the Pastoral Letter.

1. Option for the Poor and the Common Good

Some critics charge that the Bishops, in their expression of the option for the poor, ignore the essential thrust of social justice toward the common good. But the Pastoral Letter does indeed give clear recognition to the central place of the common good. It makes its own Pius XI's statement, "It is of the very essence of social justice to demand from each individual all that is necessary for the common good" (71). So there is some sense in which achieving the common good is indeed the primary option of a community. It is also in and from the creation of this common good—these commons—that all society may share and should share. Nevertheless, the Bishops—as John Paul II, other episcopal conferences, and many religious congregations—insist strongly on the priority of the option for the poor. They agree with the Synod of 1971's "Justice in the World" that this was also the option of Jesus.[2]

The Economic Pastoral has an important way of linking option for the poor with the common good. In their introductory "Pastoral Message," the Bishops state that the option for the poor is a way of "strengthening the whole community by assisting those who are most vulnerable" ("Pastoral Message," 16).[3] In a key passage the Pastoral seeks to meet directly the objection that the option for the poor hurts the common good. This deserves to be quoted in full: "The prime purpose of this special commitment to the poor is to enable them to become active participants in the life of society. It is to enable all persons to share in and contribute to the common good. The 'option for the poor,' therefore, is not an adversarial slogan that pits one group against another. Rather it states that the deprivation and powerlessness of the poor wounds the whole community. The extent of their suffering is a measure of how far we are from being a true community of persons. These wounds will be healed only by greater solidarity with the poor and among the poor themselves" (88).

This formulation is a strong echo of the response given to the same question by John XXIII in his "Peace on Earth" He calls for "the common good of all without preference for any single citizen or group." But he adds the qualification, "Considerations of justice and equity can and sometimes do demand…that more attention be given to the less fortunate members of the community."[4] In no way does the option for the poor undercut the promotion of the common good. Rather, the option amplifies its scope and strengthens its bonds.

2. Option for the Poor and the Middle Class

It is true that many of the middle class, especially the lower middle class, have felt left out of the consideration of the Bishops. There is not in the Pastoral, they believe, enough concern for "the common good of all without preference." Many in this group are struggling to keep their children in school and meet the tuition demands of college. Even two-earner families can be working extra hard not to lose mortgaged homes and to do a bit of saving for the future. Some face large medical bills for their aging parents. Numbers of them are only a lost job or an expensive medical treatment away from poverty. Divorce or separation has thrust many middle class women into the labor market at wages near or below the poverty line.

The Institute for Social Research at the University of Michigan, which has studied poverty for many years, has discovered that the permanently poor turn out to be—at least up to recent times—a very low percentage of the total U.S. society.[5] The largest number of people below the poverty line are those who have spent—and will spend—time out of poverty. Indeed, it is estimated that one-fourth of the U.S. population has at one time or another been below the poverty line. Because of these statistics, some argue that the option for the poor would make more sense if the Pastoral were being written in Brazil, where 80 percent of the people are poor.

What the U.S. Bishops have in mind, however, touches two important points relevant to U.S. society. First, they do recognize the economic pressures felt by the middle class, especially the lower middle class who "are barely getting by and fear becoming victims of economic forces over which they have no control" (85). The Bishops are sensitive to middle class concerns. Second, they also acknowledge that the middle class in U.S. society needs to be challenged. Archbishop Weakland, chair of the Pastoral drafting committee, addressed this issue: "The phrase 'preferential option for the poor' is not meant as a slogan to polarize our society, but as a challenge to all—including the middle class. In attempting to build bridges of responsibility between the poor, the middle class and the affluent classes, one must also challenge many middle class values in the United States, and not leave the impression that all is well."[6]

The Pastoral does present a challenge for all in the United States to examine life-style in the face of the needs of the poor. The "American Dream" needs to be re-evaluated, since "Christian faith and the norms of justice impose distinct limits on what we consume and how we view material goods" (75). Moreover, the Pastoral, in the name of the option for the poor, calls for more sharing on the part of those who currently possess economic power and privilege. In so doing, it echoes the strong words of Paul VI: "In teaching us charity, the Gospel instructs us in the preferential respect due the poor and the special situation they have in society. The more fortunate should renounce some of their rights so as to place their goods more generously at the service of others" (87)

It is simply not fair to criticize the Bishops' endorsement of the option for the poor by saying that it goes against the middle class in this country. But it is also necessary to be honest in admitting that this option does have serious consequences for the business activities and life style of the middle class. This will be one of the significant challenges in the implementation of the Pastoral.

II. SUBSIDIARITY

The principle of subsidiarity is central to the Economic Pastoral, where it appears as a fundamental instrument in addressing welfare issues. It is a principle deeply grounded in Church social thought. As seen in Chapter

VIII, it states two things. First, action should, wherever possible, be taken at lower levels of social or institutional structures, avoiding an overpowering, overburdening structure that controls all action. Second, the state has its legitimate and necessary role in social action which promotes the common good.

Although it is a key principle in Catholic theology, subsidiarity is not very well understood by contemporary U.S. Catholics. But its importance is evident if one seeks to defend the Pastoral from those who criticize the Bishops of "statism," i.e., an over-reliance on government action.

One major critic, Father Andrew Greeley, contended that the first draft of the Pastoral (which appeared in November, 1984) was seriously flawed in its failure to give more than scant attention to this central theme subsidiarity.[8] What Greeley saw as the absence of adequate reference to the tradition of subsidiarity was evidence to him that the drafters felt that this theory really has nothing at all to contribute to the solution of contemporary problems in U.S. society. In addition, Greeley accused the Bishops of believing that the way to solve problems was to throw money at them. Equally he charged a failure to stress "participation in decision-making."

Greeley rightly perceives that subsidiarity is a principle that has much more to say about constituting society than is acknowledged by most interpretations of Pius XI's famous dictum: nothing should be done by a higher and larger institution that can be done by a lower and smaller one. He also is correct in shifting the proper emphasis from doing to being. Nothing should be bigger than necessary. Hence, the bias is in favor of localized networks—familial, geographic, religious, economic, political. Such an approach creates the environment where "people matter for who and what they are and not merely for what they can do." Greeley wants subsidiarity also to result in more decision-making at local levels.

So the challenge: does the Pastoral fail to give centrality to the principle of subsidiarity and thus fall open to the charge of being "statists"? (1) Does it incorporate the understanding of subsidiarity found in Pius XI's "Reconstruction of the Social Order"as an emphasis on "No bigger than necessary"? (2) Does it promote an environment where people are important? (3) Does it give due weight to decision-making by smaller groups and by the poor themselves, whether at the local level or at higher levels?

On all three points the Pastoral is fully supportive of Catholic social thought on subsidiarity. Whatever may be the validity of Greeley's charges of inadequacies regarding the treatment of subsidiarity in the first draft, the subsequent drafts and especially the final document are very clear in their use of this principle.

1. Respect for Smallness

The two aspects of subsidiarity—doing and being—are substantially treated in the second, third and final drafts of the Pastoral. It may even

have been that Greeley's early challenge persuaded the drafters to aug-
ment explicit reference to the classic statement of subsidiarity found in
"Reconstruction of the Social Order" Here is the first appearance of four
in the Pastoral of that classis statement: "Just as it is gravely wrong to
take from individuals what they can accomplish on their own initiative
and industry and give it to the community, so also is it an injustice...to
assign to a greater and higher association what lesser and subordinate
organizations can do. For every social activity ought of its very nature to
furnish help [subsidium] to the members of the body social, and never
destroy or absorb them" (99).

The Bishops, in Chapter IV of the Pastoral, "The New American
Experiment: Partnership for the Public Good," note that three of the four
"partnerships" directly involve government (local/regional, national, and
international). But each of these endorsements of government action is
prefaced by an explicit statement of subsidiarity. For example, speaking of
local/regional cooperation, the document reads: "In the principle of subsidiarity, Catholic social teaching has long stressed the importance of
small and intermediate-sized communities or institutions exercising of
moral responsibility." (308) National cooperation is similarly introduced
by explicit statement of the subsidiarity principle that emphasizes what the
larger society must do: "The principle of subsidiarity calls for government
intervention when small or intermediate groups in society are unable or
unwilling to take the steps needed to promote basic justice"(314). The
principle gets the same treatment at the international level (323).

Earlier on, the Pastoral places heavy emphasis on the role of local
associations in support of "institutional pluralism" as creative of the
common good (100). This perspective then is applied to problems of
unemployment and poverty. Emphasis here is placed upon the individual
and small group that ought to be helped. The most appropriate programs
(government) for poverty are "those that enable people to take control of
their own lives" and "to help themselves" (188). Programs, therefore,
should be "small in scale, locally based and oriented toward empowering
the poor to become self-sufficient." (200) The section on unemployment
abundantly attests that for the Bishops the first line of action is to allow
the private sector to do as much as possible. Only after that is there a
place for the state, with the government supporting private efforts with
appropriate policy measures (154).

In short, the bipolarity—individual/intermediary groups on the one
side and state on the other—on which the Bishops rest their call for
action shows an eminently satisfactory understanding and practice of the
principle of subsidiarity.

2. An Environment That Respects People

The previous section stressed the Pastoral's bipolar treatment of government as helper of individuals and small groups to empower them to do

for themselves. But further attention needs to be paid to the aspect of being rather than doing. Greeley rightly observes that subsidiarity is based on being small, on an "environment where people matter," on "networks of cooperative relations and smaller organizations more generally—nothing bigger than necessary."

It is clearly the message of the Economic Pastoral that an environment must be created where people matter and where their contributions are seen to be building up a fruitful economy. Community is essential in the Bishops' perspective. The very first paragraph of the Pastoral says that "The economy is a human reality: men and women working together to develop and care for the whole of God's creation" (1). Again, people shape the economy and in turn are shaped by it (5). "Through hard work, self-sacrifice and cooperation, families have flourished; towns, cities and a powerful nation have been created" (6). In dealing with persons and institutions working for justice, the Bishops emphasize the U.S. economy has been built by the labor of human hands and minds. The economy is not a machine and "persons are not mere objects tossed about by economic forces"(96).

Thus the Pastoral frequently focuses on the individual as incorporated in local, intermediary societies which create that environment of smallness that is supportive of individuals. A strong example of this, of course, is the emphasis on the family (93).

3. Participation In Decision-making

The Bishops strongly emphasize the decision-making dimension of subsidiarity. This is abundantly evidenced in their section on "A New American Experiment: Partnership for the Public Good" (295-325). The Bishops note, for example, the aspect of empowering people to enter the decision-making process. On workplace cooperation the document calls for: "a new experiment in bringing democratic ideals to economic life" and "new patterns of partnership" (298). The call is made for "granting employees greater participation in determining the conditions of work" (300; see also 301-303).

The part of "A New American Experiment" called "Partnership in the Development of National Policies" is one more application of partnership with explicit or implicit share in decision-making. The Bishops see the need to "build new forms of effective citizenship and cooperation" (312). "The challenge of today is to move to creative ways of enabling government and private groups to work together effectively" (314). As for the economic planning which will proceed under guidance of the state, "Effective decisions in these matters will demand greater cooperation among all citizens" (317). Several other passages in this section serve only to confirm the strong role assigned to individuals, small groups, local entities and other intermediary groups in the process of decision-making.

Greeley viewed the Pastoral in the early draft as "statist," meaning that it gave too much role and power to the state (government) in fashioning and directing the economic life of society. This is viewed as akin to a tendency toward socialism. That judgment has been shared by many critics who have accused the Bishops of favoring "big government." But careful analysis of the final document simply does not support the charges either of statism or of failure to present properly the principle of subsidiarity.

III. ECONOMIC RIGHTS

Another central theme for both the Bishops and their critics is the issue of economic rights. For the Bishops, these "rights" are more than the business-type of economic rights such as the right of contract, the right of freedom to do business in other lands, the right to form free economic associations, etc. Rather, in the Pastoral Letter economic rights are rights to basic needs and to participation in the economy. Thus economic rights include the right to eat, to education, to a job, to a livable wage, to a safe and clean working environment, to health care, and to economic participation. These economic rights were introduced earlier as a norm for welfare in the chapter on Catholic social principles. Here two things need to be added: first, how the Bishops use economic rights in the Pastoral; and second, how the critics of economic rights are responded to.

1. The Pastoral's Use of Economic Rights

Early attacks did not deter the Bishops from retaining economic rights in the vocabulary of the Pastoral. In the final text, a long section is devoted to this topic (79-84). This begins with the assertion that the right to "fulfillment of material needs" is "not created by society" but is "bestowed by God and grounded in the nature and dignity of human persons" (79). The Pastoral cites approvingly John XXIII for having included economic rights in his enumeration of human rights in *Peace on Earth:* "A number of human rights also concern human welfare and are of a specifically economic nature. First among these are the rights to life, food, clothing, shelter, rest, medical care and basic education" (80).

Since in modern industrial societies these personal needs can be met normally only through remunerative work, there is also a right to such work. But some of these rights can only be attained through state intervention in some form of collective insurance, e.g. security in sickness, unemployment, old age. The possibility of such insurance becomes an economic empowerment (81). The Pastoral calls for positive action on the part of the state "to create the social and political institutions that enable all persons to become active members of society" (82).

Linking these social and economic rights to civil and political rights, the document asserts: "These fundamental personal rights...state the minimum conditions for social institutions that respect human dignity, social solidarity and justice" (80). While stressing economic rights, the Bishops in no way downplay the more traditional civil and political rights. All the Bishops ask for is a willingness to make the effort to meet these basic demands of justice and solidarity. The first step must be "development of a new cultural consensus that the basic economic conditions of human welfare are essential to human dignity and are due persons by right" (83). Economic rights must be seen to be as important as political rights.

2. Critics of Economic Rights

Michael Novak is a chief opponent of the concept of economic rights and his views are representative of the critiques made against the Pastoral's use of the term.[9] Novak argued that citizens in the United States are at different levels of discourse when they speak of civil and political rights on the one hand and social and economic rights on the other. To the former they accord an exalted status. Civil and political rights—e.g., right to free speech—are in the realm of the courts and the constitution. But this is not so with what some choose to call economic rights. For their part, the Bishops are prepared to accord economic rights the same reverence as political rights—on the basis that both stem equally, if differently, from the sanctity of human nature. For Novak, this is unacceptable, dangerous and un-American. Talk, he says, that elevates economic rights to the same level as civil and political rights pulls down the sanctity of what he calls the "American Proposition."

Another critic of this concept, former Secretary of Health, Education and Welfare, Joseph Califano, has made a similar argument: "The Constitution guarantees many precious rights—to speak and publish, to travel and worship—but it does not require that those rights be publicly funded. By contrast, the alleged new right to food empowers the state to see to it that every person does have food...And so with other welfare rights."[10]

The most serious charge made by Novak, however, is that by ignoring clear papal teaching in order to push economic rights the Bishops dangerously run the nation into the risky waters of excessive state intervention. Novak uses this dramatic language: "The extensive effort to commit the Church to 'economic rights' has the potential to become an error of classic magnitude. It might well position the Catholic Church in a preferential option for the state that will more than rival that of the Constantinian period."[11] This challenge received very wide coverage, becoming gospel truth for many of the critics of the Pastoral during its early drafting. Some felt that the Bishops would have to modify their position in the light of this sharp critique.

Novak begins his case against the Bishops with the assertion that the second draft (1985) misstates the teaching of John XXIII in *Peace on Earth*. According to the Bishops, a number of the rights mentioned in *Peace on Earth* are of a specifically economic nature, such as the rights to life, food, clothing, shelter, rest and medical care. But according to Novak, "this assertion will not be found in *Pacem in Terris [Peace on Earth]*.[12] He argues that where these rights are listed by John XXIII they are described, not as economic rights, but as "rights to life." Moreover, they are said to be a responsibility of government only when—here Novak quotes from *Peace on Earth*—"through no fault of their own some are incapable of having them realized."[13] He says further that where the Pope does address economic rights he does so in a section of the encyclical bearing the explicit title "Economic Rights."[14]

Clearly, concludes Novak, John XXIII intended a distinction between "economic rights" and "rights of life." The economic rights affirmed by the Pope are not the Bishops's assumed rights, but "the classically American" ones such as the right to initiative and enterprise, the right to (not be prevented from) work, the right to human working conditions, the right to private property. Moreover, unlike the rights to life listed in *Peace on Earth*—which are only for those who "through no fault of their own...are incapable of having them realized"—the economic rights listed in the encyclical are of universal coverage. These two sets of rights should not be confused.

The Bishops, however, were not impressed by Novak's argument. They strongly reiterated their position in the Pastoral's final text: "A number of human rights also concern human welfare and are of a specifically economic nature." And what are these? The very ones Novak claims cannot be economic rights: "First among these are the rights to life, food, clothing, shelter, rest, medical care and basic education" (80). These are said to belong to the "full range of human rights" enumerated by John XXIII, including "the civil and political rights to freedom of speech, worship and assembly" (80).

These economic rights, furthermore and in contradiction to Novak's position, "are empowerments that call for positive action by...society at large" (81). "Society at large" is made more specific: "the securing of these rights will make demands on...government." Toward realization of these economic rights there is a need for "a new cultural consensus" which will affirm that "the basic economic conditions of human welfare are essential to human dignity and due persons by right" (83). True, individual and private sector activity is also necessary. But government action is to be expected.

It is clear that the Bishops ignored Novak's strong disapproval of economic rights. Correctly so, since their position is not at all out of line with papal thought, specifically John XXIII's. To better appreciate the Bishops' use of the encyclical's treatment of economic rights, it is important to review carefully the case attempted by Novak. Because his critique is so strong against such a key teaching in the Pastoral—a teaching which has great significance for welfare—considerable attention needs to be paid to it.

First of all, whatever John XXIII had in mind as a situation in which persons were deprived of employment "through no fault of their own," he gave no specific example of such. Indeed, all his examples are cases not of personal fault and thus are covered by the right that the state will help to secure its citizens in such situations. These include "sickness, inability to work, widowhood, old age, unemployment." To this list, of those eligible for aid, the Pope adds "or in any other case in which persons are deprived of the means of subsistence through no fault of their own." Just how all-encompassing the list of those eligible now becomes is further seen if one reflects on all the types and situations of unemployment: frictional unemployment, cyclical unemployment, local plant closing, communities abandoned as industries flee to cheap labor markets, etc. Then, too, there is a wide range in the causes of inability to work: poor health, lack of education, inadequate training for new technologies, or simply a refusal because it is unacceptable to pull up stakes and seek work in another part of the country.

Next, Novak should not make so much of the title "Economic Rights" which introduces the English text of the encyclical's section (16-22). That title is not of the Pope's doing but is the work of the editor of the English edition. The official Latin text for that section, as it appears in the Vatican's official record, *Acta Apostolicae Sedis*, does not have this or any other sub-heading.[15]

Still more to the point is to compare the list of rights given in the encyclical in paragraph number 11—the "rights to life"—with those in paragraph numbers 18-22—the rights "in the economic sphere." From such a comparison it appears that, apart from the addition in the second set of the rights of initiative, enterprise, and property, the two lists correspond.[16] Both are substantively economic and both are to be guaranteed by the State.

Novak could draw some vindication from one difference in the two listings of rights in *Peace on Earth*. The first list, viewed by Novak as "rights to life," goes on in its enumeration of rights to embrace "necessary social services." These latter do not appear in the second list, viewed by Novak as "economic rights." Novak clearly had his eye on the rights of initiative, enterprise and property listed in numbers 18-22, while ignoring the rest of those paragraphs which parallel the rights listed in number 11. But with the exception of initiative, enterprise and property, the two lists of rights are substantially parallel. One can properly assume that "necessary social services"—government guaranteed security for individuals—applies to the second list as well as to the first.

That the rights are indeed parallel, including that of government guaranteed security, becomes most explicit in a later section of the encyclical to which, astonishingly, Novak makes no reference in any of his treatment of this topic. In a key section of *Peace on Earth*, John XXIII treats the role of the state in promoting what are precisely the economic rights noted by the Bishops.[17] "The whole reason for the existence of the state is the realization of the common good without preference for any single citizen or group," though "justice and equity can at times demand...more attention to the less fortunate." This common good embraces "the sum total of those conditions of social living whereby persons are able to achieve their own integral perfection more fully and more easily."

Linking the common good to rights, *Peace on Earth* emphasizes that the common good is chiefly guaranteed when personal rights and duties are maintained: "The chief concern of civil authority must be to ensure that those rights are acknowledged, respected, coordinated, defended and promoted." And lest one might imagine that this activity of government does not apply in the economic sphere, the encyclical asserts further the "obligation of civil authorities to take suitable action with regard to economic, political, cultural matters." To achieve this, the state must see to the creation of essential services—nine are mentioned.[18] It must also see to the existence of insurance and has further roles regarding employment and unemployment benefits. In still further ways the state will serve economic rights, including: wages, social benefits, health care, pension, old age insurance, etc., and "within the sphere of these principle rights a whole system of particular rights."

That Novak does not refer to this full and important discussion of economic rights in this later section of *Peace on Earth* is evidence of the shallowness of his charge that the Pastoral is out of line with papal teaching. Similarly weak is his complaint that the Bishops endorse the United Nations Universal Declaration of Human Rights, which contains economic rights. But here again the Bishops are in line with papal support of the UN Declaration. John XXIII in *Peace on Earth* had already made this point and John Paul II repeated it in his 1979 *Redeemer of Humankind*.[19] John Paul II returned to praise the United Nations for its initiative in describing economically-related human rights in his October 2, 1979 address to the 34th Session of the United Nations General Assembly. In that address, he treats on equal footing civil/political rights and economic/social rights. In listing rights "universally acknowledged," the Pope mixes together these two sets.

To sum up, rather than being outside the thrust of papal documents and other Church social teaching with regard to economic rights, the Economic Pastoral is fully within the mainstream. How the United States will view economic rights and whether they are to occupy the same position as civil and political rights are among the crucial questions seeking answer in coming decades.

IV. ECONOMIC DEMOCRACY

Sometime during the preparation of the Pastoral, Archbishop Weakland remarked that the heart of the document is "economic democracy." With that achieved, Weakland asserted, the people of the United States will have matched our political democracy. This use of the term "economic democracy" raised a tremendous furor in more conservative Catholic circles. For many, the term is nearly synonymous with "socialism."

Once again, Michael Novak was a principle spokesperson for the critics. For example, in a debate with former Congressman Robert Drinan, Novak made these strong remarks about economic democracy: "Explain why they [the Bishops] use Tom Hayden and Jane Fonda's slogan 'economic democracy'? There's a program attached to that. Do they buy the whole program? Or do they mean what Olaf Palme, the Swedish socialist, meant by it? He's been arguing for 15 years and he says exactly what the Bishops say."[20]

Concerned that use of the language of economic democracy would, in the eyes of many, prejudice what they wanted to say about the fullest possible economic participation at every level, the Bishops chose to omit the phrase from subsequent drafts. But it is very clear that they in no way pulled back from the fullness of content that the term "economic democracy" had for them.

Here is the original language of the first draft (November, 1984); it is prefaced by pointing out the greatness of the U.S. achievement in establishing the concept of political rights for all. "We believe the time has come for a similar experiment in economic democracy: the creation of an order that guarantees the minimum conditions of human dignity in the economic sphere for every person" (1st draft, 89). This, the Bishops add, would be the topic of a later section on the "New American Experiment."

Just why such strong and fearful reaction should have been generated by this language is not easy to understand. What could be wrong or threatening with the simple proposition: the United States has achieved, even if imperfectly, political democracy; now let's begin to work on the same fullness of participation for everyone in the economic field. Whatever might be meant by the term "economic democracy," it is clear that for the Bishops it meant nothing more than full participation in economic life, something that also entails participation in decision-making at all levels.

Note the language introducing the same idea in the Pastoral's final draft: "The nation's founders took daring steps to create structures of participation, mutual accountability and widely distributed power to ensure the political rights and freedoms of all. We believe that similar steps are needed today to expand economic participation, broaden the sharing of economic power and make economic decisions more accountable to the common good" (297). There certainly has been no "watering down" of the commitment to economic democracy.

Toward this economic empowerment of all, the Bishops propose "The New American Experiment." At the level of the local work place this calls for a new partnership between workers and managers, cooperation of all in discovering new businesses and new jobs, and such standard items of Catholic tradition as sharing in management, profits or stock. Within industries and plants collective bargaining—again very traditional Catholic teaching—should be less adversarial. Further, there should be reduction of power exclusively or disproportionately possessed by one group, e.g., a group whose power renders it immune from sharing sacrifices in plant closures (303). What will efforts at more democratic participation in the economy amount to at the national level? The Pastoral suggests the cooperation of individuals and groups along with government in the development of national policies.

It is at this point of the discussion, perhaps, that there occurs one element which could conceivably generate conservative fears. This is the urging that "society make provision for overall planning" in the economic domain (315). The Pastoral notes that those words are borrowed from John Paul II.[21] It adds: "The Pope's words cannot be construed as an endorsement of a highly centralized form of economic planning, much less a totalitarian one" (316). It is a question, rather, of "a just and rational coordination" of the endeavors of many economic actors to create new forms of partnership and participation in shaping national economic policies. Planning does exist. The challenge is to make sure that it is planning begun and carried through democratically, with the full and effective participation of all those involved.

The four philosophical/theological principles examined in this chapter—option for the poor, subsidiarity, economic rights, and economic democracy—provide a solid foundation for the Economic Pastoral's positions on welfare. Criticism of these principles has usually been based on a mis-reading of the text, a mis-interpretation of the tradition, and/or a distaste for the consequences. The Bishops have contributed significantly to the welfare debate in the United States by being so straightforward in the Pastoral Letter about the principles which guide them.

ENDNOTES FOR CHAPTER X

[1] See, e.g., Latin America's 1968 Medellin Conference and its 1979 Puebla Conference. Both of these meetings are examined in Chapter VIII.

[2] *Justice in the World*, 31 ff.

[3] The Pastoral Message is a separate and independent section of 29 paragraphs, introducing the themes of the Pastoral Letter.

[4] *Peace on Earth*, 56.

[5] See G. J. Duncan et al., *Years of Poverty, Years of Plenty: The Changing Economic Fortunes of American Workers and their Families* (Ann Arbor: Institute for Social Research, University of Michigan, 1984).

[6] *America*, September 21, 1985.

[7] *Call to Action*, 23.

[8] *America*, November 9, 1985.

[9] "Economic Rights: The Servile State," in *Catholicism in Crisis*, October, 1985.

[10] *America*, January 5-12, 1985.

[11] Novak, loc. cit. Novak has other arguments against economic rights. For example, whereas the recognition by government of political and civil rights does not entail monetary costs, economic rights will impose financial burdens on the state and on citizens in the form of higher taxes.

[12] Ibid.

[13] Peace on Earth, 11.

[14] Ibid., 18-22.

[15] LV, No. 4, (April 20, 1963), 257-304.

[16] The "rights to life" of no. 11 are first, bodily integrity, means to life (food, clothes, shelter, rest, medical care), and second, necessary social services to provide security against sickness, inability to work, widowhood, old age, unemployment, or "other cases."

The rights "in the economic sphere" of nos. 18-22 embrace working conditions in which physical health is not endangered and in which morals are safeguarded and the normal development of young people is not impaired. In addition, women must have working conditions which respect their duties as wives and mothers. Most important is to compare the next right with those listed in no. 11. This is the right to a just wage, described as one giving workers and their families the provisions for a standard of living in keeping with human dignity. This surely must be equated with all the rights listed in no. 11.

17 *Peace on Earth*, 63-65.

18 Here is the full listing from the encyclical (64) of economic activities on the part of government missed by Novak:

It is therefore necessary that the administration give wholehearted and careful attention to the social as well as to the economic progress of citizens, and to the development, in keeping with the development of the productive system, of such essential services as the building of roads, transportation, communications, water supply, housing, public health, education, facilitation of the practice of religion, and recreational facilities. It is necessary also that governments make efforts to see that insurance systems are made available to the citizens, so that, in case of misfortune or increased family responsibilities, no person will be without the necessary means to maintain a decent standard of living.

The government should make similarly effective efforts to see that those who are able to work can find employment in keeping with their aptitudes, and that each worker receives a wage in keeping with the laws of justice and equality. It should be equally the concern of civil authorities to insure that workers be allowed their proper responsibility in the work undertaken in industrial organization, and to facilitate the establishment of intermediate groups which will make social life richer and more effective. Finally, it should be possible for all citizens to share as far as they are able in their country's cultural advantages.

19 In Latin, *Divini Redemptoris*, 1979.

20 "The American Debate," transcript (Washington D.C.: Roosevelt Center for American Studies, no date).

21 *On Human Work*, 18.

POSTSCRIPT

In this postscript I want to introduce an element of the current welfare debate which, however important, did not seem necessary to the main lines of this book. Still, it is extremely significant within the fullness of the welfare debate—or debates. This concerns a choice to be made between reforms—"first-best" and "second-best"—on the one hand, and transformation or decisive alternatives on the other. I hinted at the importance of this discussion in my Introduction.

The Reform Debate

An understanding of the debate over welfare reform has already been developed in the preceding chapters. I cited, for instance, M.I.T.'s Lester Thurow as an authority who illustrates well the terms of the reform debate. The "first-best" solution to poverty, Thurow argues, is through income earned by employment. "Second-best" is through transfer of income by government programs, e.g., AFDC payments, food stamps, unemployment insurance and the like.

The "first-best" approach pushes for full employment, and that at wages and hours that lift workers and their families above the poverty line. The hope expressed in this approach is that adequate wage-income—and here government would have its role, e.g., minimum wage requirements—would obviate all need for welfare, except for rare cases requiring safety-net treatment.

Unfortunately, the reality of our industrial world, enmeshed as it is in world competition, is one of recurring, even deepening unemployment with each successive recession. It is true that there currently is a moment of sharply falling unemployment rates. The actual dollar-value of much of the new employment is certainly subject to question. But the mood of many in the United States is one of questioning whether the U.S. may not in fact face a future of falling out of first-class world competition and into deeper unemployment, or of creating new jobs, many of which provide inadequate incomes. (The fact of a declining number of "baby boomers" entering the workforce can be supposed eventually to ease pressure on the job market. Indeed, there is even the eventual prospect that a smaller supply of workers will push wages up.)

Another reality is the rapid rise of the number of singles, especially women, in U.S. society. Perhaps under ideal conditions within an industrial order, families could take care of all their needs, present and future. But in the social reality of the century coming up, an appalling number of women, in particular, will live at or below the poverty line. There is no obvious possibility of their taking care of all their future needs—even through whatever insurance may be available to them.

But to return to the employment picture as currently experienced more generally, the immediate prospect remains that of adopting programs which correct for unemployment or employment at less that adequate incomes. Accordingly, it will be necessary to make do with "second-best" solutions—even while working for "first-best." But lets's not deceive ourselves. "First-best" will never be universally attainable, and therefore we shall still need "second-best."

The Alternative Transformation

This sub-title combines two schools of opposition to any reform, be it "second-best" or "first-best" or whatever. For the transformation school, reform is rejected because it does not get down to radical change. However deep-going the reform, it is alleged to stick within the system. The call therefore is for transformation in order to move away from the existing order to another very different form. The alternative school says further that this transformation must itself be guided by a new vision and a new philosophy of the human.

Before turning to the alternative transformation version which rejects the industrial order, it is necessary to explore the proposition that welfare and welfare reform presuppose the continuance of the present industrial order—indeed, are substantial sustainers of it. To begin with, the welfare function of the state presumes no particular ideology: not capitalist, not marxist, not socialist. But it does presume an advanced industrial order with all its complexities of alternating swings of recession and prosperity, cycles of full employment and underemployment and unemployment, unfortunate victims of the system, inadequate income to carry one through retirement and old-age, etc. Welfare supposes that all that is inevitable in the system of the industrial order. But in addition, it supposes a necessary role of the state in correcting and compensating for the failures and inadequacies of the system.

Welfare reform thus acts upon the system, ameliorating its operation. It is not necessary to recall the several reforms discussed in the preceding chapters. Suffice it here to observe that the U.S. Catholic Bishops Economic Pastoral, despite its insightful probing for new ideas in the chapter on "The New-American Experiment," is substantially a reform program.

In contrast to this stands the alternative transformation program which calls for rejection of the system, however reformed. Thus, to take just one example of rejected reform, welfare assistance introduced to compensate for market failures is rejected because—according to this school of radical transformation—it inevitably brings in its wake a degrading and unacceptable dependency. Moreover the system, no matter how much reformed, will never embody a truly human vision of work and earning a living.

What would an alternative transformation vision of the new economy embrace? First, negatively, it would turn its back on the prevailing Newtonian mechanistic model that permeates the current industrial order. Indeed, this particular approach finds exceedingly transformative in physics the gradual erosion of the dominance of the Newtonian model and therefore its application to the economy in terms, for example, of the "natural laws" of the market.

Economics in the alternative transformation vision would be returned to what the original Greek entails: "oikos" standing for house and "nomos" for ordering—in a word, household management. Hence economics must function "as if people mattered" and—extending the meaning of household—"as if community mattered."

Another aspect of this vision adds in its embrace "as if earth mattered." That is, the economy should be regenerative. Not simply productive or generative, this transformed economy brings new, renewed energies into the human community and into the earth community, and weds these two together in creative symbiosis. Such an economic order will be celebrative of hope, life, matter, spirit, energy, earth. It will seek to carry into human life and work the alternating rhythm in nature of activity and repose.

An emphasis on economics as household management also suggests the "small," a theme explored earlier in Chapter X in the discussion of suubsidiarity. This emphasis includes small work places, work in homes, cooperatives, local farming and produce markets, small or appropriate technology. This concept is, of course, cogently presented in E. F. Schumacher's Small is Beautiful and in the vast exploration of and experimentation with Schumacher's seminal ideas by others in many different parts of the globe.

Linked in the vision to the regenerative is the feminist. This perspective challenges male, patriarchal, aggressive competitiveness, and the ensuing climbing over those in the way in the ragged scramble to get to the top. By contrast, the feminine principle emphasizes caring, respect, cooperation and mutuality. This has important consequences for the economic order.

Some feminists may rightly be concerned that my emphasis on the "household" dimension of economics might suggest that women's place is in the home. Their concern would certainly be justified, if this indeed were my thrust. But I have no intention at all to so limit women that those working outside the home get defined in terms of lacking the completeness of the home-making woman. That caution taken, it can still be recognized that women bring to home-making and community building the regenerative forces so greatly needed today, and so central to the alternative transformation vision.

What, then, would an alternative to welfare look like? I know no place where this is adequately spelled out. Certainly, it would build on the elements of the new economic order just described. It would have analogical relation to what has been described in other fields, for example, alternative medicine with its stress on health-creation rather than sickness-repairing. The alternative to welfare would look to the wholeness of the subject, in particular women and children.

The alternative would also have an important dimension of "as if community mattered." This would suggest that the community could find within itself sufficient resources to care for the many needs which are currently shifted to governmental and other agencies. This offers significant possibilities of de-centralization. One thinks of communities caring for the children of working mothers. Or of community organization of home visits to the elderly, preparing meals for them, accompanying then to doctors, etc. Experiments already abound of community-financing of cooperative projects. Many churches and religious congregations are now devoting part of their portfolios to encourage such community ventures.

Alternative thinkers have noted that communities across the Third World had the experience of being able to care for their people before the destructive advent of the colonizers. Get the neo-colonizers with their cultural and industrial impositions out for once and for all, and the Third World might be able to replicate that earlier experience of providing a living and security for their people. And this would provide wonderful instruction for First World societies.

Such sweeping alternatives are not the stuff of the Bishops Economic Pastoral. From their perspective, the Bishops felt that in endorsing the family farm, cooperatives, more local initiative and workplace democracy they were going about as far as they dared—or cared—to go. Any more radical ideas would draw from already hostile critics the heavy charge of "Utopianism." Had the Bishops pursued any such line of alternative transformation, their Pastoral would simply have been consigned to oblivion.

Conclusion

By way of conclusion, I have two statements to make—statements which may seem to go in opposite directions. First, the alternative transformation approach does indicate seeds of change and glimpses of a future that should be respected. Pursuing the vision offered in this approach within the Christian community can be considered an exercise in the "forward-looking imagination" that Paul VI summons us to in his 1971 "Call to Action" (37). There indeed will be significant gains ahead for alternative transformation thinking and acting. This will have substantial consequences for the welfare debate.

Second, however, I return to my ambivalence about the long-term reality of the industrial society. It is hoped that the current economic order will be reshaped. But generations ahead will, at least in the industrial countries, have to live and work within that economic order—even as many will be seeking to transform it. That long-term reality will entail all the problems which have been surveyed in these pages: pockets of deep poverty, serious unemployment, jobs with inadequate income, persistently high inequalities of income, and so forth.

For the foreseeable future, these problems will have to be met within a welfare system. What kind of welfare system is the focus of the serious moral and political debate in which the citizens of the United States must engage. What can be recognized now more clearly is that the U.S. Catholic Bishops, in writing their Pastoral Letter "Economic Justice for All", have opened space for a more worthwhile welfare debate. Extreme conservatives had viewed the debate as closed and were determined that it should remain closed. But the substantial contribution of the Bishops to the emerging welfare consensus has assured a keen awareness of the poor, a sensitive commitment to the dignity of all people, and a strong appreciation of the positive role of the state.

In the administration of the new U.S. president to be inaugurated in 1989, the welfare debate will continue. The Bishops' Economic Pastoral has contributed in significant fashion to that debate and to the political action which must necessarily follow if our nation is to deal with our needy sisters and brothers.

APPENDIX

The discussion of welfare and the role of the state by the Bishops' Pastoral Letter, "Economic Justice for All: Catholic Social Teaching and the U.S. Economy" is found principally in two places. First, in Chapter 3, "Selected Economic Policy Issues," the Bishops explore the topics of employment (136-169) and poverty (170-215). Second, in Chapter 4, "A New American Experiment: Partnership for the Public Good," they examine cooperation at the levels of business and local, regional and national communities (295-321).

To assist the reader of this study, these pertinent sections of the Economic Pastoral are reprinted here.

CHAPTER III

SELECTED ECONOMIC POLICY ISSUES

A. Employment

136. Full employment is the foundation of a just economy. The most urgent priority for domestic economic policy is the creation of new jobs with adequate pay and decent working conditions. We must make it possible as a nation for every one who is seeking a job to find employment within a reasonable amount of time. Our emphasis on this goal is based on the conviction that human work has a special dignity and is a key to achieving justice in society.

137.Employment is a basic right, a right which protects the freedom of all to partici- pate in the economic life of society. It is a right which flows from the principles of jus- tice which we have outlined above. Corresponding to this right is the duty on the part of society to ensure that the right is protected. The importance of this right is evident in the fact that for most people employment is crucial to self-realization and essential to the ful- fillment of material needs. Since so few in our economy own productive property, employment also forms the first line of defense against poverty. Jobs benefit society as well as workers, for they enable more people to contribute to the common good and to the productivity required for a healthy economy.

1. The Scope and Effects of Unemployment

138. Joblessness is becoming a more widespread and deep-seated problem in our nation. There are about 8 million people in the United States looking for a job who cannot find one. They represent about 7 percent of the labor force. The official rate of unemployment does not include those who have given up looking for work or those who are working part-time, but want to work full-time. When these categories are added, it becomes clear that about one-eighth of the workforce is directly affected by unemployment. The severity of the unemployment problem is compounded by the fact that almost three-fourths of those who are unemployed receive no unemployment insurance benefits.

139. In recent years there has been a steady trend toward higher and higher levels of unemployment, even in good times. Between 1950 and 1980 the annual unemployment rate exceeded current levels only during the recession years of 1975 and 1976. Periods of economic recovery during these three decades brought unemployment rates down to 3 and 4 percent. Since 1979, however, the rate has generally been above 7 percent.

140. Who are the unemployed? Blacks, Hispanics, Native Americans, young adults, female heads of households, and those who are inadequately educated are represented disproportionately among the ranks of the unemployed. The unemployment rate among minorities is almost twice as high as the rate among whites. For female heads of households the unemployment rate is over 10 percent. Among black teenagers, unemployment reaches the scandalous rate of more than one in three.

141. The severe human costs of high unemployment levels become vividly clear when we examine the impact of joblessness on human lives and human dignity. It is a deep conviction of American culture that work is central to the freedom and well-being of people. The unemployed often come to feel they are worthless and without a productive role in society. Each day they are unemployed our society tells them: We don't need your talent. We don't need your initiative. We don't need you. Unemployment takes a terrible toll on the health and stability of both individuals and families. It gives rise to family quarrels, greater consumption of alcohol, child abuse, spouse abuse, divorce, and higher rates of infant mortality. People who are unemployed often feel that society blames them for being unemployed. Very few people survive long periods of unemployment without some psychological damage even if they have sufficient funds to meet their needs. At the extreme, the strains of job loss may drive individuals to suicide.

142. In addition to the terrible waste of individual talent and creativity, unemployment also harms society at large. Jobless people pay little or no taxes, thus lowering the revenues for cities, states, and the federal government. At the same time, rising unemployment requires greater expenditures for unemployment compensation, food stamps, welfare, and other assistance. It is estimated that in 1986, for every one percentage point increase in the rate of unemployment, there will be roughly a $40 billion increase in the federal deficit. The costs to society are also evident in the rise in crime associated with joblessness. The Federal Bureau of Prisons reports that increases in unemployment have been followed by increases in the prison population. Other studies have shown links between the rate of joblessness and the frequency of homicides, robberies, larcenies, narcotics arrests, and youth crimes.

143. Our own experiences with the individuals, families, and communities that suffer the burdens of unemployment compel us to the conviction that as nation we simply cannot afford to have millions o able-bodied men and women unemployed. We cannot afford the economic costs, the social dislocation, and the enormous human tragedies caused by unemployment. In the end, however, what we can least afford is the assault on human dignity that occurs when millions are left without adequate employment. Therefore, we cannot but conclude that current levels of unemployment are intolerable, and they impose on us a moral obligation to work for policies that will reduce joblessness.

2. Unemployment in a Changing Economy

144. The structure of the U.S. economy is undergoing a transformation that affects both the quantity and the quality of jobs in our nation. The size and makeup of the workforce, for example, have changed markedly in recent years. For a number of reasons, there are now more people in the labor market than ever before in our history. Population growth has pushed up the supply of potential workers. In addition, large numbers of women have entered the labor force not only in order to put their talents and education to greater use, but also out of economic necessity. Many families need two salaries if they are to live in a decently human fashion. Female-headed households often depend heavily on the mother's income to stay off the welfare rolls. Immigrants seeking a better existence in the United States have also added to the size of the labor force. These demographic changes, however, cannot fully explain the higher levels of unemployment.

145. Technological changes are also having dramatic impacts on the employment picture in the United States. Advancing technology brings many benefits, but it can also bring social and economic costs, including the downgrading and displacement of workers. High technology and advanced automation are changing the very face of our nation's industries and occupations. In the 1970s, about 90 percent of all new jobs were in service occupations. By 1990, service industries are expected to employ 72 percent of the labor force. Much of the job growth in the 1980s is expected to be in traditionally low-paying, high-turnover jobs such as sales, clerical, janitorial, and food service. Too often these jobs do not have career ladders leading to higher skilled, higher paying jobs. Thus, the changing industrial and occupational mix in the U.S. economy could result in a shift toward lower paying and lower skilled jobs.

146. Increased competition in world markets is another factor influencing the rate of joblessness in our nation. Many other exporting nations have acquired and developed up-to-the-minute technology, enabling them to increase productivity dramatically. Combined with very low wages in many nations, this has allowed them to gain a larger share of the U.S. market to cut into U.S. export markets. At the same time many corporations have closed plants in the United States and moved their capital, technology, and jobs to foreign affiliates.

147. Discrimination in employment is one of the causes for high rates of joblessness and low pay among racial minorities and women. Beyond the normal problems of locating a job, blacks, Hispanics, Native Americans, immigrants, and other minorities bear this added burden of discrimination. Discrimination against women is compounded by the lack of adequate child care services and by the unwillingness of many employers to provide flexible employment or extend fringe benefits to part-time employees.

148. High levels of defense spending also have an effect on the number of jobs in our economy. In our pastoral letter, The Challenge of Peace, we noted the serious economic distortions caused by the arms race and the disastrous effects that it has on society's ability to care for the poor and the needy. Employment is one area in which this interconnection is very evident. The hundreds of billions of dollars spent by our nation each year on the arms race create a massive drain on the U.S. economy as well as a very serious "brain drain." Such spending on the arms race means a net loss in the number of jobs created in the economy, because defense industries are less labor-intensive than other major sectors of the economy. Moreover, nearly half of the American scientific and engineering force works in defense-related programs and over 60 percent of the entire federal research and development budget goes to the military. We must ask whether our nation will ever be able to modernize our economy and achieve full employment if we continue to devote so much of our financial and human resources to defense-related activities.

149. These are some of the factors that have driven up the rate of unemployment in recent years. Although our economy has created more than 20 million new jobs since 1970, there continues to be a chronic and growing job shortage. In the face of this challenge, our nation's economic institutions have failed to adapt adequately and rapidly

enough. For example, failure to invest sufficiently in certain industries and regions, inadequate education and training for new workers, and insufficient mechanisms to assist workers displaced by new technology' have added to the unemployment problem.

150. Generating an adequate number of jobs in our economy is a complex task in view of the changing and diverse nature of the problem. It involves numerous trade-offs and substantial costs. Nevertheless, it is not an impossible task. Achieving the goal of full employment may require major adjustments and creative strategies that go beyond the limits of existing policies and institutions, but it is a task we must undertake.

3. Guidelines for Action

151. We recommend that the nation make a major new commitment to achieve full employment. At present there is nominal endorsement of the full employment ideal, but no firm commitment to bringing it about. If every effort were now being made to create the jobs required, one might argue that the situation today is the best we can do. But such is not the case. The country is doing far less than it might to generate employment.

152. Over the last decade, economists, policy makers, and the general public have shown greater willingness to tolerate unemployment levels of 6 to 7 percent or even more. Although we recognize the complexities and trade-offs involved in reducing unemployment, we believe that 6 to 7 percent unemployment is neither inevitable nor acceptable. While a zero unemployment rate is clearly impossible in an economy where people are constantly entering the job market and others are changing jobs, appropriate policies and concerted private and public action can improve the situation considerably, if we have the will to do so. No economy can be considered truly healthy when so many millions of people are denied jobs by forces outside their control. The acceptance of present unemployment rates would have been unthinkable twenty years ago. It should be regarded as intolerable today.

153. We must first establish a consensus that everyone has a right to employment. Then the burden of securing full employment falls on all of us-policy makers, business, labor, and the general public-to create and implement the mechanisms to protect that right. We must work for the formation of a new national consensus and mobilize the necessary political will at all levels to make the goal of full employment a reality.

154. Expanding employment in our nation will require significant steps in both the private and public sectors, as well as joint action between them. Private initiative and entrepreneurship are essential to this task, for the private sector accounts for about 80 percent of the jobs in the United States, and most new jobs are being created there. Thus, a viable strategy for employment generation must assume that a large part of the solution will be with private firms and small businesses. At the same time, it must be recognized that government has a prominent and indispensable role to play in addressing the problem of unemployment. The market alone will not automatically produce full employment. Therefore, the government must act to ensure that this goal is achieved by coordinating general economic policies, by job creation programs, and by other appropriate policy measures.

155. Effective action against unemployment will require a careful mix of general economic policies and targeted employment programs. Taken together, these policies and programs should have full employment as their number one goal.

a. General Economic Policies

156. The general or macroeconomic policies of the federal government are essential tools for encouraging the steady economic growth that produces more and better jobs in the economy. We recommend that the fiscal and monetary policies of the nation-such as federal spending, tax, and interest rate policies-should be coordinated so as to achieve the goal of full employment.

157. General economic policies that attempt to expand employment must also deal with the problem of inflation. The risk of inflationary pressures resulting from such expansionary policies is very real. Our response to this risk, however, must not be to abandon the goal of full employment, but to develop effective policies that keep inflation under control.

158. While economic growth is an important and necessary condition for the reduction of unemployment, it is not sufficient in and of itself. In order to work for full employment and restrain inflation, it is also necessary to adopt more specific programs and policies targeted toward particular aspects of the unemployment problem.

b. Targeted Employment Programs

159. (1) We recommend expansion of job-training and apprenticeship programs in the private sector administered and supported jointly by business, labor unions, and government. Any comprehensive employment strategy must include systematic means of developing the technical and professional skills needed for a dynamic and productive economy. Investment in a skilled work force is a prerequisite both for sustaining economic growth and achieving greater justice in the United States. The obligation to contribute to this investment falls on both the private and public sectors. Today business, labor, and government need to coordinate their efforts and pool their resources to promote a substantial increase in the number of apprenticeship programs and to expand on-the-job training programs. We recommend a national commitment to eradicate illiteracy and to provide people with the skills necessary to adapt to the changing demands of employment.

160. With the rapid pace of technological change, continuing education and training are even more important today than in the past. Businesses have a stake in providing it, for skilled workers are essential to increased productivity. Labor unions should support it, for their members are increasingly vulnerable to displacement and job loss unless they continue to develop their skills and their flexibility on the job. Local communities have a stake as well, for their economic well-being will suffer serious harm if local industries fail to develop and are forced to shut down.

161. The best medicine for the disease of plant closings is prevention. Prevention depends not only on sustained capital investment to enhance productivity through advanced technology but also on the training and retraining of workers within the private sector. In circumstances where plants are forced to shut down, management, labor unions, and local communities must see to it that workers are not simply cast aside. Retraining programs will be even more urgently needed in these circumstances.

162. (2) We recommend increased support for direct job creation programs targeted on the long-term unemployed and those with special needs. Such programs can take the form of direct public service employment and also of public subsidies for employment in the private sector. Both approaches would provide jobs for those with low skills less expensively and with less inflation than would general stimulation of the economy. The cost of providing jobs must also be balanced against the savings realized by the government through decreased welfare and unemployment insurance expenditures and increased revenues from the taxes paid by the newly employed.

163. Government funds, if used effectively, can also stimulate private sector jobs for the long-term unemployed and for groups particularly hard to employ. Experiments need to be conducted on the precise ways such subsidies would most successfully attract business participation and ensure the generation of permanent jobs.

164. These job generation efforts should aim specifically at bringing marginalized persons into the labor force. They should produce a net increase in the number of jobs rather than displacing the burden of unemployment from one group of persons to another. They should also be aimed at long-term jobs and should include the necessary supportive services to assist the unemployed in finding and keeping jobs.

165. Jobs that are created should produce goods and services needed and valued by society. It is both good common sense and sound economics to create jobs directly for the purpose of meeting society's unmet needs. Across the nation, in every state and locality, there is ample evidence of social needs that are going unmet. Many of our parks and recreation facilities are in need of maintenance and repair. Many of the nation's bridges and highways are in disrepair. We have a desperate need for more low-income housing. Our educational systems, day-care services, senior citizen services, and other community programs need to be expanded. These and many other elements of our national life are areas of unmet need. At the same time, there are more than 8 million Americans looking for productive and useful work. Surely we have the capacity to match these needs by giving Americans who are anxious to work a chance for productive employment in jobs that are waiting to be done. The overriding moral value of enabling jobless persons to achieve a new sense of dignity and personal worth through employment also strongly recommends these programs.

166. These job creation efforts will require increased collaboration and fresh alliances between the private and public sectors at all levels. There are already a number of examples of how such efforts can be successful. We believe that the potential of these kinds of partnerships has only begun to be tapped.

c. Examining New Strategies

167. In addition to the actions suggested above, we believe there is also a need for careful examination and experimentation with alternative approaches that might improve both the quantity and quality of jobs. More extensive use of job sharing, flex time, and a reduced work week are among the topics that should continue to be on the agenda of public discussion. Consideration should also be given to the possibility of limiting or abolishing compulsory overtime work. Similarly, methods might be examined to discourage the overuse of part-time workers, who do not receive fringe benefits. New strategies also need to be explored in the area of education and training for the hard-to-employ, displaced workers, the handicapped, and others with special needs. Particular attention is needed to achieve pay equity between men and women, as well as upgrading the pay scale and working conditions of traditionally low-paying jobs. The nation should renew its efforts to develop effective affirmative action policies that assist those who have been excluded by racial or sexual discrimination in the past. New strategies for improving job placement services at the national and local levels are also needed. Improving occupational safety is another important concern that deserves increased attention.

168. Much greater attention also needs to be devoted to the long-term task of converting some of the nation's military production to more peaceful and socially productive purposes. The nation needs to seek more effective ways to retool industries, to retrain workers, and to provide the necessary adjustment assistance for communities affected by this kind of economic conversion.

169. These are among the avenues that need to be explored in the search for just employment policies. A belief in the inherent dignity of human work and in the right to employment should motivate people in all sectors of society to carry on that search in new and creative ways.

B. Poverty

170. More than 33 million Americans-about one in every seven people in our nation-are poor by the government's official definition. The norms of human dignity and the preferential option for the poor compel us to confront this issue with a sense of urgency. Dealing with poverty is not a luxury to which our nation can attend when it finds the time and resources. Rather, it is a moral imperative of the highest priority.

171. Of particular concern is the fact that poverty has increased dramatically during the last decade. Since 1973 the poverty rate has increased by nearly a third. Although the recent recovery has brought a slight decline in the rate, it remains at a level that is higher than at almost any other time during the last two decades.

172. As pastors we have seen firsthand the faces of poverty in our midst. Homeless people roam city streets in tattered clothing and sleep in doorways or on subway grates at night. Many of these are former mental patients released from state hospitals. Thousands stand in line at soup kitchens because they have no other way of feeding themselves. Millions of children are so poorly nourished that their physical and mental development are seriously harmed. We have also seen the growing economic hardship and insecurity experienced by moderate-income Americans when they lose their jobs and their income due to forces beyond their control. These are alarming signs and trends. They pose for our nation an urgent moral and human challenge: to fashion a society where no one goes without the basic material necessities required for human dignity and growth.

173. Poverty can be described and defined in many different ways. It can include spiritual as well as material poverty. Likewise, its meaning changes depending on the historical, social, and economic setting. Poverty in our time is different from the more severe deprivation experienced in earlier centuries in the U.S. or in Third World nations today. Our discussion of poverty in this chapter is set within the context of present-day American society. By poverty, we are referring here to the lack of sufficient material resources required for a decent life. We use the government's official definition of poverty, although we recognize its limits.

1. Characteristics of Poverty

174. Poverty is not an isolated problem existing solely among a small number of anonymous people in our central cities. Nor is it limited to a dependent underclass or to specific groups in the United States. It is a condition experienced at some time by many people in different walks of life and in different circumstances. Many poor people are working but at wages insufficient to lift them out of poverty. Others are unable to work and therefore dependent on outside sources of support. Still others are on the edge of poverty; although not officially defined as poor, they are economically insecure and at risk of falling into poverty.

175. While many of the poor manage to escape from beneath the official poverty line, others remain poor for extended periods of time. Long-term poverty is concentrated among racial minorities and families headed by women. It is also more likely to be found in rural areas and in the South. Of the long-term poor, most are either working at wages too low to bring them above the poverty line or are retired, disabled, or parents of preschool children. Generally they are not in a position to work more hours than they do now.

a. Children in Poverty

176. Poverty strikes some groups more severely than others. Perhaps most distressing is the growing number of children who are poor. Today one in every four American children under the age of six, and one in every two black children under six, are poor. The number of children in poverty rose by four million over the decade between 1973 and 1983, with the result that there are now more poor children in the United Stated than at any time since 1965. The problem is particularly severe among female-headed families, where more than half of all children are poor. Two-thirds of black children and nearly three-quarters of Hispanic children in such families are poor.

177. Very many poor families with children receive no government assistance, have no health insurance, and cannot pay medical bills. Less than half are immunized against preventable diseases such as diphtheria and polio. Poor children are disadvantaged even before birth, their mothers' lack of access to high quality prenatal care leaves them at

much greater risk of premature birth, low-birth weight, physical and mental impairment, and death before their first birthday.

b. Women and Poverty

178. The past twenty years have witnessed a dramatic increase in the number of women in poverty. This includes women raising children alone as well as women with inadequate income following divorce, widowhood, or retirement. More than one-third of all female-headed families are poor. Among minority families headed by women the poverty rate is over 50 percent.

179. Wage discrimination against women is a major factor behind these high rates of poverty. Many women are employed but remain poor because their wages are too low. Women who work outside their homes full-time and year-round earn only 61 percent of what men earn. Thus, being employed full-time is not by itself a remedy for poverty among women. Hundreds of thousands of women hold full-time jobs but are still poor. Sixty percent of all women work in only ten occupations, and most new jobs for women are in areas with low pay and limited chances of advancement. Many women suffer discrimination in wages, salaries, job classifications, promotions, and other areas. As a result, they find themselves in jobs that have low status, little security, weak unionization, and few fringe benefits. Such discrimination is immoral and efforts must be made to overcome the effects of sexism in our society.

180. Women's responsibilities for childrearing are another important factor to be considered. Despite the many changes in marriage and family life in recent decades, women continue to have primary responsibility in this area. When marriages break up, mothers typically take custody of the children and bear the major financial responsibility for supporting them. Women often anticipate that they will leave the labor force to have and raise children, and often make job and career choices accordingly. In other cases they are not hired or promoted to higher paying jobs because of their childrearing responsibilities. In addition, most divorced or separated mothers do not get child support payments. In 1983, less than half of women raising children alone had been awarded child support, and of those, only half received the full amount to which they were entitled. Even fewer women (14 percent) are awarded alimony, and many older women are left in poverty after a lifetime of homemaking and childrearing. Such women have great difficulty finding jobs and securing health insurance.

c. Racial Minorities and Poverty

181. Most poor people in our nation are white, but the rates of poverty in our nation are highest among those who have borne the brunt of racial prejudice and discrimination. For example, blacks are about three times more likely to be poor than whites. While one out of every nine white Americans is poor, one of every three blacks and Native Americans and more than one of every four Hispanics are poor. While some members of minority communities have successfully moved up the economic ladder, the overall picture indicates that black family income is only 55 percent of white family income, reflecting an income gap that is wider now than at any time in the last fifteen years.

182. Despite the gains which have been made toward racial equality, prejudice and discrimination in our own time as well as the effects of past discrimination continue to exclude many members of racial minorities from the mainstream of American life. Discriminatory practices in labor markets, in educational systems, and in electoral politics create major obstacles for blacks, Hispanics, Native Americans, and other racial minorities in their struggle to improve their economic status. Such discrimination is evidence of the continuing presence of racism in our midst. In our pastoral letter, Brothers and Sisters to Us, we have described this racism as a sin - "a sin that divides the human family, blots out the image of God among specific members of that family, and violates the fundamental human dignity of those called to be children of the same Father."

2. Economic Inequality

183. Important to our discussion of poverty in America is an understanding of the degree of economic inequality in our nation. Our economy is marked by a very uneven distribution of wealth and income. For example, it is estimated that 28 percent of the total net wealth is held by the richest 2 percent of families in the United States. The top ten percent holds 57 percent of the net wealth. If homes and other real estate are excluded, the concentration of ownership of "financial wealth" is even more glaring. In 1983, 54 percent of the total net financial assets were held by 2 percent of all families, those whose annual income is over $125,000. Eighty-six percent of these assets were held by the top 10 percent of all families.

184. Although disparities in the distribution of income are less extreme, they are still striking. In 1984 the bottom 20 percent of American families received only 4.7 percent of the total income in the nation and the bottom 40 percent received only 15.7 percent, the lowest share on record in U.S. history. In contrast, the top one-fifth received 42.9 percent of the total income, the highest share since 1948. These figures are only partial and very imperfect measures of the inequality in our society. However, they do suggest that the degree of inequality is quite large. In comparison with other industrialized nations, the United States is among the more unequal in terms of income distribution. Moreover, the gap between rich and poor in our nation has increased during the last decade. These inequities are of particular concern because they reflect the uneven distribution of income and wealth. Some degree of inequality not only is acceptable, but also may be considered desirable for economic and social reasons, such as the need for incentives and the provision of greater rewards for greater risks. However, unequal distrubtion should be evaluated in terms of several moral principles we have enunciated: the priority of meeting the basic needs of the poor and the importance of increasing the level of participation by all members of society in the economic life of the nation. These norms establish a strong presumption against extreme inequality of income and wealth as long as there are poor, hungry, and homeless people in our midst. They also suggest that extreme inequalities are detrimental to the development of social solidarity and community. In view of these norms we find the disparities of income and wealth in the United States to be unacceptable. Justice requires that all members of our society work for economic, political, and social reforms that will decrease these inequities.

3. Guidelines for Action

186. Our recommendations for dealing with poverty in the United States build upon several moral principles that were explored in chapter two of this letter. The themes of human dignity and the preferential option for the poor are at the heart of our approach; they compel us to confront the issue of poverty with a real sense of urgency.

187. The principle of social solidarity suggests that alleviating poverty will require fundamental changes in social and economic structures that perpetuate glaring inequalities and cut off millions of citizens from full participation in the economic and social life of the nation. The process of change should be one that draws together all citizens, whatever their economic status, into one community.

188. The principle of participation leads us to the conviction that the most appropriate and fundamental solutions to poverty will be those that enable people to take control of their own lives. For poverty is not merely the lack of adequate financial resources. It entails a more profound kind of deprivation, a denial of full participation in the economic, social, and political life of society and an inability to influence decisions that affect one's life. It means being powerless in a way that assaults not only one's pocketbook but also one's fundamental human dignity. Therefore, we should seek solutions that enable the poor to help themselves through such means as employment. Paternalistic programs which do too much for and too little with the poor are to be avoided.

189. The responsibility for alleviating the plight of the poor falls upon all members of society. As individuals, all citizens have a duty to assist the poor through acts of charity and personal commitment. But private charity and voluntary action are not sufficient. We also carry out our moral responsibility to assist and empower the poor by working collectively through government to establish just and effective public policies.

190. Although the task of alleviating poverty is complex and demanding, we should be encouraged by examples of our nation's past successes in this area. Our history shows that we can reduce poverty. During the 1960s and early 1970s, the official poverty rate was cut in half, due not only to a healthy economy, but also to public policy decisions that improved the nation's income transfer programs. It is estimated, for example, that in the late 1970s federal benefit programs were lifting out of poverty about 70 percent of those who would have otherwise been poor.

191. During the last twenty-five years, the Social Security Program has dramatically reduced poverty among the elderly. In addition, in 1983 it lifted out of poverty almost 1.5 million children of retired, deceased, and disabled workers. Medicare has enhanced the life expectancy and health status of elderly and disabled people, and Medicaid has reduced infant mortality and greatly improved access to health care for the poor.

192. These and other successful social welfare programs are evidence of our nation's commitment to social justice and a decent life for everyone. They also indicate that we have the capacity to design programs that are effective and provide necessary assistance to the needy in a way that respects their dignity. Yet it is evident that not all social welfare programs have been successful. Some have been ill-designed, ineffective, and wasteful. No one has been more aware of this than the poor themselves, who have suffered the consequences. Where programs have failed, we should discard them, learn from our mistakes, and fashion a better alternative. Where programs have succeeded, we should acknowledge that fact and build on those successes. In every instance, we must summon a new creativity and commitment to eradicate poverty in our midst and to guarantee all Americans their right to share in the blessings of our land.

193. Before discussing directions for reform in public policy, we must speak frankly about misunderstandings and stereotypes of the poor. For example, a common misconception is that most of the poor are racial minorities. In fact, about two-thirds of the poor are white. It is also frequently suggested that people stay on welfare for many years, do not work, could work if they wanted to, and have children who will be on welfare. In fact, reliable data show that these are not accurate descriptions of most people who are poor and on welfare. Over a decade people move on and off welfare, and less than 1 percent obtain these benefits for all ten years. Nor is it true that the rolls of Aid to Families with Dependent Children (AFDC) are filled with able-bodied adults who could but will not work. The majority of AFDC recipients are young children and their mothers who must remain at home. These mothers are also accused of having more children so that they can raise their allowances. The truth is that 70 percent of AFDC families have only one or two children and that there is little financial advantage in having another. In a given year, almost half of all families who receive AFDC include an adult who has worked full or part-time. Research has consistently demonstrated that people who are poor have the same strong desire to work that characterizes the rest of the population.

194. We ask everyone to refrain from actions, words, or attitudes that stigmatize the poor, that exaggerate the benefits received by the poor, and that inflate the amount of fraud in welfare payments. These are symptoms of a punitive attitude towards the poor. The belief persists in this country that the poor are poor by choice or through laziness, that anyone can escape poverty by hard work, and that welfare programs make it easier for people to avoid work. Thus, public attitudes toward programs for the poor tend to differ sharply from attitudes about other benefits and programs. Some of the most generous subsidies for individuals and corporations are taken for granted and are not even called benefits but entitlements. In contrast, programs for the poor are called handouts and

receive a great deal of critical attention, even though they account for less than 10 percent of the federal budget.

195. We now wish to propose several elements which we believe are necessary for a national strategy to deal with poverty. We offer this not as a comprehensive list but as an invitation for others to join the discussion and take up the task of fighting poverty.

196. a). The first line of attack against poverty must be to build and sustain a healthy economy that provides employment opportunities at just wages for all adults who are able to work. Poverty is intimately linked to the issue of employment. Millions are poor because they have lost their jobs or because their wages are too low. The persistent high levels of unemployment during the last decade are a major reason why poverty has increased in recent years. Expanded employment especially in the private sector would promote human dignity, increase social solidarity, and promote self reliance of the poor. It should also reduce the need for welfare programs and generate the income necessary to support those who remain in need and cannot work: elderly, disabled, and chronically ill people, and single parents of young children. It should also be recognized that the persistence of poverty harms the larger society because the depressed purchasing power of the poor contributes to the periodic cycles of stagnation in the economy.

197. In recent years the minimum wage has not been adjusted to keep pace with inflation. Its real value has declined by 24 percent since 1981. We believe Congress should raise the minimum wage in order to restore some of the purchasing power it has lost due to inflation.

198. While job creation and just wages are major elements of a national strategy against poverty, they are clearly not enough. Other more specific policies are necessary to remedy the institutional causes of poverty and to provide for those who cannot work.

199. b). Vigorous action should be undertaken to remove barriers to full and equal employment for women and minorities. Too many women and minorities are locked into jobs with low pay, poor working conditions, and little opportunity for career advancement. So long as we tolerate a situation in which people can work full time and still be below the poverty line-a situation common among those earning the minimum wage-too many will continue to be counted among the "working poor." Concerted efforts must be made through job training, affirmative action, and other means to assist those now prevented from obtaining more lucrative jobs. Action should also be taken to upgrade poorer paying jobs and to correct wage differentials that discriminate unjustly against women.

200. c). Self-help efforts among the poor should be fostered by programs and policies in both the private and public sectors. We believe that an effective way to attack poverty is through programs that are small in scale, locally based, and oriented toward empowering the poor to become self-sufficient. Corporations, private organizations, and the public sector can provide seed money, training and technical assistance, and organizational support for self-help projects in a wide variety of areas such as low-income housing, credit unions, worker cooperatives, legal assistance, and neighborhood and community organizations. Efforts that enable the poor to participate in the ownership and control of economic resources are especially important.

201. Poor people must be empowered to take charge of their own futures and become responsible for their own economic advancement. Personal motivation and initiative, combined with social reform, are necessary elements to assist individuals in escaping poverty. By taking advantage of opportunities for education, employment, and training, and by working together for change, the poor can help themselves to be full participants in our economic, social, and political life.

202. d) The tax system should be continually evaluated in terms of its impact on the poor. This evaluation should be guided by three principles. First, the tax system should raise adequate revenues to pay for the public needs of society, especially to meet the basic needs of the poor. Secondly, the tax system should be structured according to the principle of progressivity, so that those with relatively greater financial resources pay a

higher rate of taxation. The inclusion of such a principle in tax policies is an important means of reducing the severe inequalities of income and wealth in the nation. Action should be taken to reduce or offset the fact that most sales taxes and payroll taxes place a disproportionate burden on those with lower incomes. Thirdly, families below the official poverty line should not be required to pay income taxes. Such families are, by definition, without sufficient resources to purchase the basic necessities of life. They should not be forced to bear the additional burden of paying income taxes.

203. e) All of society should make a much stronger commitment to education for the poor. Any long-term solution to poverty in this country must pay serious attention to education, public and private, in school and out of school. Lack of adequate education, especially in the inner city setting, prevents many poor people from escaping poverty. In addition, illiteracy, a problem that affects tens of millions of Americans, condemns many to joblessness or chronically low wages. Moreover, it excludes them in many ways from sharing in the political and spiritual life of the community. Since poverty is fundamentally a problem of powerlessness and marginalization, the importance of education as a means of overcoming it cannot be overemphasized.

204. Working to improve education in our society is an investment in the future, an investment that should include both the public and private school systems. Our Catholic schools have the well-merited reputation of providing excellent education, especially for the poor. Catholic inner-city schools provide an otherwise unavailable educational alternative for many poor families. They provide one effective vehicle for disadvantaged students to lift themselves out of poverty. We commend the work of all those who make great sacrifices to maintain these inner-city schools. We pledge ourselves to continue the effort to make Catholic schools models of education for the poor.

205. We also wish to affirm our strong support for the public school system in the United States. There can be no substitute for quality education in public schools, for that is where the large majority of all students, including Catholic students, are educated. In Catholic social teaching, basic education is a fundamental human right. In our society a strong public school system is essential if we are to protect that right and allow everyone to develop to their maximum ability. Therefore, we strongly endorse the recent calls for improvements in and support for public education, including improving the quality of teaching and enhancing the rewards for the teaching profession. At all levels of education we need to improve the ability of our institutions to provide the personal and technical skills that are necessary for participation not only in today's labor market but also in contemporary society.

206. f) Policies and programs at all levels should support the strength and stability of families, especially those adversely affected by the economy. As a nation, we need to examine all aspects of economic life and assess their effects on families. Employment practices, health insurance policies, income security programs, tax policy, and service programs can either support or undermine the abilities of families to fulfill their roles in nurturing children and caring for infirm and dependent family members.

207. We affirm the principle enunciated by John Paul II that society's institutions and policies should be structured so that mothers of young children are not forced by economic necessity to leave their children for jobs outside the home. The nation's social welfare and tax policies should support parents' decisions to care for their own children and should recognize the work of parents in the home because of its value for the family and for society.

208. For those children whose parents do work outside the home, there is a serious shortage of affordable, quality day care. Employers, governments, and private agencies need to improve both the availability and the quality of child care services. Likewise, families could be assisted by the establishment of parental leave policies that would assure job security for new parents.

209. The high rate of divorce and the alarming extent of teenage pregnancies in our

nation are distressing signs of the breakdown of traditional family values. These destructive trends are present in all sectors of society: rich and poor; white, black, and brown; urban and rural. However, for the poor they tend to be more visible and to have more damaging economic consequences. These destructive trends must be countered by a revived sense of personal responsibility and commitment to family values.

210. g). A thorough reform of the nation's welfare and income-support programs should be undertaken. For millions of poor Americans the only economic safety net is the public welfare system. The programs that make up this system should serve the needs of the poor in a manner that respects their dignity and provides adequate support. In our judgment the present welfare system does not adequately meet these criteria. We believe that several improvements can and should be made within the framework of existing welfare programs. However, in the long run, more far-reaching reforms that go beyond the present system will be necessary. Among the immediate improvements that could be made are the following:

211. (1) Public assistance programs should be designed to assist recipients, wherever possible, to become self-sufficient through gainful employment. Individuals should not be worse off economically when they get jobs than when they rely only on public assistance. Under current rules, people who give up welfare benefits to work in low-paying jobs soon lose their Medicaid benefits. To help recipients become self-sufficient and reduce dependency on welfare, public assistance programs should work in tandem with job creation programs that include provisions for training, counseling, placement, and child care. Jobs for recipients of public assistance should be fairly compensated so that workers receive the full benefits and status associated with gainful employment.

212. (2) Welfare programs should provide recipients with adequate levels of support. This support should cover basic needs in food, clothing, shelter, health care, and other essentials. At present only 4 percent of poor families with children receive enough cash welfare benefits to lift them out of poverty. The combined benefits of AFDC and food stamps typically come to less than three-fourths of the official poverty level. Those receiving public assistance should not face the prospect of hunger at the end of the month, homelessness, sending children to school in ragged clothing, or inadequate medical care.

213. (3) National eligibility standards and a national minimum benefit level for public assistance programs should be established. Currently welfare eligibility and benefits vary greatly among states. In 1985 a family of three with no earnings had a maximum AFDC benefit of $96 a month in Mississippi and $558 a month in Vermont. To remedy these great disparities, which are far larger than the regional differences in the cost of living, and to assure a floor of benefits for all needy people, our nation should establish and fund national minimum benefit levels and eligibility standards in cash assistance programs. The benefits should also be indexed to reflect changes in the cost of living. These changes reflect standards that our nation has already put in place for aged and disabled people and veterans. Is it not possible to do the same for the children and their mothers who receive public assistance?

214. (4) Welfare programs should be available to two-parent as well as single-parent families. Most states now limit participation in AFDC to families headed by single parents, usually women. The coverage of this program should be extended to two-parent families so that fathers who are unemployed or poorly paid do not have to leave home in order for their children to receive help. Such a change would be a significant step toward strengthening two-parent families who are poor.

4. Conclusion

215. The search for a more human and effective way to deal with poverty should not be limited to short-term reform measures. The agenda for public debate should also

include serious discussion of more fundamental alternatives to the existing welfare system. We urge that proposals for a family allowance or a children's allowance be carefully examined as a possible vehicle for ensuring a floor of income support for all children and their families. Special attention is needed to develop new efforts that are targeted on long-term poverty, which has proven to be least responsive to traditional social welfare programs. The "negative income tax" is another major policy proposal that deserves continued discussion. These and other proposals should be part of a creative and ongoing effort to fashion a system of income support for the poor that protects their basic dignity and provides the necessary assistance in a just and effective manner.

CHAPTER IV

A NEW AMERICAN EXPERIMENT: PARTNERSHIP FOR THE PUBLIC GOOD

295. For over two hundred years the United States has been engaged in a bold experiment in democracy. The founders of the nation set out to establish justice, promote the general welfare, and secure the blessings of liberty for themselves and their posterity. Those who live in this land today are the beneficiaries of this great venture. Our review of some of the most pressing problems in economic life today shows, however, that this undertaking is not yet complete. Justice for all remains an aspiration; a fair share in the general welfare is denied to many. In addition to the particular policy recommendations made above, a long-term and more fundamental response is needed. This will call for an imaginative vision of the future that can help shape economic arrangements in creative new ways. We now want to propose some elements of such a vision and several innovations in economic structures that can contribute to making this vision a reality.

296. Completing the unfinished business of the American experiment will call for new forms of cooperation and partnership among those whose daily work is the source of the prosperity and justice of the nation. The United States prides itself on both its competitive sense of initiative and its spirit of teamwork. Today a greater spirit of partnership and teamwork is needed; competition alone will not do the job. It has too many negative consequences for family life, the economically vulnerable, and the environment. Only a renewed commitment by all to the common good can deal creatively with the realities of international interdependence and economic dislocations in the domestic economy. The virtues of good citizenship require a lively sense of participation in the commonwealth and of having obligations as well as rights within it. The nation's economic health depends on strengthening these virtues among all its people, and on the development of institutional arrangements supportive of these virtues.

297. The nation's founders took daring steps to create structures of participation, mutual accountability, and widely distributed power to ensure the political rights and freedoms of all. We believe that similar steps are needed today to expand economic participation, broaden the sharing of economic power, and make economic decisions more accountable to the common good. As noted above, the principle of subsidiarity states that the pursuit of economic justice must occur on all levels of society. It makes demands on communities as small as the family, as large as the global society and on all levels in between. There are a number of ways to enhance the cooperative participation of these many groups in the task of creating this future. Since there is no single innovation that will solve all problems, we recommend careful experimentation with several possibilities that hold considerable hope for increasing partnership and strengthening mutual responsibility for economic justice.

A. Cooperation within Firms and Industries

298. A new experiment in bringing democratic ideals to economic life calls for serious

exploration of ways to develop new patterns of partnership among those working in individual firms and industries. Every business, from the smallest to the largest, including farms and ranches, depends on many different persons and groups for its success: workers, managers, owners or shareholders, suppliers, customers, creditors, the local community, and the wider society. Each makes a contribution to the enterprise, and each has a stake in its growth or decline. Present structures of accountability, however, do not acknowledge all these contributions or protect these stakes. A major challenge in today's economy is the development of new institutional mechanisms for accountability that also preserve the flexibility needed to respond quickly to a rapidly changing business environment.

299. New forms of partnership between workers and managers are one means for developing greater participation and accountability within firms. Recent experience has shown that both labor and management suffer when the adversarial relationship between them becomes extreme. As Pope Leo XIII stated, "Each needs the other completely: capital cannot do without labor, nor labor without capital." The organization of firms should reflect and enhance this mutual partnership. In particular, the development of work patterns for men and women that are more supportive of family life will benefit both employees and the enterprises they work for.

300. Workers in firms and on farms are especially in need of stronger institutional protection, for their jobs and livelihood are particularly vulnerable to the decisions of others in today's highly competitive labor market. Several arrangements are gaining increasing support in the United States: profit sharing by the workers in a firm; enabling employees to become company stockholders; granting employees greater participation in determining the conditions of work; cooperative ownership of the firm by all who work within it; and programs for enabling a much larger number of Americans, regardless of their employment status, to become shareholders in successful corporations. Initiatives of this sort can enhance productivity, increase the profitability of firms, provide greater job security and work satisfaction for employees, and reduce adversarial relations. In our 1919 Program of Social Reconstruction, we observed "the full possibilities of increased production will not be realized so long as the majority of workers remain mere wage earners. The majority must somehow become owners, at least in part, of the instruments of production." We believe this judgment remains generally valid today.

301. None of these approaches provides a panacea, and all have certain drawbacks. Nevertheless we believe that continued research and experimentation with these approaches will be of benefit. Catholic social teaching has endorsed on many occasions innovative methods for increasing worker participation within firms. The appropriateness of these methods will depend on the circumstances of the company or industry in question and on their effectiveness in actually increasing a genuinely cooperative approach to shaping decisions. The most highly publicized examples of such efforts have been in large firms facing serious financial crises. If increased participation and collaboration can help a firm avoid collapse, why should it not give added strength to healthy businesses? Cooperative ownership is particularly worthy of consideration in new entrepreneurial enterprises.

302. Partnerships between labor and management are possible only when both groups possess real freedom and power to influence decisions. This means that unions ought to continue to play an important role in moving toward greater economic participation within firms and industries. Workers rightly reject calls for less adversarial relations when they are a smokescreen for demands that labor make all the concessions. For partnership to be genuine it must be a two-way street, with creative initiative and a willingness to cooperate on all sides.

303. When companies are considering plant closures or the movement of capital, it is patently unjust to deny workers any role in shaping the outcome of these difficult choic-

es. In the heavy manufacturing sector today, technological change and international competition can be the occasion of painful decisions leading to the loss of jobs or wage reductions. While such decisions may sometimes be necessary, a collaborative and mutually accountable model of industrial organization would mean that workers not be expected to carry all the burdens of an economy in transition. Management and investors must also accept their share of sacrifices, especially when management is thinking of closing a plant or transferring capital to a seemingly more lucrative or competitive activity. The capital at the disposal of management is in part the product of the labor of those who have toiled in the company over the years, including currently employed workers. As a minimum, workers have a right to be informed in advance when such decisions are under consideration, a right to negotiate with management about possible alternatives, and a right to fair compensation and assistance with retraining and relocation expenses should these be necessary. Since even these minimal rights are jeopardized without collective negotiation, industrial cooperation requires a strong role for labor unions in our changing economy.

304. Labor unions themselves are challenged by the present economic environment to seek new ways of doing business. The purpose of unions is not simply to defend the existing wages and prerogatives of the fraction of workers who belong to them, but also to enable workers to make positive and creative contributions to the firm, the community, and the larger society in an organized and cooperative way. Such contributions call for experiments with new directions in the U.S. labor movement.

305. The parts played by managers and shareholders in U.S. corporations also need careful examination. In U.S. law, the primary responsibility of managers is to exercise prudent business judgment in the interest of a profitable return to investors. But morally this legal responsibility may be exercised only within the bounds of justice to employees, customers, suppliers, and the local community. Corporate mergers and hostile takeovers may bring greater benefits to shareholders, but they often lead to decreased concern for the well-being of local communities and make towns and cities more vulnerable to decisions made from afar.

306. Most shareholders today exercise relatively little power in corporate governance. Although shareholders can and should vote on the selection of corporate directors and on investment questions and other policy matters, it appears that return on investment is the governing criterion in the relation between them and management. We do not believe this is an adequate rationale for shareholder decisions. The question of how to relate the rights and responsibilities of shareholders to those of the other people and communities affected by corporate decisions is complex and insufficiently understood. We, therefore, urge serious, long-term research and experimentation in this area. More effective ways of dealing with these questions are essential to enable firms to serve the common good.

B. Local and Regional Cooperation

307. The context within which U.S. firms do business has direct influence on their ability to contribute to the common good. Companies and indeed whole industries are not sole masters of their own fate. Increased cooperative efforts are needed to make local, regional, national, and international conditions more supportive of the pursuit of economic justice.

308. In the principle of subsidiarity, Catholic social teaching has long stressed the importance of small-and intermediate-sized communities or institutions in exercising moral responsibility. These mediating structures link the individual to society as a whole in a way that gives people greater freedom and power to act. Such groups include families, neighborhoods, church congregations, community organizations, civic and business associations, public interest and advocacy groups, community development corporations, and many other bodies. All these groups can play a crucial role in generating creative partnerships for the pursuit of the public good on the local and regional level.

309. The value of partnership is illustrated by considering how new jobs are created. The development of new businesses to serve the local community is key to revitalizing

areas hit hard by unemployment. The cities and regions in greatest need of these new jobs face serious obstacles in attracting enterprises that can provide them. Lack of financial resources, limited entrepreneurial skill, blighted and unsafe environments, and a deteriorating infrastructure create a vicious cycle that makes new investment in these areas more risky and therefore less likely.

310. Breaking out of this cycle will require a cooperative approach that draws on all the resources of the community. Community development corporations can keep efforts focused on assisting those most in need. Existing business, labor, financial, and academic institutions can provide expertise in partnership with innovative entrepreneurs. New cooperative structures of local ownership will give the community or region an added stake in businesses and even more importantly give these businesses a greater stake in the community. Government on the local, state, and national levels must play a significant role, especially through tax structures that encourage investment in hard hit areas and through funding aimed at conservation and basic infrastructure needs. Initiatives like these can contribute to a multilevel response to the needs of the community.

311. The Church itself can work as an effective partner on the local and regional level. First-hand knowledge of community needs and commitment to the protection of the dignity of all should put Church leaders in the forefront of efforts to encourage a community-wide cooperative strategy. Because churches include members from many different parts of the community, they can often serve as mediator between groups who might otherwise regard each other with suspicion. We urge local church groups to work creatively and in partnership with other private and public groups in responding to local and regional problems.

C. Partnership in the Development of National Policies

312. The causes of our national economic problems and their possible solutions are the subject of vigorous debate today. The discussion often turns on the role the national government has played in creating these problems and could play in remedying them. We want to point to several considerations that could help build new forms of effective citizenship and cooperation in shaping the economic life of our country.

313. First, while economic freedom and personal initiative are deservedly esteemed in our society, we have increasingly come to recognize the inescapably social and political nature of the economy. The market is always embedded in a specific social and political context. The tax system affects consumption, saving, and investment. National monetary policy, domestic and defense programs, protection of the environment and worker safety, and regulation of international trade all shape the economy as a whole. These policies influence domestic investment, unemployment rates, foreign exchange, and the health of the entire world economy.

314. The principle of subsidiarity calls for government intervention when small or intermediate groups in society are unable or unwilling to take the steps needed to promote basic justice. Pope John XXIII observed that the growth of more complex relations of interdependence among citizens has led to an increased role for government in modern societies. This role is to work in partnership with the many other groups in society, helping them fulfill their tasks and responsibilities more effectively, not replacing or destroying them. The challenge of today is to move beyond abstract disputes about whether more or less government intervention is needed, to consideration of creative ways of enabling government and private groups to work together effectively.

315. It is in this light that we understand Pope John Paul II's recommendation that "society make provisions for overall planning" in the economic domain. Planning must occur on various levels, with the government ensuring that basic justice is protected and also protecting the rights and freedoms of all other agents. In the Pope's words:

In the final analysis this overall concern weighs on the shoulders of the state, but it cannot mean one-sided centralization by the public authorities. Instead what is in question is a just and rational coordination within the framework of which the initiative of individuals, free groups, and local work centers and complexes must be safeguarded.

316. We are well aware that the mere mention of economic planning is likely to produce a strong negative reaction in U.S. society. It conjures up images of centralized planning boards, command economies, inefficient bureaucracies, and mountains of government paperwork. It is also clear that the meaning of "planning" is open to a wide variety of interpretations and takes very different forms in various nations. The Pope's words should not be construed as an endorsement of a highly centralized form of economic planning, much less a totalitarian one. His call for a "just and rational coordination" of the endeavors of the many economic actors is a call to seek creative new partnership and forms of participation in shaping national policies.

317. There are already many forms of economic planning going on within the U.S. economy today. Individuals and families plan for their economic future. Management and labor unions regularly develop both long- and short-term plans. Towns, cities, and regions frequently have planning agencies concerned with their social and economic future. When state legislatures and the U.S. Congress vote on budgets or on almost any other bill that comes before them, they are engaged in a form of public planning. Catholic social teaching does not propose a single model for political and economic life by which these levels are to be institutionally related to each other. It does insist that reasonable coordination among the different parts of the body politic is an essential condition for achieving justice. This is a moral precondition of good citizenship that applies to both individual and institutional actors. In its absence no political structure can guarantee justice in society or the economy. Effective decisions in these matters will demand greater cooperation among all citizens. To encourage our fellow citizens to consider more carefully the appropriate balance of private and local initiative with national economic policy, we make several recommendations.

318. First, in an advanced industrial economy like ours, all parts of society, including government, must cooperate in forming national economic policies. Taxation, monetary policy, high levels of government spending, and many other forms of governmental regulation are here to stay. A modern economy without governmental interventions of the sort we have alluded to is inconceivable. These interventions, however, should help, not replace, the contributions of other economic actors and institutions and should direct them to the common good. The development of effective new forms of partnership between private and public agencies will be difficult in a situation as immensely complex as that of the United States in which various aspects of national policy seem to contradict one another. On the theoretical level, achieving greater coordination will make demands on those with the technical competence to analyze the relationship among different parts of the economy. More practically, it will require the various subgroups within our society to sharpen their concern for the common good and moderate their efforts to protect their own short-term interests.

319. Second, the impact of national economic policies on the poor and the vulnerable is the primary criterion for judging their moral value. Throughout this letter we have stressed the special place of the poor and the vulnerable in any ethical analysis of the U.S. economy. National economic policies that contribute to building a true commonwealth should reflect this by standing firmly for the rights of those who fall through the cracks of our economy: the poor, the unemployed, the homeless, the displaced. Being a citizen of this land means sharing in the responsibility for shaping and implementing such policies.

320. Third, the serious distortion of national economic priorities produced by massive national spending on defense must be remedied. Clear-sighted consideration of the role of government shows that government and the economy are already closely intertwined through military research and defense contracts. Defense-related industries make up a major part of the U.S. economy and have intimate links with both the military and civilian government; they often depart from the competitive model of free-market capitalism.

Moreover, the dedication of so much of the national budget to military purposes has been disastrous for the poor and vulnerable members of our own and other nations. The nation's spending priorities need to be revised in the interests of both justice and peace.

321. We recognize that these proposals do not provide a detailed agenda. We are also aware that there is a tension between setting the goals for coherent policies and actually arriving at them by democratic means. But if we can increase the level of commitment to the common good and the virtues of citizenship in our nation, the ability to achieve these goals will greatly increase. It is these fundamental moral concerns that lead us as bishops to join the debate on national priorities.

INDEX